THE RISE OF FOOD CHARITY
IN EUROPE

Edited by
Hannah Lambie-Mumford and Tiina Silvasti

D1612588

First published in Great Britain in 2021 by

Policy Press, an imprint of
Bristol University Press
University of Bristol
1-9 Old Park Hill
Bristol
BS2 8BB
UK
t: +44 (0)117 954 5940
e: bup-info@bristol.ac.uk

Details of international sales and distribution partners are available at
policy.bristoluniversitypress.co.uk

© Bristol University Press 2021

British Library Cataloguing in Publication Data
A catalogue record for this book is available from the British Library

ISBN 978-1-4473-4756-9 paperback
ISBN 978-1-4473-4000-3 hardback
ISBN 978-1-4473-4757-6 ePdf
ISBN 978-1-4473-4758-3 ePub

Cover design: Robin Hawes
Front cover image: iStock-899116556

Bristol University Press and Policy Press use environmentally responsible
print partners.

Printed and bound in Great Britain by CPI Group (UK) Ltd, Croydon,
CR0 4YY

FSC
www.fsc.org
MIX
Paper from
responsible sources
FSC® C013604

Contents

List of figures and tables

Figures

Tables

Notes on contributors

Sabrina Arcuri is a postdoctoral research fellow at the Department of Agriculture, Food and Environment (DAFE), University of Pisa, Italy. Her research is focused on food (in)security in wealthy countries, the origins, development and governance of urban/local food strategies and sustainable food systems. Sabrina's publications include 'Food poverty, food waste and the consensus frame on charitable food redistribution in Italy', *Agriculture and Human Values*, 36: 263–75.

Gianluca Brunori is Full Professor of Food Policy at the Department of Agriculture, Food and Environment, University of Pisa, Italy. His research activity concerns innovation in agriculture and rural areas, the sustainability of food systems, and the role of small farming in rural development and in food security. He is also editor in chief of the journal *Agricultural and Food Economics*. He has authored and co-authored numerous articles and book chapters on sustainable food systems and food security, including 'Food waste reduction and food poverty alleviation: a system dynamics conceptual model', *Agriculture and Human Values*, 36(2): 289–300.

Francesca Galli is a research fellow at the Department of Agriculture, Food and Environment, University of Pisa, Italy. Her research interests are in agricultural economics, food policy, food and nutrition security, food systems and sustainability assessment. In the field of food poverty, Francesca co-authored 'Food waste reduction and food poverty alleviation: a system dynamics conceptual model', *Agriculture and Human Values*, 36(2): 289–300, and 'Addressing food poverty in systems: governance of food assistance in three European countries', *Food Security*, 10: 1353–70.

Amaia Inza-Bartolomé is an Assistant Professor at the Faculty of Labour Relations and Social Work, University of the Basque Country (UPV/EHU), Spain. She is the coordinator of the Social Work section and the First Vice Dean of the Faculty. Amaia's research focuses on social policy and social services, welfare state theory, disabilities and food poverty and food charities. She is the author of the book *El secuestro neoliberal del bienestar, ¿es posible la justicia social?* (Erasmus Ediciones, 2011) and several publications about social investment and welfare states' paradigmatic change.

Fabian Kessl is Professor of Social Work Theories and Methods at the Department of Social Work and Social Policy at University of Duisburg-Essen, Germany. His current research interests are in the transformation of the welfare state and welfare state agencies, the everyday life of service users and the institutional change of public services in general. He has published numerous papers and edited international special issues of the *European Journal of Social Work* (EJSW) and *Social Work & Society* (SW&S) on 'Knowledge transfer in social work' (2015) and 'Boundary work' (2012).

Hannah Lambie-Mumford is a Lecturer in the Department of Politics and International Relations at the University of Sheffield, UK. Hannah's research focuses on food insecurity, the rise of emergency food provision, the role of public policy and the human right to food. Hannah is the author of *Hungry Britain: The rise of food charity* (Policy Press, 2018). She is currently leading a British Academy-funded programme of empirical research in Germany, Spain and the UK entitled 'Changing nature of social care in an era of austerity: the rise of food banks across Europe'. Hannah also sits on the Child Poverty Action Group's (CPAG's) Policy Advisory Committee and the Food Standard Agency's (FSA's) Advisory Committee for Social Science.

Vesna Leskošek works at the Faculty of Social Work, University of Ljubljana, Slovenia, where she is currently a Dean. Her main research interests are in social inequality and poverty, food poverty, welfare states and child protection. Vesna was an independent expert for poverty and social exclusion at the European Commission from 2004 to 2011. She has also edited and co-authored several scientific monographs and book chapters, including 'Food poverty between charity and the human right to food: the case of urban gardens in Slovenia', in A.-L. Mathhies and K. Närhi (eds) *The ecosocial transition of societies: The contribution of social work and social policy* (Routledge, 2017).

Rachel Loopstra is a Lecturer in Nutrition at King's College London, UK, and Future Research Leader Fellow at the Economic and Social Research Council (ESRC). Her research is focused on examining how public policies and socio-economic shocks influence vulnerability to food insecurity and food bank usage in the UK and Canada. In collaboration with The Trussell Trust and funded by the Impact Acceleration Account at the University of Oxford, she led a first nationwide household survey of people receiving food from Trussell Trust food banks: 'Financial insecurity, food insecurity, and disability: the profile of people receiving emergency food assistance from The Trussell Trust Foodbank Network in Britain'. She sits on the Oxfam GB UK Programmes Policy Advisory Group.

Stephan Lorenz is a researcher and lecturer at the Institute of Sociology, Friedrich Schiller University of Jena, Germany. His core areas of research cover different aspects of food and sustainability studies. Stephan's habilitation thesis (a further academic qualification thesis after the doctoral degree in Germany) focused on the development of food banks (so-called '*Tafel*' initiatives) in Germany since the early 1990s and their strong increase in the second half of the last decade. He is interested in both the environmental claims, that is, fighting food excess, and the social claims, that is, alleviating poverty.

Amy Markus (MSc) wrote a master's thesis on the effect of food banks on local responsibility for food security under the supervision of Hilje van der Horst at Wageningen University, the Netherlands. She currently works as a policymaker in a non-governmental organisation representing the interests of the older population.

Leon Pijnenburg works as an Assistant Professor at the Department of Communication, Technology and Philosophy, Wageningen University & Research, the Netherlands. His research area covers ethics, the philosophy of science and social and political philosophy. Leon's recent project concerns food banks and the question of human rights and dignity. He has also studied the critical theory of Jürgen Habermas and translated his work into the Dutch language.

Graham Riches is Emeritus Professor and former Director of the University of British Columbia's School of Social Work. His research focuses on food insecurity, charity, the right to food and social policy within the wealthy food secure Global North. *Food banks and the welfare crisis* (CCSD, 1986) explored Canada's embrace of charitable food banking imported from the United States in the early 1980s. In the ensuing era of austerity driven neoliberalism he co-authored international texts critiquing US style food banking's transnational expansion at the expense of public policy. Most recently published is *Food bank nations, corporate charity and the right to food* (Routledge, 2018). Now living on Vancouver Island he consults widely while promoting right to food advocacy in his rural small town community.

Leire Escajedo San-Epifanio is Full Professor of Constitutional Law in the Department of Constitutional Law and History of Political Thought, University of the Basque Country, Spain. One of her main research interests is the right to food and food waste. She has co-edited the books *Envisioning a future without food waste and food poverty* (Wageningen Academics, 2015) and *Derecho a la alimentación y Despilfarro alimentario* (Tirant lo Blanch, de proxima aparición, 2018). Leire is also a member of the Executive Committee of the European Society for Food and Environmental Ethics (EURSAFE).

Holger Schoneville is an Assistant Professor for Social Work (Wissenschaftlicher Mitarbeiter) at Dortmund University, Germany. His research interests include the social conditions of poverty and social exclusion, as well as subjectivity and vulnerability in relation to social work theory. Holger has published a number of papers on poverty and food aid, including 'Poverty and the transformation of the welfare (state) arrangement: Food banks and the charity economy', *Social Work & Society*, 16(2), and (with Kessl, F.) 'Tafeln & Co. – Soziale Arbeit in der Mitleidsökonomie', *Sozial Extra. Zeitschrift für Soziale Arbeit und Sozialpolitik*, 37(5): 13–14.

Tiina Silvasti is Professor of Social and Public Policy in the Department of Social Sciences and Philosophy, University of Jyväskylä, Finland. Tiina is the co-editor of *First World hunger revisited: Food charity or the right to food?* (Palgrave Macmillan, 2014) and *The new social division. Making and unmaking precariousness* (Palgrave Macmillan, 2015). She is also the leader of the Food System Studies Research Group at the University of Jyväskylä. Her recent research interests focus on First World hunger – the rising use of charitable food assistance and food aid delivery in wealthy Western countries.

Ville Tikka is a doctoral candidate in the Department of Social Sciences and Philosophy, University of Jyväskylä, Finland. His research interests are in food system studies, including dimensions of social, ecological and economic sustainability. In relation to food aid, he has published 'Two decades of discussion on charitable food aid in Finland: analysing the framing by and through the media', *Agriculture and Human Values*, 36(2): 341–52.

Hilje van der Horst is an Assistant Professor at Wageningen University, the Netherlands, and is affiliated with the Consumption and Healthy Lifestyles (CHL) group. She is a sociologist specialising in the dynamics of inequality and exclusion in health and consumption. Her research focuses on domestic consumption practices, food aid and sustainable consumption. Hilje is an editorial board member of the *International Journal of Consumer Studies* and a board member of the Dutch Sociological Association. In relation to food banks, she co-authored 'The "dark side" of food banks? Exploring emotional responses of food bank receivers in the Netherlands', *British Food Journal*, 116(9): 1506-20.

Romana Zidar is the Migration Advocacy Officer on the National Committee of the United Nations Children's Fund (UNICEF) Slovenia and researcher of social and child protection. In addition, her fields of research include the political and personal dimensions of the (non-)take-up of monetary social benefits. In relation to food poverty, Romana co-authored (with Leskošek, V.) 'Food poverty between charity and the human right to food: the case of urban gardens in Slovenia', in A.-L. Mathhies and K. Närhi (eds) *The ecosocial transition of societies: The contribution of social work and social policy* (Routledge, 2017).

Acknowledgements

First and foremost, we would like to thank all of the authors in this volume: Sabrina Arcuri, Gianluca Brunori, Francesca Galli, Hilje van der Horst, Amaia Inza-Bartolomé, Fabian Kessell, Vesna Leskošek, Rachel Loopstra, Stephan Lorenz, Amy Markus, Leon Pijnenburg, Leire Escajedo San-Epifanio, Holger Schoneville, Ville Tikka and Romana Zidar. Thank you all for contributing your exceptional scholarship and for your dedication to this book project. Thanks also to Graham Riches for providing a thought-provoking foreword, which sets the tone of the book.

We are grateful to the Faculty of Social Sciences and Sheffield Sustainable Food Futures (SheFF) at the University of Sheffield for providing funding to bring contributing authors together in Sheffield. The discussions we held, both at the university and with members of the public, formed an invaluable foundation for the book.

Thanks also to the whole Policy Press team, especially Laura Vickers-Rendall, our commissioning editor, who has been supportive, enthusiastic and encouraging throughout this process. We are also extremely grateful to our copy-editors, Hannah Austin and Chris Stanners, for their invaluable help pulling together and polishing the manuscript.

Foreword

Professor Graham Riches

The publication of *The rise of food charity in Europe* is at once distressing yet hugely encouraging. It is distressing because of the necessity for such a book in today's wealthy but austerity-driven Europe, where widespread food poverty and food charity remain entrenched. Indeed, I first began writing about food charity in Canada in the early 1980s as a primary response to food insecurity, the official euphemism for hunger, as Janet Poppendieck once wrote. US-style food banking was quickly adopted and followed by its transatlantic spread to Europe and beyond. As Fernand Braudel, the eminent French historian wrote at the time: 'today's society is capable of feeding its poor. To do otherwise is an error of government' (1985). What lessons have gone unlearned?

An urgent reminder to rethink the food charity phenomenon was a *Guardian* letter dated 24 March 2019. Headlined 'Food banks are no solution to poverty', it was signed by 58 academics and campaigners from the UK, Finland and North America, and declared that 'charitable food aid is a sticking plaster on a gaping wound of systemic inequality in our societies'. It was responding to an international summit in London organised by the US-based and 'big food'-backed Global Foodbanking Network (GFN), founded in 2006. GFN now operates in more than 30 countries across the world, partnering with the European Food Bank Association (FEBA), established in 1986. Food banking, they claim, is the link between food waste and food poverty reduction, promoting the corporate food charity as the 'green' intervention reducing food waste while promising *zero hunger*. The questioning of the corporate capture of food charity as an effective response to rich world hunger was welcome news.

Likewise, in recent years, the burgeoning increase in interdisciplinary research and writing about the food charity phenomenon in journal articles, book chapters and national reports is heartening and much needed. Certainly, previous texts have examined the growth of food banking within the Anglo-Saxon 'liberal' welfare states across selected First World countries and the industrialised Organisation for Economic Co-operation and Development (OECD). Similarly, there is an established literature on food policy, food sovereignty, food systems and health and food inequalities.

All the more encouraging is Hannah Lambie-Mumford and Tiina Silvasti's timely new book. By offering European perspectives on what to do about widespread food poverty – domestic hunger – in the Global North, *The rise of food charity in Europe* is an original and significant contribution not only to the literature, but also to a necessary and growing international human rights and civil society debate. Its authoritative co-edited text informed and enriched by the expertise of fellow European social sciences and legal scholars uses the lens of comparative social policy analysis to shed light on the food charity landscapes of seven European Union (EU) member states with varying types of welfare state regimes: social-democratic Finland; conservative Germany and the Netherlands; the Latin Rim or Southern welfare states of Italy and Spain; post-Socialist Slovenia and the liberal UK.

The strength of its social policy analysis lies in its focus on the arrangements by which these societies choose to organise their collective health and social well-being by exploring and revealing the nuances, contradictions and institutionalisation of the differing roles played by front-line charitable food aid and its transformative implications for the welfare state and public policy in combating deep poverty. At the same time, within the context of an emergent parallel charity economy, it investigates the social justice and social rights implications for food charity practice. Who benefits and why? Where does and should collective responsibility lie?

On my side of the Atlantic back in the 1980s, I was shocked then, as today, to find in rich food-secure Canada, with its then reasonably well-structured European-style 'liberal' welfare state, that charitable food banks were needed to feed the growing numbers of people being denied access to adequate income assistance and their publicly funded social safety net. Of course, this was the time when neoliberalism, downsizing the progressive state and punitive welfare reform began to bite. Nevertheless, the Canadian prairies, like their wealthy US neighbours, were exporting countless bushels of grain to feed a hungry world. Yet, hunger in the breadbasket of the world was on our own doorstep.

Most worrying, as Canadian food banks began functioning as stopgaps to domestic hunger, the foundations were being laid for a nationally institutionalised and increasingly corporate system of food charity across the country. Hunger was being socially constructed as a matter for charity and not the primary obligation of the state. This was unremarkable in the US, where both public food aid and charitable food banking had long been normalised since the late 1960s. By 1989, this was the case in Canada. Food banks were the new food safety net for a broken welfare system. Food assistance replaced income assistance as the primary response to food deprivation and income inadequacy. Federal and provincial governments looked on.

Since the early 1990s, while welfare and workfare reforms became normalised, it is worth noting that global hunger, extreme poverty, food and nutrition security, and food assistance received the attention of a host of United Nations (UN) world food summits, declarations and conventions, the most recent being to achieve the Sustainable Development Goals target of *zero hunger* by 2030. Significantly, UN mandates establishing the offices of Special Rapporteur on Extreme Poverty (1998) and the Right to Food (2002) have advanced these commitments. The injection of international human rights law and obligations into debates and policies about global hunger even in the rich world has been a progressive step forward.

Furthermore, in 2004, the Food and Agriculture Organization's (FAO's) *Voluntary guidelines on the right to food* provided practical guidelines regarding standards and measures to be implemented by UN member states 'supporting the progressive realization of the right to food in the context of national food security'. The objective of creating 'enabling environments, assistance and accountability' was underpinned by the first guideline focused on 'democracy, governance, human rights and the rule of law'. While the Global South is the intended beneficiary of such advice, it holds equal application in the North.

I first became interested in the right to food and human rights-based approaches to poverty reduction when researching and writing about the rise of food banks in Canada. Of particular interest was the 1966 International Covenant on Economic, Social and Cultural Rights (ICESCR), a core instrument of the UN Charter of Human Rights, which recognises the right to food, clothing and shelter as core elements of the right to an adequate standard of living and social security. On coming into force, Canada ratified the ICESCR in 1976. Today, 169 UN member countries are state parties to this multilateral treaty, excepting the US and three other countries. Ratification expresses intent and obligations under international law, with governments being held accountable for ensuring domestic compliance with the right to food – together with its associated bundle of economic, social and political rights – that no one should go hungry.

However, it was not until 1999 that UN General Comment 12 clarified the meaning of the right to food. It defined the right to food as being 'when every man, woman or child, alone or in community with others have physical and economic access at all times to adequate food or the means for its procurement'. In other words, in market societies, people require sufficient money from wages or benefits to shop for food in normal and customary ways. Income poverty and unfair income distribution are the root causes of food insecurity. The state is also ultimately accountable for ensuring domestic compliance. It is '*the primary duty bearer*' obligated to 'respect, protect and fulfil' the progressive realisation of the right to food directed at achieving food security for all. The private sector and civil society have important roles to play but the government is first and foremost publicly accountable. The right to food provides not only a critical framework for analysing food poverty, but also a key international instrument for holding governments to account.

While acknowledging the right to food, *The rise of food charity in Europe* nevertheless chooses not to use it as the central organising concept for the book. Rather, its social policy analysis employs it as a tool to reflect on the normative and changing aspects of the social rights embedded in food charity itself. In other words, it not only understands human rights arguments as they relate to welfare entitlements and the obligations of the state (as essential and critical as I believe they are), but also examines the profound implications for social rights and social justice of the daily work and public actions of entrenched charitable food aid.

The seven national case studies, either on their own or taken together, are sources of critical analysis based on robust evidence-based data, contributing progressive ideas to ongoing debates within both Europe and the wider rich world about the prevalence of food poverty, its causes and the drivers and nature of food charity. Behind each study lie the questions of who benefits and why from these particular social and political arrangements as the front-line response to food poverty. What are its obligations? What are its consequences for public policy? What I learned and appreciated most from the case studies and the comparative analysis was a more enriched, nuanced and reflective understanding of food charity and its relationship to the state in the struggle against food poverty.

First, in Spain, despite the fact that there is 'startling EU data about the numbers of people unable to feed themselves' (Chapter 6), the government continues to look the other way. Indeed, in Italy, 'food poverty is not perceived as a political priority' (Chapter 3); the same can be said in Slovenia, 'where it is overlooked, hardly attracting any public attention' (Chapter 5). Indeed, by 'restricting social rights and promoting charitable assistance', Germany has avoided addressing 'deep poverty', 'what it shares with other Western "welfare" countries' (Chapter 2). Such examples of official neglect should come as no surprise. When national governments decline to measure the prevalence of food poverty, there is no doubt that it will remain a political afterthought.

While European food bank usage is evidence of widespread poverty, such data are more likely an underestimate of the true scale of the problem. In Canada, for example, where official data are collected, only one in four food-insecure people turn to food banks for assistance. Taking note, the UK has wisely decided to measure national food insecurity. Still, that is not the end of the matter. Governments only 'own' their official data when they act on the evidence. Canadian and US official food insecurity data are only as good as the public policy attention that they receive, which is little, if any. Regrettably, food bank data – usage, volumes of food and millions of meals provided – create the public illusion and political peace of mind that food charity is successfully tackling the problem.

Second, as food charity has become increasingly institutionalised within the parallel charity economy, the book argues that it is critical to understand its growth and influence upon differing European welfare state policies and practices. Especially important is food charity's embeddedness in different religious, cultural and family traditions as responses to poverty, and the implications for social justice and social rights. Historically, one should note the longstanding Catholic links to North American food banking, which influenced the founding of the first food bank in Paris in 1984. This led to the founding of FEBA two years later and the early development of food banking in Catholic Spain, Ireland, Italy and Portugal, as well as through Caritas in Slovenia more recently. Protestantism has also been active in the Netherlands, through the Lutheran Evangelican Church in Finland, Anglicanism in the UK and *Diakonie* in Germany. Such knowledge building will not only advance understanding of the forces and factors contributing to the growth of European food charity, but also inform broader questions about its moral legitimacy and effectiveness as a substitute for public policy within rich world welfare states.

Third, a critical finding is that social exclusion and exclusion from consumer society are found to be embedded within the need for, and the daily workings of, charitable food provision. The case studies find food banks to be sites of compassion and care but also of conflict, stigma and shame. Increasingly bureaucratic, digitalised and harsh welfare (workfare) eligibility criteria too often lead to the denial of income benefits. The consequent need to beg for whatever surplus food is on food charity shelves is shaming and an affront to human dignity. Food banks frequently run out of food. Supplies are limited and must be rationed. In this process, food bank volunteers serve as the de facto moral guardians of the poor, using their discretion to determine deservingness, how much and for whom. Compassion and understanding may well be shown but conflict between applicant and volunteer is never far away.

Where, one might ask, is the shame of politicians and governments that permit this state of affairs? There is certainly none in Slovenia, where reductions in social cash benefits are intentional and lead to increasing poverty. Nor in the Netherlands, where the Dutch government while claiming that food banks are a shame on society, at the same time walks away from food poverty by maintaining that its system of social security assures the right to food. Nor in Germany, where 'its welfare system, despite some continuities, has ironically failed to address the most vulnerable or rather impaired their situation ... even [being] true in times of economic prosperity' (Chapter 2). To my knowledge, only Scotland has declared its shame about the rise of food banks and is now taking comprehensive action informed by the right to food to mitigate their use.

Fourth, when all is said and done, food charity is entirely dependent on continuing supplies of surplus food – edible food waste – the final discarded product of the food value chain. Its sources are both public and private. As discussed in the case studies of Finland, Italy, the Netherlands, Spain and Slovenia, the EU's Common Agricultural Policy through the Fund for European Aid to the Most Deprived (FEAD) distributes commodity intervention stocks to participating member states. This public food aid, as in the US, falls within the mandates of the respective ministries of agriculture, thereby contributing to a confusing and disconnected food and social policy. Certainly, if FEAD's goal is market stabilisation or even food waste reduction, these are matters for national agricultural and environmental considerations. However, given that the aim is also feeding deprived people, why is such food aid not the responsibility of ministries of social security or social welfare, particularly when income inadequacy is the primary cause of food poverty?

Likewise, charitable food banks dependent on edible food waste generated along the industrial food value chain fall into the same confusing trap when big food's sense of corporate social responsibility (CSR) promotes surplus food as the 'green' 'win–win' solution to both food waste and food poverty reduction. Undoubtedly, food

waste and food poverty are significant global issues, yet their mixing
and matching is neoliberal doublespeak. Food waste is a product of a
dysfunctional industrial food system built on upstream overproduction,
overstocking and supply. Food poverty is primarily caused by income
poverty, unfair income distribution, interrupted earnings and a broken
social safety net. These are separate matters for public policy, requiring
distinct approaches and solutions. After all, if they are to be part of
the solution, food banks will require ever-increasing supplies of edible
food waste, not less. Is feeding 'left over' food to 'left behind' people
really the best we can do?

Lastly of note is the increasing support or involvement by the state in
food charity practice through: the direct or indirect referral of welfare
claimants to food banks; local authority in-kind or financial support; or
national funding to support charitable surplus food distribution. This
mirrors a pattern of longstanding legislative support in the US, where
charity and corporate food banking has long been the beneficiary
of considerable tax incentives. The federal government of Canada
demonstrates its support in somewhat more sunny but perplexing
ways. It launched its 2018 national poverty reduction plan from the
warehouse of Moisson Montreal food bank, where a YouTube video
showed Prime Minister Trudeau and his wife taking smiling selfies of
themselves with volunteers two years earlier.

Is it therefore correct to argue that governments in this gilded
neoliberal age are indifferent to charitable food banking. I think so.
Austerity, precarious underpaid work, social spending cutbacks, stricter
conditionality, workfare disciplining the poor and the denial of benefits
signal politicians' disregard for the poor. They remain untroubled
by believing that charity is doing its thing. They exploit the public
legitimacy of charitable food aid as a perceived antidote to poverty. It
is a sure way to promise ever lower taxes. As the book argues: there is
an iterative process at play here. As charitable initiatives step in to fill
the gaps left by state provision, when put alongside political discourse
that praises the efforts and import of charitable food assistance, in
taking on this role, food charity could be further entrenching state
retrenchment. Little wonder that as the social rights of citizens are
curtailed, food assistance replaces income assistance by propping up
broken social safety nets.

Social policy analysis has an unavoidable date with intervention.
What is to be done? The authors' final call is for a radical reassessment
of social policy priorities – and the consequences of environmental
policies to counter the ever-increasing provision of food charity. As
the Spanish case study laments: 'When philanthropy, CSR activity

and even individual citizens' altruism perform a function for which the state is constitutionally responsible, it is necessary to ask where the political responsibility lies (Chapter 6).' In austerity-driven First World welfare states, as the FAO *Voluntary guidelines* advise, this is surely a matter for 'democracy, governance, human rights and the rule of law'. Yet, as Oliver de Schutter has noted, the EU 'in general is weak on social rights' (2016, personal communication, 9 March). Indeed, the *European pillar of social rights* has no mention of the right to food.

Food charity therefore has crucial roles to play. The monitoring and advocacy of civil society and church organisations such as Caritas in Italy, the Evangelican Lutheran Church in Finland and The Trussell Trust in the UK, as well as that of many active organisations not included in this study, offer hope that civil society is determined to hold the state to account. Notably, the subtext of the right to food is accountability, public policy and mobilisation.

The fact that all European countries have ratified the ICESCR is a standing invitation for civil society to collectively participate in the iterative five-year Human Rights Periodic Review processes. Joined-up civil society action is a key strategy to ensure that delinquent governments implement these rights and create the necessary framework legislation and national action plans directed at ending poverty and securing food security for all.

Meanwhile, research and writing of the quality of *The rise of food charity in Europe* must be continued. It is essential reading for students, academics, policy analysts and all those wishing to fulfil the social contract.

Graham Riches
Emeritus Professor of Social Work
University of British Columbia
1 May 2019

Reference

Braudel, Fernand (1985) 'The new history', *World Press Review*, 32(3): March.

Introduction: exploring the growth of food charity across Europe

Hannah Lambie-Mumford and Tiina Silvasti

European social policy analysis of food charity

An increasing body of country-specific research demonstrates that the need for emergency food assistance is growing throughout Europe, and that rising numbers of people are being forced to turn to charitable food aid to satisfy their basic need for food. Studies on contemporary experiences of food insecurity and food charity have recently been conducted in Estonia (Kõre, 2014), Finland (Silvasti and Karjalainen, 2014), France (Rambeloson et al, 2007), Germany (Pfeiffer et al, 2011), Spain (Pérez de Armiño, 2014) and the UK (Lambie-Mumford, 2017; Loopstra and Lalor, 2017).

There is a long history of charitable food provision in Europe – the European Federation of Food Banks was established in 1986 and now has members from 24 European countries (FEBA, no date). However, the recent country-specific research suggests that the period since the year 2000 has been a particularly important juncture for both the development of the provision of food assistance and the rising need for it. Evidence suggests that the years following 2003 were particularly crucial for the development of food charity in Germany (Pfeiffer et al, 2011; see also Chapter 2 of this book), those following 2008 in Spain (Pérez de Armiño, 2014; see also Chapter 6 of this book) and those following 2010 in the UK (The Trussell Trust, no date; see also Chapter 7 of this book).

There appear to be some noteworthy parallels across these European experiences of rising food charity, in particular, relating to changing welfare states and neoliberal social policy across Europe over the last 20–30 years. Evidence suggests that the recent rise of food charity has occurred in the context of increased conditionality and reductions to entitlements in social security across the continent. In parallel, there appears to have been a delegation of responsibility for caring for those experiencing food insecurity from the state to the charitable sector (Pfeiffer et al, 2011; Silvasti and Karjalainen, 2014). These commonalities indicate that there may be important social policy dynamics at work across Europe:

- In Germany, the German Social Code II, introduced in 2005, represented a more workfare-oriented social security regime and saw a significant reduction in the buying power of the payments that people received (Pfeiffer et al, 2011).
- In Spain, since the economic crash of the mid-2000s, austerity programmes have had particular impacts on the shape of the welfare state, increasing conditionality, reducing funding for services and contributing to what Pérez de Armiño (2014: 133) refers to as the Spanish welfare state's 'progressive erosion'.
- In Finland, Silvasti and Karjalainen (2014: 83) argue that a particularly important point was the move in the 1990s away from the Nordic model of welfare towards a more means-tested model, similar to Anglo-Saxon welfare states.
- In the UK, research is beginning to demonstrate that the advent of the so-called 'era of austerity' in 2010, bringing the most significant period of welfare reform and retrenchment since the establishment of the welfare state, was closely linked to a subsequent rise in charitable food provision, particularly through The Trussell Trust Foodbank Network (The Trussell Trust, no date; Dowler and Lambie-Mumford, 2015; Loopstra et al, 2015).

The relatively recent European experiences of the growth of food charity in parallel with economic crisis, uncertainty and the retrenchment of welfare states are similar to the evolution of this sort of charitable provision on other continents. Notable cases include the US, Canada, Australia and New Zealand in the mid-1990s (Riches, 1997). In both the US and Canada, the numbers of emergency food projects and people turning to them for help grew in the context of economic recession and reforms to social security that saw reductions in entitlements and a broader programme of welfare retrenchment (Poppendieck, 1998; Riches, 2002).

While there are convergences and evident parallels, there are also differences in the developments of charitable operations that have yet to be explored. This is especially the case for differences connected to the particular political and cultural histories and welfare regimes of European nations, and their impact on the evolution of food charity in those countries.

Understanding the drivers of the rise of food charity is an urgent empirical question. Rising need and provision indicate a change in the nature of poverty in Europe and a widespread shift towards charitable responses to satisfying basic needs. Yet, there remains a lack of both comprehensive data and rigorous comparative analysis – in addition to only a limited number of empirical country case studies – of the drivers behind and consequences of the rise of food charity as a response to the growth in severe poverty. In the context of growing public, policy and academic interest in issues of food, poverty and food charity, this represents a significant gap in our knowledge.

This edited collection provides the first comprehensive qualitative cross-case study of the rise of food charity across Europe. Using food charity as a lens through which to examine the changing dynamics of poverty and social policy responses to it, the work is a key social policy text on the shifting nature of care in the context of changing social policies and welfare states. The book provides a cross-national comparative analysis of the reasons for the rise of charitable food provision as a response to contemporary poverty in Europe. Through case studies from Finland, Germany, Italy, the Netherlands, Slovenia, Spain and the UK, the book explores operational issues, including:

- how food charity has evolved;
- what food charity looks like now; and
- its current scale in these countries.

The social policy analysis focuses on questions around the role of welfare states in driving the need for food charity and shaping the nature of the charitable response. It also explores the role that food charity has in welfare provision, both independently and in relation to state-based provision. Crucially, the book draws on empirical evidence from each of the countries to explore:

- how the development of food charity may relate to welfare state traditions, for example, the role religious organisations have historically played in formal welfare provision;
- the impact of changing social policies – specifically, changes to social rights and entitlements – on recent growth in provision and the modern manifestation of food charity;
- the social justice implications of these shifts in social policy and the rise of charitable food provision; and
- where responsibilities lie for ensuring adequate access to food.

The collection offers a unique and much-needed comparative insight into the rise of food charity across Europe from a social policy perspective. This chapter first sets out the comparative concepts used by the authors throughout the book. It goes on to describe how the book will examine the debates around social and human rights, and the role of food waste in food charity. It then discusses the utility of understanding food charity as part of the 'charity economy'. It ends with an outline of the rest of the book.

Food charity, poverty and social justice: comparative concepts

Currently, there is a lack of consistent and agreed terminology surrounding food, poverty and food charity in Europe. It is important to address this issue as the lack of agreed terminology can hamper attempts to draw comparisons and make the most of the data that are currently available. Differences extend across understandings of what constitutes food charity, as well as concepts around limited access to food, including the use of terms such as 'hunger', 'food poverty' and 'food insecurity'. This section also sets out the interpretation of social justice adopted in this book.

Food charity

Terminology around emergency food provision varies between countries. For example, in the US and many European countries, the term 'food bank' usually refers to warehouses or centres that collect, store and redistribute food to charitable organisations, which then pass on the food directly to recipients (Berner and O'Brien, 2004; Costello, 2007; Pérez de Armiño, 2014). In this model, food banks effectively work as 'middlemen', collecting and redistributing food, but are not themselves client facing. The food is distributed to charitable organisations – either 'emergency' or 'non-emergency' food programmes (Mabli et al, 2010). Emergency providers include food pantries, soup kitchens, emergency shelters and breadlines (Berner and O'Brien, 2004; Mabli et al, 2010). Food pantries and breadlines distribute food for people to take home and prepare themselves (Berner and O'Brien, 2004; Mabli et al, 2010). Soup kitchens provide prepared meals, which are served on site, while emergency shelters provide both shelter and prepared meals to clients in need (Mabli et al, 2010). 'Non-emergency' programmes include, for example, day-care centres or summer holiday programmes (Mabli et al, 2010). However, in the UK and Finland, the term 'food bank' is used to describe projects that provide food to people directly in the form of food parcels for people to take home, prepare and eat (Lambie-Mumford and Dowler, 2014; Silvasti and Karjalainen, 2014).

This book adopts a broad definition of charitable food provision. This refers to all voluntary initiatives helping people to access food that they would otherwise not be able to obtain. It therefore covers a variety of provision, including projects that provide food parcels, food banks (of all kinds), soup kitchens, meal projects and social supermarkets. In these projects, food may be provided at low or no cost, with its distribution facilitated by a range of organisations (faith or non-faith) involved in delivery at various scales of operation (local, regional and national).

Food and poverty, 'food poverty' and 'food insecurity'

Similarly, there are divergences across countries in interpreting experiences of limited access to food. In Finland and Slovenia, the terms 'hunger' and 'food poverty' are often used. In the UK, 'food poverty' has long been commonly used (Dowler et al, 2001), but 'food insecurity' is increasingly referred to in policy-focused research (Loopstra et al, 2015; Loopstra and Lalor, 2017). Food security is defined as:

> access by all people at all times to enough food for an active, healthy life and includes at a minimum: a) the ready availability of nutritionally adequate and safe foods, and b) the assured ability to acquire acceptable foods in socially acceptable ways (e.g., without resorting to emergency food supplies, scavenging, stealing, and other coping strategies). Food insecurity exists whenever the availability of nutritionally adequate and safe foods or the ability to acquire acceptable foods in socially acceptable ways is limited or uncertain. (Anderson, 1990: 1560)

Limitations to the concept of food insecurity have meant that it is not used as a comparative concept in this volume. Importantly, in the Italian, Finnish and Spanish languages, 'food security' and 'food safety' are synonymous, and it is therefore problematic to use the term in those country contexts. The terminology of 'food insecurity' and 'food poverty' poses further challenges in a comparative European social policy research context. Critics of the concept of food security suggest that it may run the risk of endorsing charitable food aid as a solution to food poverty, rather than empowering sovereign actors to democratically manage their own access to food (Schanbacher, 2010). It can be seen as reductionist, running the risk of encouraging a focus on access to food specifically or even the provision of food, rather than the broader dynamic relationship between poverty and food experiences, and, crucially, the structural determinants of this.

This edited collection therefore focuses on contemporary responses to poverty, using food charity as a lens through which to explore the impact of changing social policies on how people are cared for. In this volume, access to food – or specifically 'food insecurity' in the particular case studies in some chapters – is treated as a key dynamic of poverty, one that is worthy of independent investigation and vital for understanding the impact of wider policy shifts.

This approach is in keeping with contemporary definitions of poverty. Access to food has long been a key part of understandings of relative poverty and minimum living standards in Europe. Having the resources to access a customary diet was at the forefront of Townsend's (1979: 31) definition of poverty. Elements of food experiences continue to feature in poverty measures, for example, the European Union Statistics on Income and Living Conditions (EU-SILC) (Eurostat, no date).

Social justice

In this book's examination of the impact of changing social policies on rising food charity in Europe, key social justice elements will be explored. Notably, questions relating to issues of equality, exclusion, rights and entitlements, social acceptability, solidarity, care, accountability, and responsibility will all be covered. This builds on previous food charity research, which has explored each of these dimensions.

The social unacceptability, stigma and experience of exclusion inherent in the receipt of charitable provision are increasingly well documented (Poppendieck, 1998; Garthwaite, 2016). Even where recipients of assistance are treated kindly, receiving charitable handouts is very much outside of the socially accepted or 'normal' way of acquiring food in Europe, usually through monetary exchange in the form of food shopping (Meah, 2013). Excluding people living in poverty from the primary food market and pushing them into a secondary market and charity economy also means that people are forced to consume what is left over from the affluent population, even if that is not what they really need or want. This is particularly the case where charities redistribute surplus food. It does not correspond with what is considered to be appropriate and sufficient in contemporary consumer society, where freedom of choice is an aspiration (Riches and Tarasuk, 2014: 48; Lorenz, 2015: 10–11).

The solidarity and care that are offered by charitable food projects have been revealed by previous research (Lambie-Mumford, 2017), but the specific form of different charitable providers can have implications for the particular nature of recipients' experiences of exclusion. Faith-based organisations and churches are active operators in the field of charitable food assistance all across Europe. This is consistent with their moral principles that emphasise the importance of charity. Nevertheless, it also means that recipients of charitable food assistance often have to expose themselves to religious symbols or religious activities, such as praying, services and spiritual music, whether they want to or not (Lambie-Mumford, 2017). This may create feelings of oppression or anxiety for those who are atheist or irreligious, or who belong to other religious groups (Salonen, 2016).

The lack of accountability, rights and entitlements in charitable systems is also problematic in social justice terms (Riches, 1997; Poppendieck, 1998). This is a crucial difference from social welfare measures exercised as a part of government policy relating to poverty and charitable food assistance. The public sector has obligations that are determined and regulated by formal, democratically negotiated norms based on social rights and statutory social security. In contrast, food charities are by no means obligated to provide food for people in need of food aid because charity does not involve an idea of rights (Kortetmäki and Silvasti, 2018). The third sector and business-based charitable actors decide their practices and norms on their own, and their operations depend largely on voluntary work. Charitable food provision is therefore gifted, not based on notions of entitlements, and is thus not able to offer legitimate access to food to all citizens equally.

The question of where responsibilities lie – in theory and practice – for responding to the need for help with food is critical to understanding the evolution of food charity and the implications of its existence into the future. It has been suggested that the positive cultural status of charitable work normalises poverty and legitimises personal generosity as an answer to the major social, political and economic disorder manifesting as food poverty in the first place, and, eventually, as a violation of the human right to food (Riches and Silvasti, 2014). Questions of where responsibilities lie for responding to food crisis and the respective roles of governments, charities and the private sector will be at the forefront of the analysis in this book (Riches, 2011; Riches and Silvasti, 2014).

Social rights and the human right to food

This book builds on work by several of its contributors around the human right to food (Riches, 1997; Riches and Silvasti, 2014; Lambie-Mumford, 2017). In this book, this idea is employed as an important tool for understanding perspectives on the rise of food charity, but it is not used as an organising concept. The book's broader social policy and poverty analysis allows the collection to engage with the role and changing nature of different rights. For example, it is not just human rights approaches, but – critically for social policy analysis – different understandings of social rights, that will be explored and employed. Notably, this book deals with both notions of social rights in relation to welfare state entitlements, on the one hand, and more normative interpretations of social rights as societal objectives and the levels of social protection that are or should be guaranteed, on the other (Dean, 2015).

The human right to food means:

> the right to have regular, permanent and unrestricted access, either directly or by means of financial purchases, to quantitatively and qualitatively adequate and sufficient food corresponding to the cultural traditions of the people to which the consumer belongs, and which ensures a physical and mental, individual and collective, fulfilling and dignified life free of fear. (Ziegler et al, 2011: 15)

Most importantly, rights also invoke corresponding obligations. That is to say, right-bearers are entitled to certain goods and can express related claims to the parties who have the obligation. Hence, the right to food invokes the corresponding obligation on states to ensure that all citizens have the capacity to feed themselves in dignity. This obligation involves duties to *respect*, *protect* and *fulfil* the right to food (Ziegler et al, 2011: 15–20).

Normally, people are expected to be able to feed themselves and their families; hence, in practice, the state's obligations are often limited to respecting and protecting the right to food. However, one's ability as an individual to feed oneself and one's family may fail for various reasons. Examples include unemployment, underemployment, illness, old age or becoming widowed or a single parent. Under circumstances of economic hardship and where a personal social safety net is lacking, the human right to food obliges the state to provide people in poverty with either food or resources for acquiring food. By definition, the core content of the right to food as a human right is consistent with the concept of food security (Anderson, 1990; FAO, 2005). However, while the elimination of food insecurity is a prerequisite for the right to food, it is only one aspect of this right's progressive realisation (Riches, 1999; Mechlem, 2004).

Where people are unable to acquire food for themselves and their family, and need to rely on charitable food assistance in the absence of public social security – or where that public social security turns out to be inadequate – it is justified to say that the right to food is not being fulfilled. The previous United Nations (UN) Special Rapporteur on the Right to Food described the reliance on food banks in Canada as 'symptomatic of a broken social protection system and the failure of the State to meet its obligations to its people' (De Schutter, 2012: 5).

The role of food waste

In many countries investigated in this collection, the redistribution of surplus food and food waste recovery have a role to play in the sourcing of food for charity provision. This varies between countries, playing an integral role in Italy and Slovenia and less of a role in the UK, for example. In some cases (France, Italy, Slovenia and Finland, where a legislative initiative is in process), environmental regulations and guidelines covering the management of food waste and facilitating surplus food redistribution have been enacted, moving food waste more firmly into the social policy sphere. Here, the motive is environmental: to reduce waste by donating excess food to charities.

Regardless of the scale of redistribution practices or the presence of waste redistribution laws, there is a powerful narrative around the so-called moral 'buy one, get one free' model of reducing food waste while feeding hungry people (Poppendieck, 1998). The implications of this narrative of substituting waste food for money or state provision, and, more generally, of conflating the two very distinct problems of food waste and hunger, have previously been found to be highly problematic (Riches, 2011). Donating surplus food to charitable actors, and hence redistributing it to people living in poverty, does not address the root causes of poverty and food insecurity (Riches, 2011). At its best, it offers short-term relief for the acute problem of hunger. Neither does it address the root cause of the environmental problem of excessive amounts of waste food. It may be a short-term solution to rescue edible food from landfill to give to the poor, but the real environmental problem lies in the structures of the global food system (for example, Ericksen et al, 2010), which cannot be solved by delivering excess to charities (Salonen and Silvasti, 2019).

This book considers food waste and experiences of limited access to food to be distinct phenomena, with different determinants and requiring different responses and solutions. Given the book's focus on social policy, it deals with surplus food redistribution in passing as a characteristic of the operation of some instances of food charity. There is a real danger that doing otherwise would be to conflate environmental policy questions of how to reduce food waste with distinct social policy questions around not just the need for assistance with food, but what the best and most appropriate social responses are to experiences of poverty.

Food charity and the charity economy

Growing income poverty and the rise of food charity can be connected with the emergence of the so-called 'charity economy' (Kessl, 2015; Kessl et al, 2016). It is argued that large-scale income poverty, which is increasingly characterised by precarious work due to changing labour market conditions, is creating a situation where it is more and more necessary for charities to take care of the basic needs of the most vulnerable people in European societies. The rise of food charity can be understood as one part of this expanding economy.

The charity economy (Kessl, 2015; Kessl et al, 2016) is characterised as an alternative distribution system where surplus elementary goods are donated, or sold at minimal cost, to people with no or low purchasing power. In this distribution system, necessities that have already been used, or cannot, for one reason or another, be sold on the primary market, are delivered through charity operations (generally by voluntary or low-paid workers) to recipients, who are typically people living in poverty. Through these practices, the charity economy is established as a form of 'secondary market' for used or unsaleable articles.

Charitable food assistance fits into the practice of the charity economy – particularly when the food delivered by charities is surplus food donated by farmers, food-processing industries, retailers, restaurants or catering operations. Donated food is edible and safe to eat but usually close to its expiry date or not saleable for other reasons (for example, minor quality or packaging errors). Consequently, this food becomes the waste of primary market actors and is redistributed on the secondary market.

The charity economy is tightly connected with the prevailing capitalist economic model. Private actors are able to save money on waste management. Delivering excess to a secondary market also allows the current capitalistic system of food production to continue systematic overproduction by presenting donations of surplus as a benevolent philanthropic act benefiting people in poverty. This, in turn, promotes a positive image of private corporate social responsibility (Salonen and Silvasti, 2019). Another consequence of these practices is that charities become dependent on these food sources and the private companies that donate their excess (Tarasuk and Eakin, 2005). The functions of food charities redistributing surplus are dependent on both vulnerable people in need of food assistance due to poverty and surplus production in the primary market.

The expanding charity economy can be understood as an expression of the transformation of European welfare states. It is an indication of a move away from the former politics of poverty alleviation and earlier social policy goals to truly eradicate the structural root causes of poverty (Kessl et al, 2016). Instead, responsibility for the most vulnerable people in society is being passed from states to the third sector and charities. However, at best, the charitable provision of food and other necessities can serve as a means to alleviate the immediate consequences of poverty; it cannot serve as a means to eradicate poverty.

Overview of this book

Case study selection

The case studies in this book are drawn from across Europe and represent key points of difference and commonality in terms of the types of welfare states and histories of charitable and faith-based provision for those in poverty. The book includes case-study chapters on Finland, Germany, Italy, the Netherlands, Slovenia, Spain and the UK.

Decisions and directives at the European Union (EU) level certainly have considerable impact on the operation of social welfare in EU member countries. However, in the EU – in fact, in the whole continent of Europe – there is no common social policy comparable, for example, to the Common Agricultural Policy. This means that responsibility for social and poverty policies lies primarily with national governments. Historically, there have been remarkable regional differences in the ways of organising welfare responsibilities in Europe. According to the classification by Gösta Esping-Andersen (1990), the Western welfare states can be divided into three categories of welfare capitalism: liberal (for example, the UK and anglophone countries), conservative (for example, Germany and Continental Europe) and social-democratic (for example, Scandinavian countries). Later, this typology was supplemented by the Latin Rim or Southern welfare states, also called a rudimentary regime (for example, Mediterranean countries) (Leibfried, 1993), and to some extent the contested post-socialist welfare regime (Aidukaite, 2004; Polese et al, 2015). The public sector has significantly different functions in combating poverty within each of these welfare policy regimes. Consequently, the role of charitable work also varies considerably.

However, the notion of welfare state regimes is not unproblematic. The original typology is based on a comparative historical analysis of social policy development in 18 Organisation for Economic Co-operation and Development (OECD) countries up to the 1980s (Esping-Andersen, 1990). Over time, it has inspired an array of alternative welfare state typologies, often including more than the three types of regimes noted previously in this section, or using different kinds of criteria for classification. In addition, the typology neglects the gender and care dimensions of social policy (Arts and Gelissen, 2002). Furthermore, given the rapid changes over the last few decades, there is also a question of how well this typology can be applied today. For these reasons, welfare state types were not used as a sampling strategy to identify case studies. However, given the variety of welfare states covered, the typology can still provide interesting analytical insight.

Other key points of similarity and difference between the selected cases are also important to note. Welfare policies are embedded in the different political and cultural histories of European regions. Religious actors played a major role in the histories of welfare state development and hence also in the present-day operations of charitable food assistance across Europe (Bäckström et al, 2016). In Spain and Italy, the Catholic Church had a strong impact on the development of the welfare regime and in the development of national social policy systems (for example, Manow, 2015), which, in turn, define the responsibilities of the public sector and the role of charity. During the period of socialist rule, religion was ousted from public life in Slovenia, but in the post-socialist era, the influence of the Christian religion, especially Catholicism, has strengthened. Consequently, in Slovenia, both the political and cultural contexts of the development of charitable food assistance are interesting. In Germany, the Church has played a long-standing role in the delivery of state services (Zehavi, 2013). These cases contrast with Finland, the Netherlands and the

UK, where the state has traditionally provided services directly, with faith-based organisations and other charities more commonly acting as informal voluntary providers that are peripheral in the practice of welfare. The growth of extensive faith-based emergency food provision therefore represents a marked change in the practice of welfare delivery in these countries (for example, Silvasti and Karjalainen, 2014).

This volume therefore includes seven national case studies from a mix of European welfare states usually categorised as having different welfare policy regimes and divergent political and cultural histories, but where charitable food assistance is established. Finland represents the Lutheran Scandinavian welfare state, whereas Germany is an example of a country that is traditionally classified as a representative of the conservative welfare regime. Italy and Spain are Southern welfare states and Catholic countries with a specific cultural background to the delivery of food aid. The Netherlands is often described as a country with a low poverty rate and a successful hybrid of welfare regimes, with strong characteristics from both the social-democratic and conservative models. Yet, there are also people in the Netherlands in need of charitable food assistance. Slovenia is a post-socialist country with one of the lowest levels of income inequality in Europe, as measured by the Gini coefficient. Nonetheless, about 17 per cent of people live at risk of poverty or social exclusion, and charitable food assistance has been introduced as an instrument to combat food poverty. In the final case study, the UK offers an example of a more liberal model, which has seen the rapid expansion in recent years of neoliberal social policies that are increasingly being shown to act as a driver of rising need for charitable food assistance.

Structural outline

Academic experts from each of the case-study countries have provided empirical chapters (Chapters 1–7). In order to enable comparisons to be drawn, each chapter adopts a common approach, providing evidence on the dynamics and implications of the rise of food charity in the particular case-study country. Each chapter is a country case study involving a secondary review of existing data and literature. The chapters will focus on several key themes: the history of food charity in the national context and the relationship between the welfare state and charities; the nature of and drivers behind contemporary food charity provision; key changes in social policy and their impact on rising charitable food provision; and the social justice implications of increasing need for charitable assistance with food. Each chapter concludes with critical reflections on where the authors think developments will go next.

This common approach enables comparative analyses to be drawn in the book's final chapter. However, the chapters are also designed to form stand-alone, authoritative case studies on the rise of food charity in different countries. The authors draw on a wealth of relevant evidence and data from their countries and provide insight into the unique circumstances of the national context.

In Chapter 1, Silvasti and Tikka explore the changes in social policy and the organisation of charitable food aid since the mid-1990s in Finland in order to understand the rise, establishment and legitimisation of charitable food provision there. In Chapter 2, Kessl et al highlight the importance of the notion of the shadow welfare state in understanding the role that food charity increasingly plays in plugging gaps in state welfare provision. In Chapter 3, Arcuri et al highlight the importance of austerity policies in Italy after the euro crisis in driving the need for food charity. In Chapter 4, Van der Horst et al discuss where responsibilities lie in theory and practice for solving food insecurity in the Netherlands. In Chapter 5, Leskošek and Zidar discuss the roles of post-socialist social policies, increasing conditionality and reduced entitlements in paving the way for the rise of food charity in Slovenia. In Chapters 6 and 7, Inza-Bartolomé and San-Epifanio, and Lambie-Mumford and Loopstra, respectively, highlight the importance of the post-2008 austerity and welfare reform policies enacted as a response to the financial crisis in driving the rise of food charity in Spain and the UK.

The Conclusion (Chapter 8) brings together analysis from all seven case-study countries. It argues that while manifested in different ways and on different timescales, reductions in state entitlements appear to have an important role to play in determining the need for and shape of food charity across Europe. This has important implications for social justice as systems move away from being based on universal rights and entitlements towards ad hoc provision that is vulnerable, unreliable and exclusionary.

This is an important juncture at which to take stock of the implications of the rise of food charity across Europe. Social policy and other researchers are now beginning to ask about the long-term effects of these projects on our welfare landscapes. This book provides urgently needed social policy insight into the drivers of the rise of food charity and the nature of the charitable responses being developed across Europe. The findings indicate that a radical reassessment of social policy priorities is urgently needed if the ever-increasing provision of food charity is to be abated or reversed.

References

Aidukaite, J. (2004) *The emergence of the post-socialist welfare state. The case of the Baltic states: Estonia, Latvia and Lithuania*, Stockholm: University College of South Stockholm/Elanders Gotab.

Anderson, S.A. (1990) 'Core indicators of nutritional state for difficult-to-sample populations', *The Journal of Nutrition*, 120(11): 1555–600.

Arts, W. and Gelissen, J. (2002) 'Three worlds of welfare capitalism or more? A state-of-the-art report', *Journal of European Social Policy*, 12(2): 137–58.

Bäckström, A., Davie, G., Edgardh, N. and Petterson, P. (2016) *Welfare and religion in 21st century Europe: Volume 1: Configuring the connections*, London and New York, NY: Routledge.

Berner, M. and O'Brien, K. (2004) 'The shifting pattern of food security support: food stamp and food bank usage in North Carolina', *Nonprofit and Voluntary Sector Quarterly*, 33(4): 655–72.

Costello, H.E. (2007) 'Hunger in our own backyard: the face of hunger in the United States', *Nutrition in Clinical Practice*, 22(6): 587–90.

Dean, H. (2015) *Social rights and human welfare*, Abingdon: Routledge.

De Schutter, O. (2012) *Report of the Special Rapporteur on the right to food on his mission to Canada (6 to 16 May 2012)*, Geneva: United Nations.

Dowler, E. and Lambie-Mumford, H. (2015) 'How can households eat in austerity? Challenges for social policy in the UK', *Social Policy and Society*, 14(3): 417–28.

Dowler, E., Turner, S.A. and Dobson, B. (2001) *Poverty bites: Food, health and poor families*, London: Child Poverty Action Group.

Ericksen, P., Bohle, H.-G. and Stewart, B. (2010) 'Vulnerability and resilience of food systems', in J. Ingram, P. Ericksen and D. Liverman (eds) *Food security and global environmental change*, Oxon: Earthscan, pp 67–77.

Esping-Andersen, G. (1990) *The three worlds of welfare capitalism*, Princeton, NJ: Princeton University Press.

Eurostat (no date) 'European Union Statistics on Income and Living Conditions (EU-SILC)', http://ec.europa.eu/eurostat/web/microdata/european-union-statistics-on-income-and-living-conditions

FAO (Food and Agriculture Organization) (2005) *Voluntary guidelines to support the progressive realisation of the right to adequate food in the context of national food security*, Rome: United Nations, www.fao.org/3/a-y7937e.pdf

FEBA (European Federation of Food Banks) (no date) 'Who we are – membership', www.eurofoodbank.org/en/members-network

Garthwaite, K. (2016) 'Stigma, shame and "people like us": an ethnographic study of foodbank use in the UK', *Journal of Poverty and Social Justice*, 24(3): 277–89.

Kessl, F. (2015) 'Charity economy – a symbol of fundamental shift in Europe', *Tidsskrift for Socialpedagogik*, 18(1): 147–52.

Kessl, F., Oechler, M. and Schroeder, T. (2016) 'Charity economy', in F. Kessl, W. Lorenz, H.-U. Otto and S. White (eds) *European social work – A compendium*, Leverkusen and Farmington Hills: Barbara Budrich Publishers, pp 365–81.

Kõre, J. (2014) 'Hunger and food aid in Estonia: a local authority and family obligation', in G. Riches and T. Silvasti (eds) *First world hunger revisited: Food charity or the right to food?*, London: Palgrave Macmillan, pp 57–71.

Kortetmäki, T. and Silvasti, T. (2018) 'Food assistance', in P.B. Thompson and D.M. Kaplan (eds) *Encyclopedia of food and agricultural ethics* (2nd edn), New York, NY: Springer, https://doi.org/10.1007/978-94-007-6167-4_613-1

Lambie-Mumford, H. (2017) *Hungry Britain: The rise of food charity*, Bristol: Policy Press.

Lambie-Mumford, H. and Dowler, E. (2014) 'Rising use of "food aid" in the United Kingdom', *British Food Journal*, 116(9): 1418–25.

Leibfried, S. (1993) 'Towards a European welfare state? On integrating poverty regimes into the European community', in C. Jones (ed) *New perspectives on the welfare state in Europe*, London: Routledge, pp 133–56.

Loopstra, R. and Lalor, D. (2017) 'Financial insecurity, food insecurity, and disability: the profile of people receiving emergency food assistance from The Trussell Trust Foodbank Network in Britain', www.trusselltrust.org/wp-content/uploads/sites/2/2017/07/OU_Report_final_01_08_online2.pdf

Loopstra, R., Reeves, A., Taylor-Robinson, D., McKee, M. and Stuckler, D. (2015) 'Austerity, sanctions, and the rise of food banks in the UK', *BMJ*, 350(1775), https://doi.org/10.1136/bmj.h1775

Lorenz, S. (2015) 'Having no choice: social exclusion in the affluent society', *Journal of Exclusion Studies*, 5(1): 1–17.

Mabli, J., Cohen, R., Potter, F. and Zhao, Z. (2010) *Hunger in America 2010: National report prepared for Feeding America*, Princeton, NJ: Mathematica Policy Research Inc.

Manow, P. (2015) 'Workers, farmers and Catholicism: a history of political class coalitions and the South-European welfare state regime', *Journal of European Social Policy*, 25(1): 32–49.

Meah, A. (2013) 'Shopping', in P. Jackson (ed) *Food words*, London: Bloomsbury, pp 197–200.

Mechlem, K. (2004) 'Food security and the right to food in the discourse of the United Nations', *European Law Journal*, 10(5): 631–48.

Pérez de Armiño, K. (2014) 'Erosion of rights, uncritical solidarity and food banks in Spain', in G. Riches and T. Silvasti (eds) *First world hunger revisited: Food charity or the right to food?*, London: Palgrave Macmillan, pp 131–45.

Pfeiffer, S., Ritter, T. and Hirseland, A. (2011) 'Hunger and nutritional poverty in Germany: quantitative and qualitative empirical insights', *Critical Public Health*, 21(4): 417–28.

Polese, A., Morris, J. and Kovacs, B. (2015) 'Introduction: the failure and future of the welfare state in post-socialism', *Journal of Eurasian Studies*, 6(1): 1–5.

Poppendieck, J. (1998) *Sweet charity? Emergency food and the end of entitlement*, New York, NY: Penguin Group.

Rambeloson, Z.J., Darmon, N. and Ferguson, E.L. (2007) 'Linear programming can help identify practical solutions to improve the nutritional quality of food aid', *Public Health Nutrition*, 11(4): 395–404.

Riches, G. (1997) 'Hunger and the welfare state: comparative perspectives', in G. Riches (ed) *First world hunger: Food security and welfare politics*, Basingstoke: Macmillan Press, pp 1–13.

Riches, G. (1999) 'Advancing the human right to food in Canada: social policy and the politics of hunger, welfare, and food security', *Agriculture and Human Values*, 16(2): 203–11.

Riches, G. (2002) 'Food banks and food security: welfare reform, human rights and social policy. Lessons from Canada?', *Social Policy & Administration*, 36(6): 648–63.

Riches, G. (2011) 'Thinking and acting outside the charitable food box: hunger and the right to food in rich societies', *Development in Practice*, 21(4/5): 768–75.

Riches, G. and Silvasti, T. (eds) (2014) *First world hunger revisited: Food charity or the right to food?*, Second Edition, Hampshire: Palgrave Macmillan.

Riches, G. and Tarasuk, V. (2014) 'Canada: thirty years of food charity and public policy neglect', in G. Riches and T. Silvasti (eds) *First world hunger revisited: Food charity or the right to food?*, Basingstoke: Palgrave Macmillan, pp 42–56.

Salonen, A.S. (2016) 'Food for the soul or the soul for food? Users' perspectives on religiously affiliated food charity in a Finnish city', https://helda.helsinki.fi/bitstream/handle/10138/166534/FOODFORT.pdf?sequence=1

Salonen, A.S. and Silvasti, T. (2019) 'Faith-based organizations as actors in the charity economy: a case study of food assistance in Finland', in H. Gaisbauer, G. Schweiger and C. Sedmak (eds) *Absolute poverty in Europe: Interdisciplinary perspectives on a hidden phenomenon*, Bristol: Policy Press, pp 267–89.

Schanbacher, W.D. (2010) *The global conflict between food security and food sovereignty*, Santa Barbara, CA: Praeger.

Silvasti, T. and Karjalainen, J. (2014) 'Hunger in a Nordic welfare state: Finland', in G. Riches and T. Silvasti (eds) *First world hunger revisited: Food charity or the right to food?*, Basingstoke: Palgrave Macmillan, pp 72–86.

Tarasuk, V. and Eakin, J.M. (2005) 'Food assistance through "surplus" food: insights from an ethnographic study of food bank work', *Agriculture and Human Values*, 22(2): 177–86.

The Trussell Trust (no date) 'Trussell Trust foodbank stats', www.trusselltrust.org/news-and-blog/latest-stats/

Townsend, P. (1979) *Poverty in the UK*, Middlesex: Pelican.

Zehavi, A. (2013) 'Religious supply, welfare state restructuring and faith-based social activities', *Political Studies*, 61(3): 561–79.

Ziegler, J., Golay, C., Mahon, C. and Way, S.A. (2011) *The fight for the right to food: Lessons learned*, Basingstoke: Palgrave Macmillan.

1

New frames for food charity in Finland

Tiina Silvasti and Ville Tikka

Introduction

In 2017 in Finland, approximately 1,843 tons of food aid was delivered by initiatives financed by the Fund for European Aid to the Most Deprived (FEAD) alone. Nationally, the FEAD's operational programme is focused exclusively on combating food poverty. It works to distribute food aid to the most deprived people throughout the country using 650 distribution centres run by partner organisations. These are usually parishes, faith-based organisations (FBOs) or non-governmental organisations (NGOs). Altogether, 271,723 food parcels and 55,754 meals were provided to recipients within the year. However, it is estimated that only 23 per cent of all food distributed by partner organisations is funded by the FEAD. Donations are another source of food, and some partner organisations also buy food for distribution using their own resources. There are no up-to-date official statistics on the use of charitable food aid in Finland. According to the FEAD's partner organisations, out of Finland's population of 5.5 million, 284,352 people received food assistance at least once during 2017 (Mavi, 2018). Furthermore, based on an extensive survey conducted as part of the hard-to-survey-populations strategy during 2012/13, it is estimated that over 22,000 people have been turning to charitable food assistance every week (Ohisalo, 2014: 40; 2017: 51).

These figures prove that there is a need for charitable food aid in Finland. According to earlier research, the primary reason for this need is income poverty (Riches and Silvasti, 2014). Where people lack sufficient earned income to provide a decent standard of living, they are entitled to social security. However, the European Committee of Social Rights[1] has repeatedly criticised the minimum level of basic social security benefits in Finland. In particular, the labour market subsidy,[2] sick leave allowance and income assistance have been highlighted as being too low to provide an adequate standard of living (European Social Charter, 2018).

It may be claimed that in monetary terms, as well as numbers of recipients of charitable food aid, the phenomenon is a minor factor in undermining the foundations of the Nordic welfare regime compared, for example, to an increasingly unequal public health-care system. However, in a wealthy country such as Finland, satisfying the basic human need for food and nutrition should be regarded as a matter of social principle. Furthermore, if we accept the argument that the problem is insignificant, it could be claimed that it is surely trivial enough to easily be solved. The solution can simply be implemented within the existing social security system by raising the minimum level of basic social security benefits, as the European Committee of Social Rights has suggested. Given the relatively small number of people in need of food aid, the budget required to put these poverty policy measures into effect should not be prohibitive. Yet, the political will and appetite to tackle the poverty problem seem to be lacking.

Even in the absence of effective political action to fight hunger, public interest and research concerning food poverty and voluntary emergency food provision have varied over the last 25 years. The initial wave of media interest dates back to the 1990s, when breadlines and food banks appeared on the nation's streets for the first time (Karjalainen, 2008). At about the same time as this media debate, the first studies on the topic were also published (for example, Kontula and Koskela, 1993; Hänninen, 1994; Heikkilä and Karjalainen, 1998).

The focus of discussion in both the media and research was on the escalating poverty problem as a welfare paradox in the context of a Nordic welfare state regime. Finland definitely identifies itself as a Nordic welfare state, together with Sweden and other Scandinavian countries. The overall picture presented in the media discussion was contradictory. The obvious inconsistency between a Nordic welfare regime and rising food aid delivery conducted by charitable actors was certainly identified, but there was still no serious political debate about the fundamental basis or future direction of welfare policy in Finland. Over time, the subject became less newsworthy, and media interest ceased. Gradually, people became used to the phenomenon. Charitable food aid received a kind of tacit approval, and it was normalised (Silvasti, 2015). Under these circumstances, little by little, food aid as a means to fight food poverty became embedded as a concern of the realm of charity (Silvasti and Karjalainen, 2014).

Although both media and academic interest in charitable food provision had temporarily fallen at the beginning of the 2010s (Tikka,

2019), the situation has changed in more recent times, with plenty of research on food aid being published, especially in the field of social policy (for example, Silvasti and Karjalainen, 2014; Ohisalo, 2017; Laihiala, 2018). In addition, the scope of research has expanded to encompass several disciplines and approaches. These include: theological examination of the Christian underpinnings of the motives and practices of charitable actors, conducted by ethnographic methods (Salonen, 2016); philosophical reflection on the social and environmental injustice of charitable food aid (Kortetmäki and Silvasti, 2017); and social-scientific media analysis from an environmental perspective, framing food aid not only as a social issue of poverty, but also as an environmental 'solution' to food waste (Tikka, 2019).

Similarly, the focus of media discussion has also varied. During the 1990s and early 2000s, charitable food aid was understood to be a social policy issue. As such, it was connected to topics such as increasing income inequalities, cuts in social security and deepening poverty. In the context of a Nordic welfare regime and a strong public commitment to the ideal of state responsibility, increasing social inequality and deepening poverty were regarded as social evils. This offered a negative interpretational frame through which to view charitable food aid (Silvasti and Karjalainen, 2014). However, during the 2010s, interest in charitable food provision as a means to reduce food waste in the name of environmental protection has increased. Framing food aid (Arcuri, 2019; Tikka, 2019) as a means to recover otherwise wasted food, and, as such, as an environmental act, provides a new positive frame for interpreting charitable food provision. Combining these two frames, the new line of discussion celebrates the win–win situation, where 'the planet is saved by fighting food poverty' and surplus food is delivered to people afflicted with food insecurity. This combination of frames constitutes a new form of legitimisation for charitable responses to poverty.

Furthermore, over the quarter of a century of modern food aid provision in Finland, the administrative framework for such action has changed. There has been the will and an active tendency to develop – rather than shut down – the practices of charitable food aid delivery. This chapter asks: what does this kind of entrenchment of charitable food aid provision tell us about the Finnish welfare state? The chapter begins with a short history of the development of modern charitable food aid provision in Finland. That is followed by an examination of poverty, and food poverty in particular, in the context of Finnish social policy. There is then a discussion of the new interpretational frames for charitable food provision, such as food aid as an environmental act preventing food waste, and charitable food delivery as part of an emerging charity economy. In the conclusions, the Finnish case is summarised with reflections on the social justice implications of reliance on food charity in the context of a Nordic welfare regime.

A short history of modern food aid in Finland

After the Second World War, Finland was a poor, war-torn country in need of foreign food aid. The United Nations International Children's Emergency Fund (UNICEF) was founded in 1946 to provide emergency food and health care to children in countries that had been devastated by the war. As one of the first beneficiaries, Finland received food aid between 1947 and 1951 (UNICEF Finland, 2019). The pace of reconstruction was fast during the 1950s, and the Finnish economy developed strongly throughout the 1960s. The most intense period of building the country's welfare state, mainly following the Nordic model and the example of Sweden, dates back to the 1970s and 1980s. During those decades, people in Finland were convinced that in the name of universalism, the welfare state should satisfy the basic needs of all citizens. The old social evil of hunger was thought to have been eradicated for good (Silvasti and Karjalainen, 2014).

However, this turned out not to be the case, and in the early 1990s, the need for emergency food assistance unexpectedly returned during an exceptionally deep economic recession. The first indication of 'the hunger problem' came about as a by-product of a survey exploring the health impacts of the economic slump. According to this survey, 100,000 Finnish people were experiencing an extreme situation where 'the fridge was empty and there was no money to buy food' (Kontula and Koskela, 1993). The first charitable food distributor, and the biggest actor in the field to this day, was the Evangelical Lutheran Church of Finland (ELCF). It has been organising food provision with the help of voluntary workers since 1993. The first operation in Myllypuro in Helsinki was originally named according to the way in which it practically functioned: 'the breadline'. The first food bank was initiated two years later by the ELCF in Tampere. In the Finnish context, the term 'food bank' does not refer to the central warehouse or stock of donated food. Instead, food banks operate as sites to deliver food directly to recipients.

The 1990s' slump was recognised as a transient state of economic emergency. Thus, originally, charitable food provision was meant to be nothing more than a temporary solution to the short-term food poverty caused by that specific situation. It was thought by deacons working within the ELCF that the Christian voluntary work community could meet the immediate food needs of people sooner than the public sector. It was not their intention that responsibility for people suffering severe poverty should be permanently delegated to the ELCF and the third sector (Malkavaara, 2002).

Policymakers' initial reactions to rising income insecurity and food poverty were typically disbelief and denial. For example, in 1990, then Prime Minister Harri Holkeri criticised Finnish citizens for favouring expensive food when cheaper alternatives were available: 'the use of herring should be increased and tenderloin reduced', he advised (YLE, 1990). Generally, it was argued that the problem of hunger was being exaggerated. Hunger in Finland was belittled by comparing it with famines in the developing world. The problem was also minimised by insisting that the supply of free food from charities inevitably created demand for it. If the problem of food poverty was recognised at all, the reason for the situation was readily attributed to the hungry people themselves. Through blaming and shaming victims, it was concluded that the reason for food poverty was essentially individual: people in need of food aid were deemed incapable in some way, for example, drug abusers, the 'new poor' or 'new helpless'. By contrast, cumulative weaknesses in the social security system were never seriously discussed (Karjalainen, 2008).

In the end, the existence of food poverty was acknowledged in public discussion, if not officially recognised in any political statement. It was widely accepted that the level of income assistance (the very last resort of means-tested income security) was too low to sustain an adequate standard of living. However, at the same time, it was argued that the state could not afford to increase spending on social security, even when the national economy was recovering. In fact, during the early 2000s, charitable food aid provision as a solution to the hunger problem was tacitly accepted as being a task for religious actors and the third sector while there was simultaneously exceptionally strong growth in Finland's gross domestic product. This development clearly indicates the way in which Finnish basic social security moved away from a traditional Nordic welfare regime, based on public responsibility, in the direction of a liberal welfare regime and the Anglo-Saxon model (Silvasti and Karjalainen, 2014).

Economic recession and social security cuts, motivated by a neoliberal direction in economic policy, were not the only factors that contributed to the establishment of food aid. Finland joined the European Union (EU) in 1995, and the very next year, in 1996, as the only Nordic welfare state in the bloc, it also joined the EU's

Food Distribution Programme for the Most Deprived Persons of the Community (MDP). It is fair to say that the decision to accept MDP assistance reinforced and institutionalised the concept of charitable food aid delivery in Finland. Back in the early 1990s, there was no nationwide distribution system to deliver food aid to recipients, nor were there systems for regular large-scale corporate food donations from retailers and the food industry to charities. Both systems have grown up and become established since the implementation of the MDP programme, when food from the EU provided the first basic stock that enabled regular and continual food aid provision for many parishes, FBOs and NGOs.

The peculiarity of this process is that the MDP was not an integral part of social and poverty reduction policy. Rather, it was part of the Common Agricultural Policy (CAP) and therefore classified as marketing support. Consequently, from 1996 to 2013, social and poverty policy and the governance of EU food assistance were the responsibilities of different domains within the Finnish administration. There was no cooperation or coordination of food aid between the Ministry of Social Affairs and Health (MSAH) and the Ministry of Agriculture and Forestry. The practical outcome of this inconsistency was that even though poverty policy definitely came within the remit of the MSAH, the ministry opted out of food aid activity completely (Ohisalo, 2013; Silvasti and Karjalainen, 2014).

Moreover, the MSAH still maintains only a vague connection with charitable food aid. It certainly acknowledges food aid activities; yet, it explicitly states that they are not part of national social security, but a form of 'civic activity' (MSAH, 2017a). This can be interpreted as a desperate attempt to maintain the ideals of the Nordic welfare regime and public responsibility. However, in the 2016 and 2017 government budgets, the MSAH – having had little or no previous connection to food aid practices – allocated around €1.8 million to food aid, with another €1.2 million of grants available to food aid providers on application (MSAH, 2016, 2017b, 2019a).

In addition to the direct funding from the MSAH, between 2017 and 2019, food aid organisers received over €2.5 million from the Funding Centre for Social Welfare and Health Organisations (STEA), a funding operator that functions in connection with the MSAH.[3] In fact, by funding such activities, the MSAH, together with the Ministry of Economic Affairs and Employment (the government ministry responsible for FEAD activities), is actively involved in entrenching food aid in Finland and shaping its future. Most notably, by allocating funding to a limited number of organisers for specific purposes (cold storage facilities, refrigerated vehicles and so on), the MSAH influences both who can provide food aid and how the practice is organised. Thus, it is reasonable to say that the MSAH has a major role in actively building a new private–public model of food aid in Finland.

In retrospect, striking incoherence can be seen in the interpretation of the way in which charitable food aid has been established. On the one hand, delivering food as a charitable act has been represented as an illegitimate form of social security in the framework of Nordic welfare state policies. On the other hand, food provision has been construed as a legitimate form of charity and kindness for the ELCF and FBOs. Therefore, the general view in Finland about establishing charitable food aid as a permanent part of the social security of last resort is contradictory. This contradiction is repeated in practice since it is common knowledge that people who are not eligible for income assistance or for whom income assistance is inadequate to provide any standard of living are referred to charities for additional aid by social workers from the public sector (Ohisalo and Määttä, 2014). Hence, food charity appears to be simultaneously a suitable solution to an awkward but undeniable hunger problem and a matter of national shame because of its conflict with the Finnish welfare model based on the Nordic ethos of welfare (Karjalainen, 2008). This double standard can still be seen in public discussion of the issue (Silvasti and Karjalainen, 2014; Salonen and Silvasti, 2019) and particularly in the contradictory behaviour of the MSAH. Overall, this contradiction appears to reflect a collective interpretation of the fundamental nature of charity as a form of philanthropy – charity seems to be immune to serious critique, making political debate about the topic extremely difficult (McMahon, 2011; Riches and Silvasti, 2014).

Eventually, the MDP was phased out at the end of 2013 and replaced by the FEAD programme. This does not come under the CAP, but is part of the EU's Cohesion Policy; in Finland, it is administered by the Ministry of Economic Affairs and Employment. The main focus of the FEAD programme is on supporting national programmes that distribute material assistance, like food, clothing and other necessities for personal use. However, in contrast to the MDP, the scope of the programme extends beyond material assistance to activities that promote social inclusion.

In practice, Finland's FEAD programme is focused exclusively on combating food poverty. Social inclusion activities, such as giving information about the services and projects available in the public and third sectors, as well as guidance, advice and support on using these services, are all delivered alongside food provision (Mavi, 2018).

Basically, the FEAD programme continues the food aid measures that started with the MDP. From the point of view of recipients of assistance, there is no practical difference from the earlier food aid provision (Ministry of Economic Affairs and Employment, 2019).

The transition period from the MDP to the FEAD lasted roughly a year, leading to temporary disruptions in the availability of food to charities (European Commission, 2018). In principle, the temporary shortage of food to be distributed could have offered an opportunity for serious political discussion and consideration of the future of charitable food aid. However, this opportunity was neglected. Instead, during the transition period, the food authorities loosened the regulations on the distribution of expiring food from retailers to charities by relaxing the rules governing expiration dates. This is in line with and motivated by the EU-led efforts to reduce food waste and promote food waste recovery as part of a so-called 'circular economy' (European Commission, 2017). Consequently, as part of these efforts to combat food waste, charities are now allowed to freeze donated food on the expiry date or offer it as a hot meal one day after expiration (Evira, 2013).

This chain of events clearly shows how different policy actors that have influence over food aid delivery interact without explicit leadership and proper communication between discrete parts of the administration. This leaves the development of food aid provision as a more or less arbitrary and obscure process, with similarly arbitrary consequences for people afflicted by food poverty. Moreover, the development of this new kind of private–public charitable system of poverty relief is happening without a transparent democratic process, and in the shadow of the public and institutional arrangements that constitute the welfare state.

Under these circumstances, donated food is becoming increasingly important to charitable operations. According to the latest annual implementation report summary of the FEAD in Finland (Mavi, 2018), less than a quarter (23 per cent) of all food delivered by FEAD partner organisations is now financed by the fund. More than half of all distribution locations provide donated food in addition to EU food. Moreover, most of the biggest food aid distributors in urban areas – for example, in the Helsinki metropolitan area – receive no EU food at all, relying solely on donations (Kirkko ja kaupunki, 2017).

Consequently, during the 2010s, Finnish food aid provision has become increasingly connected with food system surplus and food waste recovery. In addition, the emphasis of such aid has shifted from the mere alleviation of hunger to focus more on communality, and the activation and agency of food aid recipients. Public funding from the MSAH has been allocated to initiatives such as Yhteinen keittiö (Communal Kitchen) and also directly to food aid providers as 'Christmas presents' – unallocated funds from the ministry's budget – during the 2015–19 government's term of office (MSAH, 2017b; Yhteinen keittiö, 2019). Yhteinen keittiö is a prime example of simultaneously emphasising communal activity and the individual agency of food aid recipients. The direct funding of food aid providers is another nudge towards the institutionalisation of food aid practices as the redistribution system for food surplus, with funds allocated to acquisitions such as refrigerated transports rather than personnel costs, salaries or overheads (MSAH, 2017b).

As well as being in line with the aforementioned EU-level efforts to minimise waste (European Union, 2010), focusing on food waste reduction through charitable food aid fits with the national agenda of promoting a circular economy as a form of sustainability (Valtioneuvosto, 2015; Sitra, 2016). The government's key project – 'Breakthrough to a circular economy and adoption of clean solutions to promote circular economy and reduce waste' – has provided particularly fertile ground for the development of food waste recovery practices (Valtioneuvosto, 2017). While many individual food aid providers have established bilateral collaborations with retailers, Yhteinen pöytä (Shared Table) and the city of Vantaa have been organising a centralised redistribution network (Yhteinen pöytä, 2019) – a model that is now being piloted across Finland in ten additional cities, with funding from the Finnish Innovation Fund Sitra (Sitra, 2019).

Building on, for example, the Berliner Tafel (Berlin Table) model (see Chapter 2), Yhteinen pöytä aims to support existing food aid providers with centralised, large-scale food surplus collection and redistribution via its network of food factories, retailers and food aid distributors. Logistically, this means that the Yhteinen pöytä initiative transports food surplus to a central facility from where it is quickly distributed, with no long-term storage. It is a unique model in the Nordic countries insofar as it is the only city-led food aid scheme in the region. The enterprise is funded and owned by the city of Vantaa and Vantaa Parish Union, and thus operates with substantial public funding (Yhteinen pöytä, 2016, 2019).[4]

The model is also noteworthy in that it is primarily focused not on the recipients, but on the providers of aid. Finnish food aid has been called a 'patchwork quilt of aid' (Ohisalo et al, 2014): a loose network of practices with little or no coordination between them, despite the existence of an association for food aid organisers[5] Finland does not have an umbrella organisation that would coordinate and bring all the organisers together. Therefore, while Yhteinen pöytä may not be the first, it is providing a strong and comprehensive link between organisers of food aid in the region.

In addition to Yhteinen pöytä being piloted or implemented in multiple regions, three publicly funded, nationwide initiatives are under way:

- 'From Breadlines to Participation' (Ruokajonoista osallisuuteen), 2018–20, led by Sininauhaliitto (Blue Ribbon Union – a central association for FBOs working with substance abusers) and funded by the European Social Fund (ESF);
- 'Food Aid Network' (Ruoka-apuverkosto), 2019–21, led by KOA ry (Association for Domestic Relief Work) and funded by STEA (a standalone state-aid authority operating in connection with the MSAH, as mentioned previously in this chapter); and
- 'Enabling Community' (Osallistava yhteisö), 2019/20, led by Kirkkopalvelut (an Evangelical Lutheran central organisation) and funded by STEA.

Together, these initiatives represent an unprecedented level of coordination for food aid in Finland. They also strongly emphasise the social and communal aspects of such aid, shifting the focus from offering hunger relief to providing opportunities for recipients to engage with the community and society. Therefore, the social problem addressed is not so much food or income poverty, but social exclusion. Paradoxically, as a part of food aid, food should be understood, first and foremost, as a 'lead item' or attraction but not the focal point of these practices. This also marks a potential shift away from breadlines and queuing for food – the hitherto emblematic forms of food aid in Finland – to other, perhaps more humane practices.

Poverty and food poverty in the context of Finnish social policy

During the economic recession that first triggered the need for modern food aid in the early 1990s, basic social security and minimum supplementary benefits were cut or frozen as part of austerity measures. This hard-line social policy practised during the recession radically weakened the social security of the most vulnerable people in society. With the economic recession over by the end of the 1990s, economic growth in Finland was strong during the first years of the new millennium. In spite of that, no improvements of note were introduced in the area of social policy. Significantly, basic social security benefits remained frozen for more than ten years. Consequently, income inequality between socio-economic groups grew substantially (Silvasti and Karjalainen, 2014).

Simultaneously, Finland's basic social security moved away from the Nordic welfare model towards the traditional liberal model, entailing more means testing. At the beginning of the 1990s, this change was motivated mainly by economic recession. Nevertheless, as the end of the decade approached, there was an increasingly explicit effort to actively transform social and labour policies in concert with arguments that endorsed greater income inequality as a precondition for future economic growth and stronger international competitiveness. In Finland, as in many other European countries, work was emphasised as the best solution to numerous social problems. Since the mid-1990s, the development and implementation of the government's activation policy has been one of the key tools in reforming social policy. This development followed the so-called 'activation paradigm' and was inspired by the goals and instruments of the international trend towards activation policies.

The rationale behind activation measures is to link social benefits for the unemployed to work obligations. This manifests as a strong tendency towards ever stricter work requirements for recipients of unemployment benefits (Keskitalo, 2008). The latest reform – 'the activation model for unemployment security' – was implemented in 2018. As part of the government's key strategy on employment and competitiveness, the activation model 'incorporates measures to encourage people to actively seek work and use employment services at all stages of their unemployment'. If unemployed people fail to meet the requirements of the activation model, they will be subject to sanctions, including a reduction in their unemployment benefit (MSAH, 2019b).

The status of income assistance has also changed. Originally, it was meant to be a supplementary means-tested social security benefit of very last resort. However, it has gradually become an indispensable supplement to plug the gaps left by falling levels of basic social security. In fact, it is now the primary source of basic social security for a growing number of people. As a result, this means-tested form of social assistance, meant as a last resort and supposed to be a marginal form of social welfare in the Nordic model, is now practically an integral part of basic social security. Essentially, the minimum level of basic social security in Finland has repeatedly been proven to be too low to provide a decent standard of living (Kuivalainen, 2010; European Social Charter, 2018; THL, 2019).

The latest indication of an alarmingly low level of basic social security is presented in the recent 'Evaluation report on the adequacy of basic social security 2015–2019' published by the National Institute for Health and Welfare (THL, 2019).[6] The report states that 'the income levels of those receiving unemployment benefit, home care allowance, minimum sick leave allowance or parental daily allowance were not sufficient to cover the reasonable minimum consumption budget. Student social security covers the reasonable minimum consumption budget only if supplemented by a student loan' (THL, 2019). Moreover, the basic level of social security for unemployed people has fallen as a consequence of reductions in benefits resulting from the new activation model implemented in 2018. This reveals the core of the harsh, sanction-based activation policy measures targeted at the unemployed. Overall, during the evaluation period 2015–19, the role of means-tested, last-resort income assistance in filling the gaps in basic social security provision has increased significantly. There can be no doubt that this kind of long-term hard-line social policy development will further exacerbate the need for charitable food aid provision.

Despite the various weaknesses in the social security system, in comparison with other European countries, the income level provided by basic social security in Finland ranks either at the top or in the middle, depending on the circumstances of the recipient's family and life (THL, 2019). Also, as measured by the Gini coefficient, income differentials in Finland (Gini index: 25.3) remain well below the European average (Gini index: 30.7) (Eurostat, 2019a).

According to the European Statistics on Income and Living Conditions (EU-SILC), 23.7 per cent of citizens of the EU's 28 member states were living at risk of poverty or social exclusion in 2015. In Finland, the corresponding figure was 16.6 per cent (896,000 people). This is the fourth-lowest figure in Europe, after Iceland, the Czech Republic and Norway. Furthermore, in 2016, the percentage of people at risk of poverty or social exclusion had further reduced, to 15.7 per cent (849,000 people). This is the lowest figure in the whole of the available 11-year reference period. According to the Official Statistics of Finland (2018), the percentage of people at risk of poverty or social exclusion has varied between 15.7 per cent and 17.9 per cent during the 2005–16 period.

The 'at risk of poverty or social exclusion' (AROPE) indicator, used in the EU-SILC survey to measure the level of risk, corresponds to the number of people who are either at risk of poverty, severely materially deprived or living in a household with very low work intensity. Accordingly, people are classified as being at risk of poverty and social exclusion on three dimensions:

- They live in a household whose disposable monetary income per consumption unit is below 60 per cent of the national median income.
- People living in a household with low work intensity are all persons aged under 60 who work less than 20 per cent of their potential in the survey year.
- People are considered to be in a household that suffers deprivation if it meets at least four of the following nine indicators: experiencing payment difficulties, difficulty coping with unexpected financial expenses or cannot afford a telephone, washing machine, television, car, protein-rich meal every other day, one week's holiday per year outside the home or keep the home warm enough.

This classification helps to illustrate the overall picture of poverty in Finland. In 2016, 68.5 per cent of people at risk of poverty or social exclusion were disadvantaged on one of those three dimensions. Most of them (378,000) were low-income earners; 159,000 people were members of underemployed households, and 44,000 people (2 per cent) suffered severe material deprivation. Only 0.5 per cent of the population were disadvantaged on all three dimensions of the AROPE indicator (Official Statistics of Finland, 2018). In addition, as measured by the food component of the EU–SILC indicators on material deprivation, the percentage of individuals in Finland who are not able to afford a protein-rich meal – with meat, chicken, fish or a vegetarian equivalent – every second day has varied between 2.5 per cent and 3.3 per cent over the period 2009–17, against the EU average of 7.9 per cent (Eurostat, 2019b).

Even if, statistically, the poverty rate looks relatively good in European comparisons of income inequality and the AROPE rate, there are still people in need of food aid. Who are these people and how have they ended up in such a situation? Although the public social security system has adopted more means testing in its procedures, there is no authoritative means testing for food aid delivery. Consequently, no accurate official statistics or reliable time series of the numbers of people receiving food assistance are available. Also, the depth of poverty that the recipients are suffering is obscure.

Practices in the field vary considerably. Some charities – for example, the ELCF in its welfare work – may survey potential recipients about their individual needs and circumstances before giving them food aid. However, in many cases, recipients of food aid are not required to prove their need for assistance by using any official document or referral. On the other hand, some actors request a Finnish passport or a Social Insurance Institution of Finland (Kela) card (personal health insurance card). This is done mostly to ensure that recipients are registered under the Finnish welfare system and to avoid the misuse of aid. The practice excludes potential recipients of aid who do not hold Finnish citizenship, official documentation or a right of residence (a Kela card is issued to all permanent residents of Finland). The latest data available are from 2014, when one in ten food aid distributors reportedly requested a Kela card or other form of identification. However, it is impossible to obtain up-to-date numbers as these requests for identification do not result in any publicly available records (Ohisalo et al, 2014).

In the absence of official statistics, there are multiple estimates about Finnish food aid, though these figures do not encompass all of the country's food aid operations. This is due to the fragmentation of the field, which means that numbers and estimates often either cover only a portion of operations or may overlap. According to FEAD partner organisations, 284,352 people received food aid in 2017 (Mavi, 2018). In addition to the FEAD statistics, the ELCF – as one of the biggest food aid distributors – has produced some figures relating to its own food delivery. According to the Church Research Agency (Kirkkopalvelut, 2014, 2018), parishes alone distribute food aid to approximately 100,000 people in need every year. Moreover, according to the extensive information collected under the hard-to-survey-populations strategy during 2012/13, over 22,000 people turn to charitable food assistance every week (Ohisalo, 2014: 40; 2017: 51). Many individual organisers also provide estimates on aspects such as the amount of donated food that they receive (for example, Samaria, 2018).

Recipients of food assistance are a very heterogeneous group, consisting of single parents, families with several children and people outside or on the periphery of the labour market, for example, under- and unemployed people, low-income pensioners, people with mental health problems and/or substance abuse problems, students, and immigrants (Ohisalo, 2014; Kotimaanapu, 2019; Mavi, 2018). In 2017, there was disruption to income assistance payments as a result of administrative reorganisation in which income assistance was transferred from municipal social services to Kela. As a result, there were serious delays in the processing and payment of benefits (Kela, 2017). According to food charities, this disruption led to 'an avalanche of people' in need of food aid (Samaria, 2018). This clearly indicates the high level of risk of food insecurity among people living on benefits.

In a food aid user survey conducted at FEAD partner organisation distribution sites in 2017, most of the respondents (57 per cent) were women, with 34 per cent of them under 49 years old and 66 per cent aged 50 years or older. Up to 95 per cent of the respondents were living without earned income, and 90 per cent of them had Finnish citizenship (Mavi, 2018). When considering these figures, it is important to keep in mind that many of the biggest food aid distributors in urban areas rely totally on donated food and are therefore not included in this survey of FEAD partners' food aid users.

Furthermore, the demographic and socio-economic structures in cities are different from those of rural Finland. It has previously been reported that in sparsely populated Northern and Eastern Finland, access to food is becoming more difficult for many elderly people without a car and driving licence due to the closure of village shops and the ever-lengthening distances involved in shopping for groceries (Kirkkopalvelut, 2014). Consequently, EU food aid funded by the FEAD is especially important in remote rural areas in these parts of Finland, where no large-scale food industry and big supermarkets are present to donate food to charitable actors. In some of those rural localities, food aid delivery is fully dependent on the FEAD (Kirkko ja kaupunki, 2017). Naturally, this has an impact on the quality and quantity of the food available for charity provision. From an equality perspective, this kind of geographical variation in the availability of donated food highlights one of the weaknesses of the charitable relief of food poverty. There may be a burning need for food assistance in a certain region but no food available for provision.

Preventing food waste as part of the emerging charity economy

In the Finnish context, there are two intertwining new trends of development in charitable food provision that reflect the current transformation of the welfare state and indicate a shift in the organisation of social security. These trends connect charitable food provision to food waste recovery as part of a circular economy (Hanssen et al, 2014; FEBA, 2016), and emerging forms of the so-called charity economy (Kessl, 2015; Kessl et al, 2016). From a social policy perspective, it is symptomatic that food poverty – meaning a situation where the basic human right to food and nutrition is endangered – has permanently returned to the social welfare agenda, and that there is no serious political effort to find a solution to this enduring problem based on state welfare responsibilities.

Therefore, charitable food provision serves as an excellent example of the shift from public forms and practices of poverty reduction to a mixed model of private–public poverty relief. In turn, emerging 'alternative forms of economy' – the circular economy and the charity economy – are employed to manage, not solve, the stubborn food poverty problem. Within this mixed private–public model of poverty relief, distressed people cannot rely on public social support. Instead, they are dependent on the voluntary donations of those with surplus who are willing to give. This kind of social policy evolution seriously undermines the fundamental promise of welfare universalism specific to the traditional Nordic welfare regime.

In summary, a circular economy is proposed as a more sustainable alternative to the linear economic model of 'take–make–dispose' or 'take–produce–consume–discard', though the concept is still highly contested (for example, Korhonen et al, 2018; Prieto-Sandoval et al, 2018). A common definition is the three, or increasingly four,[7] Rs: 'reuse–repair–refurbish/repurpose/rethink–recycle'. In scientific literature, a multitude of definitions has been suggested in recent years within various disciplines (Kirchherr et al, 2017). Arguably the most widely used definition is that of the Ellen MacArthur Foundation (2013: 14), which introduced the concept as 'an industrial system that is restorative or regenerative by intention and design', being based on three principles: designing out waste and pollution; keeping products and materials in use; and regenerating natural systems (Ellen MacArthur Foundation, 2019). From a food system perspective, the redistribution of edible surplus via food aid, in fact, bypasses the principle of designing out waste, focusing instead on keeping food in use. Hierarchically, waste prevention should be the primary objective in waste management, with redistribution or food donation second (for example, European Union, 2010; Zero Waste Europe, 2019).

Yet, during the 2010s, the focus of media discussion about food aid has slowly moved from regarding it as a poverty-related problem towards regarding it as a means of environmental protection by preventing food waste. It is often argued that charitable food aid based on food waste recovery solves two problems: food waste and food poverty. Donating expiring food to charities seems to offer a genuine win–win situation as it evokes a strong feeling of doing good – saving the planet by fighting food poverty. Essentially, the environmental motive behind emergency food aid delivery offers a positive interpretational framework for food charities, in contrast to the earlier image of labelling food poverty as an iniquitous societal problem (Tikka, 2019). The significance of this shift is in its potential to guide public opinion even further from defending state welfare responsibilities towards accepting a more liberal welfare regime that includes mixed private–public solutions to structural social problems like food poverty (Tikka, 2019).

Furthermore, food waste recovery is explicitly endorsed by the FEAD, which supports schemes that collect and distribute food donations with the intention of reducing food waste. Actually, one of the main principles of the programme is 'considering the possible impact of the earth's climate when purchasing food, and making an effort to reduce food waste' (European Commission, 2015). Thus, the programme directly encourages the redistribution of expiring food and market excess to food charities. Again, this connects the FEAD to the disposal end of the prevailing food system and, finally, to a circular economy (Salonen and Silvasti, 2019).

The ramifications of framing food aid for the poor as food waste recovery can already be seen at the policy level. For example, France banned large shops from throwing away or destroying unsold food in 2016. Instead, retailers are obliged to donate this food to charities or send it away for animal feed. Once again, the rationale behind the legislation is tackling food waste and food poverty in tandem (Chrisafis, 2015). Similar laws are being advocated all over Europe, and in 2016, over 100 members of the Finnish Parliament signed a corresponding legislative initiative (Lakialoite, 2016). The initiative was positively received by the media, but retailers have opposed the proposed legislation, pointing out that bilateral agreements with charities already address the issue adequately and that these practices, relying heavily on volunteer work, might not be able to handle the sudden influx of donations (Kärppä, 2016). At the time of writing, the initiative is still going through the parliamentary process.

Reducing food waste is necessary both ethically and on the grounds of environmental protection. However, in the context of charitable food poverty relief, food waste recovery as part of a circular economy needs to be critically explored. Basically, food waste recovery means transforming food once classified as 'inedible' (for example, expiring or otherwise unmarketable food) back into 'edible' food in order to prevent food waste. In the case of food charity, food classified as inedible for wealthy consumers, who can afford to satisfy their basic need for food in the market, is transformed back into being edible for people suffering food poverty.

Food charities usually depend on donations consisting mostly of expiring and surplus food. The supply varies according to market conditions, and charities can distribute only what is donated to them. This means that the only way to guarantee charitable food provision for the people in need of food aid is to guarantee the availability of market excess. From an environmental point of view, this is absolutely unsustainable because securing charitable food delivery is, in fact, based on overproduction and oversupply in the primary market. For environmental protection, minimising overproduction is the only satisfactory solution. Again, from a social policy perspective, charitable food provision can, at best, be a temporary remedy for acute hunger; it does not contribute in any way to solving the structural root causes of poverty. Thus, food charity as part of a circular economy is an indication of, rather than a solution to, the stubborn problems of food poverty as well as food waste (Kortetmäki and Silvasti, 2017; Salonen and Silvasti, 2019). Food waste recovery can be used in the management and rerouting of surplus food but, in the end, it does not offer a proper tool for environmental protection. Instead, it raises concerns over social justice and equity.

Alongside the circular economy, emerging forms of the so-called charity economy bring up new ways to frame charitable food provision as part of a social security system, as well as part of the general economic system. The prevailing food system is part of the market economy. The charity economy forms a kind of 'secondary market', distributing surplus produced in the primary market to people whose lack of purchasing power excludes them from this primary market. Thus, a charity economy is mostly based on donations. Basically, it creates an alternative distribution system where donated necessities – which are in demand to satisfy basic needs – are distributed further down the line to people in need (Kessl, 2015; Kessl et al, 2016). Food donations mainly comprise products that remain unsold in the primary market. Other consumer goods, like clothes and shoes, may be personal donations consisting of used or useless goods. These usually unwanted or discarded consumer goods are then redistributed from primary markets or primary users for charitable purposes. In charities, the logistics and delivery of donated necessities are often arranged by volunteers and low-paid workers – for example, supported rehabilitees – or by people performing community or civilian services.

The charity economy serves and seamlessly supplements the contemporary capitalist business model based on supply-side economics by organising new ways to get rid of system-based market excess while saving money on waste management. As donors, private businesses can pose as benefactors and report the positive outcomes of their corporate social responsibility activities because, as previously mentioned, donating surplus food to charities evokes a strong feeling of contributing to saving the planet while fighting food poverty. The people who rely on food aid benefit the primary market by utilising its excess. The more dependent poverty relief efforts are on charity, the more necessary donations are. Furthermore, by taking care of surplus produced in the primary market, a charity economy paves the way for the continuation of systematic overproduction in the prevailing unsustainable production system (Kortetmäki and Silvasti, 2017; Salonen and Silvasti, 2019).

The rise of the charity economy is based on changes in public welfare responsibilities and, especially, on giving up the former social policy goal of eradicating poverty. Actually, charities operate, grow and develop their functions in awareness of the fact that there are a permanently large enough number of people who live constantly or repeatedly in poverty deep enough to threaten their ability to satisfy their basic needs. As a result of austerity policies connected to growing income inequalities and harsh activation policy measures, an increasing number of people living on basic social security cannot cope without charitable assistance. What is more, work is evidently not the best social policy as the breakdown of the traditional connection between poverty and unemployment is becoming more apparent (Tanner, 2019). The permanent precariousness of paid work – in the form of temporary positions and jobs without a living wage – increases the poverty that leads to the need for charity.

Conclusions

Within the Nordic welfare state model, distributing non-monetary social assistance, such as food, has always been considered to be disrespectful. In the current consumer society, the replacement of monetary benefits with goods is construed as patronising poor people by restricting their freedom of choice (Lorenz, 2015). Even though providing charitable food aid as a means to alleviate poverty is incompatible with the Nordic welfare regime, over the last 25 years, charitable food aid provision has become established as part of the poverty relief of last resort in Finland.

Retrospectively, it can be seen that during the 1990s and 2000s, the development of food aid provision was haphazard and poorly coordinated. The most important policy sectors to have an impact on cementing the position of charitable food aid were agriculture (the ministry with executive responsibility for the MDP) and social affairs (the ministry with executive responsibility for poverty policy). Decision-making on food aid happened without explicit leadership, or proper coordination and communication between these policy sectors. Given the differing goals and contexts of different policies, no government department made any informed drive to permanently establish charity food provision in Finland. Rather, this establishment was the outcome of a confused situation, involving different policy actions and economic developments that took place simultaneously but were independent in practice.

Once established, charitable food provision seems to be very hard to abolish, and there has been no serious attempt in Finland to do so. Instead, food aid – originally interpreted as a symptom of poverty – is nowadays often framed as food waste recovery and, as such, a positive environmental act as part of a circular economy. This interpretative combination of a poverty frame and an environmental frame constitutes a new form of legitimisation for charitable responses to the issue of poverty as they promise to solve two problems at the same time: food poverty and food waste. The relevance of this shift lies in its potential to guide public opinion from defending public welfare responsibilities to accepting charity-based, mixed private–public solutions to the structural social problem of poverty (Tikka, 2019).

The circular economy is intertwined with emerging forms of the charity economy as food charities are utilised in redistributing market excess by delivering market surplus to people afflicted with poverty. Charities actually operate, grow and develop in awareness of the fact that there are a permanently large enough number of people living precariously in poverty deep enough to threaten their ability to satisfy their basic needs. The most serious problem in presenting charity as a solution to poverty is social injustice. The right to food is a basic human right. People afflicted by food poverty do not have any legal right to charitable food aid. It is not possible to fully respect, protect and fulfil this human right to food through charitable gifts (Poppendieck, 1999; Ziegler et al, 2011). Thus, food waste recovery performed as part of a circular economy and relying on charities can be used in the management of surplus food; however, they do not provide a solution to the root causes of environmental problems or poverty. Instead, they raise concerns over social justice and equity.

Recent developments in charitable food provision in Finland have been characterised by the introduction of various private–public solutions to poverty relief. The process behind this situation is still obscure. The MSAH publicly maintains its commitment to a Nordic welfare state regime and the ideal of public responsibility by explicitly stating that charitable food aid is not part of the national social security system, but a form of 'civic activity' (MSAH, 2017a). However, between 2016 and 2019, the MSAH allocated funding for charitable food aid provision for the first time. This proves that the MSAH is actively taking part in building new charity-based private–public food aid provision models in Finland.

Many of these new initiatives emphasise the social and communal aspects of the aid, shifting the focus from hunger alleviation to providing opportunities for people in need to engage in society. Therefore, the primary social problem addressed is not so much poverty, but social exclusion. Food provision is presented as more of an initial incentive for prospective recipients, not the main focus of these practices. These new developments also present an unprecedentedly high level of coordination in the otherwise patchy field of food aid in Finland. The changes may foreshadow a shift away from spartan breadlines towards more humane practices, where food aid provision is a kind of secondary element behind other social policy measures aiming to boost social inclusion. On the other hand, this mode of operation is likely to exclude some of the people in need of food aid as they are not able or willing to partake in social interaction.

Furthermore, the development of this mixed private–public charitable system of poverty relief still falls disturbingly between administrative sectors as the FEAD (which replaced the MDP in 2014) comes under the administrative domain of the Ministry of Economic Affairs and Employment. This fragmentation of the administration, funding and leadership of food aid provision leads to a situation where no one has overall control. Instead, the development of future food aid provision actually takes place in the shadow of the public institutional arrangements of the welfare state without any transparent democratic process. This increases the risk of future policy mismatches and arbitrary end results. In addition, the role of emerging intermediary organisations – such as Yhteinen pöytä and its regional counterparts, and the planned Food Aid Network – is not yet fully known. Currently, the fragmented food aid sector as a whole is poorly documented, lacks coordination and arguably does not cover the nation fairly, comprehensively or inclusively. It remains to be seen whether the new initiatives can provide solutions to these issues.

Since the Second World War, the Finnish welfare state has been developed in the spirit of the Nordic ethos of welfare. The course of development has been from individual responsibility to collective social insurance and risk management, from Church and philanthropy to public sector and state responsibility, and, notably, from charity to social rights. In an apparently Nordic welfare state, leaving people afflicted by poverty to the mercy of charity represents a clear change in the development of social policy. Food aid provision can be interpreted as a form of residual social policy supplemented by private charity that is the opposite of the universalism integral to the Nordic welfare model. From a social justice perspective, charitable actors delivering food aid actually jeopardise social rights by taking an active part in dismantling the welfare state and public responsibility for the most vulnerable. In the end, rooting a charitable response to the basic need for food in 'civic activity' inevitably violates universal social rights. Respecting social rights universally, as has previously been emphasised, is a cornerstone of the Nordic welfare state model.

Notes

[1] The European Committee of Social Rights is an impartial investigative body working within the Council of Europe that examines whether the countries that have accepted the European Social Charter are adhering to its requirements.

[2] The labour market subsidy is a means-tested benefit intended for unemployed persons who enter the labour market for the first time or who can no longer receive basic or earnings-related unemployment allowance since the maximum payment period for these benefits has been reached.

[3] Data gathered on 25 March 2019 from the STEA grant database (see: http://avustukset.stea.fi/).

[4] Food aid enterprises do receive substantial public funding from cities and municipalities as grants, but Yhteinen pöytä is still a first, being founded, funded and partly owned by the city.

[5] The Kotimaisen avustustyön liitto KOA ry (Association for Domestic Relief Work), formerly the Ruoka-apu Yhdistysten Liitto RAYL ry (Food Aid Organisations' Union).

[6] A research and development institute working under the MSAH.

[7] At the high end of the R-scale, the 'six Rs of sustainability' – prominently used by NGOs – adds 'reduce' and 'refuse' to the list (for example, Practical Action, 2019).

References

Arcuri, S. (2019) 'Food poverty, food waste and the consensus frame on charitable food redistribution in Italy', *Agriculture and Human Values*, 36(2): 263–75, https://doi.org/10.1007/s10460-019-09918-1

Chrisafis, A. (2015) 'France to force big supermarkets to give unsold food to charities', www.theguardian.com/world/2015/may/22/france-to-force-big-supermarkets-to-give-away-unsold-food-to-charity

Ellen MacArthur Foundation (2013) 'Towards the circular economy. Vol. 1: an economic and business rationale for an accelerated transition', www.ellenmacarthurfoundation.org/publications/towards-the-circular-economy-vol-1-an-economic-and-business-rationale-for-an-accelerated-transition

Ellen MacArthur Foundation (2019) 'What is a circular economy?', www.ellenmacarthurfoundation.org/circular-economy/concept

European Commission (2015) *The Fund for European Aid to the Most Deprived (FEAD): Breaking the vicious circle of poverty and deprivation*, Luxembourg: Publications Office of the European Union.

European Commission (2017) 'Report from the Commission to the European Parliament, the Council, the European Economic and Social Committee and the Committee of the Regions: on the implementation of the Circular Economy Action Plan', https://ec.europa.eu/commission/publications/report-implementation-circular-economy-action-plan-1_en

European Commission (2018) 'Annual implementation report summary – Finland', https://ec.europa.eu/social/main.jsp?catId=1239&langId=en&intPageId=3611

European Social Charter (2018) 'European Committee of Social Rights: conclusions 2017 Finland', https://um.fi/documents/3573 2/0/12.+uudistettu+raportti%2C+lokakuu+2016+p%C3%A4%C3%A4telm%C3%A4t.pdf/333396f8-8b5b-2f8f-e1ac-aa572135925d

European Union (2010) *Being wise with waste: The EU's approach to waste management*, Luxembourg: Publications Office of the European Union.

Eurostat (2019a) 'Gini coefficient of equivalised disposable income – EU-SILC survey', http://appsso.eurostat.ec.europa.eu/nui/show.do?dataset=ilc_di12

Eurostat (2019b) 'Inability to afford a meal with meat, chicken, fish (or vegetarian equivalent) every second day – EU-SILC survey', http://appsso.eurostat.ec.europa.eu/nui/show.do?dataset=ilc_mdes03&lang=en

Evira (2013) 'Foodstuffs donated to food aid', www.ruokavirasto.fi/globalassets/tietoa-meista/asiointi/oppaat-ja-lomakkeet/yritykset/elintarvikeala/food-lomakkeet---ohjeet/eviran_ohje_16035_2_uk.pdf

FEBA (European Federation of Food Banks) (2016) 'Circular economy in favour of the most deprived: addressing food waste through food redistribution', FEBA position paper, www.eurofoodbank.org/images/cont/position-paper-circular-economy---review_file.pdf

Hänninen, S. (1994) 'Nälästä' ['On Hunger'], in M. Heikkilä, S. Hänninen, J. Karjalainen, O. Kontula and K. Koskela (eds) *Nälkä* [*Hunger*], Helsinki: Stakes and STM, pp 3–13.

Hanssen, O.J., Ekegren, P., Gram-Hanssen, I., Korpela, P., Langevad-Clifforth, N., Skov-Olsen, K., Silvennoinen, K., Stare, M., Stenmarck, Å. and Svanes E. (2014) *Food redistribution in the Nordic region: Experiences and results from a pilot study*, Copenhagen: Nordic Council of Ministers.

Heikkilä, M. and Karjalainen, J. (1998) *Leaks in the safety net: The role of civil dialogue in the Finnish inclusion policy*, Helsinki: Stakes.

Karjalainen, J. (2008) 'Nälkä-äläkästä Nälkäryhmään. Tutkimus, ruokapankit ja politiikka lehdistössä' ['From hunger-uproar to the Hunger Group: research, food banks and politics in media'], in S. Hänninen, J. Karjalainen, K.-M. Lehtelä and T. Silvasti (eds) *Toisten Pankki. Ruoka-apu Hyvinvointivaltiossa* [*A bank for the others: Food aid in a welfare state*], Helsinki: Stakes, pp 69–114.

Kärppä, H. (2016) 'Kaupat tyrmäävät hävikkiruuan pakollisen jakelun' ['Stores shoot down mandatory redistribution of food waste'], www. hs.fi/talous/art-2000002903241.html

Kela (Social Insurance Institution of Finland) (2017) 'Perustoimeentulotuen siirto Kelaan, Kelan sisäinen arviointi 2017' ['Transfer of basic income support to Kela, Internal assessment 2017'], www.kela.fi/documents/10180/3571044/toturaportti0806. pdf/06f4fd6b-50de-4302-b6ea-ac5c2adb0ae9

Keskitalo, E. (2008) 'Balancing social citizenship and new paternalism: Finnish activation policy and street-level practice in a comparative perspective', PhD dissertation, University of Helsinki.

Kessl, F. (2015) 'Charity economy – a symbol of fundamental shift in Europe', *Tidsskrift for Socialpedagogik*, 18(1): 147–52.

Kessl, F., Oechler, M. and Schroeder, T. (2016) 'Charity economy', in F. Kessl, W. Lorenz, H.-U. Otto and S. White (eds) *European social work – A compendium*, Leverkusen and Farmington Hills: Barbara Budrich Publishers.

Kirchherr, J., Reike, D. and Hekkert, M. (2017) 'Conceptualizing the circular economy: an analysis of 114 definitions', *Resources, Conservation & Recycling*, 127: 221–32.

Kirkko ja kaupunki (2017) 'Seurakuntien ruoka-apua tarvitsee paljon enemmän kuin 100 000 suomalaista' ['More than 100,000 Finns in need of food assistance from parishes'], www.kirkkojakaupunki.fi/-/seurakuntien-ruoka-apua-tarvitsee-paljon-enemman-kuin-100-000-suomalaista

Kirkkopalvelut (2014) 'EU-elintarviketuki – Ruokaa tarvitseville' ['EU food aid – food for those in need'], Wayback Machine, https://web.archive.org/web/20140718111213/http:/www.kirkkopalvelut.fi/eu-elintarviketuki

Kirkkopalvelut (2018) 'Ruoka-avusta loppukuun oljenkorsi: Seurakunnat jakoivat ruokaa 100 000 ihmiselle' ['Getting by with food aid: parishes distributed food to 100,000 people'], www.kirkkopalvelut.fi/Ruoka-avusta+loppukuun+oljenkorsi%3A+Seurakunnat+jakoivat+ruokaa+100+000+ihmiselle

Kontula, O. and Koskela, K. (1993) *Taloudellisen laman terveysvaikutuksia 1992–1993* [*Impact of economic recession on health during 1992–1993*], Sosiaali- ja terveysministeriön julkaisuja, Helsinki: STM.

Korhonen, J., Nuur, C., Feldmann, A. and Birkie, S.E. (2018) 'Circular economy as an essentially contested concept', *Journal of Cleaner Production*, 175: 544–52.

Kortetmäki, T. and Silvasti, T. (2017) 'Charitable food aid in a Nordic welfare state: a case for environmental and social injustice', in A.-L. Matthies and K. Närhi (eds) *The ecosocial transition of societies: The contribution of social work and social policy*, Abingdon: Routledge, pp 219–33.

Kotimaanapu (2019) 'Ruokaturva' ['Food security'], https://kotimaanapu.fi/ruokaturva/

Kuivalainen, S. (2010) 'Kestääkö suomalainen vähimmäisturva pohjoismaisen vertailun? Vertaileva analyysi vähimmäisturvan tasosta ja sen köyhyyttä ehkäisevästä vaikutuksesta neljässä Pohjoismaassa 1990–2005' ['Does Finnish basic social security stand up to Nordic comparison? Comparative analysis of the level of basic social security and its anti-poverty impact in four Nordic countries in 1990–2005'], *Yhteiskuntapolitiikka*, 75(4): 377–88.

Laihiala, T. (2018) *Kokemuksia ja käsityksiä leipäjonoista: Huono-osaisuus, häpeä ja ansaitsevuus* [*Disadvantagedness, shame and deservingness among the recipients of charity food aid in Finland*], Kuopio: Publications of the University of Eastern Finland.

Lakialoite (2016) 'Lakialoite laiksi elintarvikelain muuttamiseksi' ['Bill to amend Food Act'], www.eduskunta.fi/FI/vaski/KasittelytiedotValtiopaivaasia/Sivut/LA_29+2016.aspx

Lorenz, S. (2015) 'Having no choice: social exclusion in the affluent society', *Journal of Exclusion Studies*, 5(1): 1–17.

Malkavaara, M. (2002) 'Nälkä ja köyhyys kirkon asiaksi. Näkökulmia laman ja markkinakilpailun aikaan' ['Hunger and poverty into churches' agenda. Perspectives on the era of recession and market competition'], in V. Mäkinen (ed) *Lasaruksesta leipäjonoihin. Köyhyys kirkon kysymyksenä* [*From Lazarus to breadlines: Church and the question of poverty*], Jyväskylä: Atena, pp 283–312.

Mavi (2018) 'Tiivistelmä komission 17.07.2018 hyväksymästä Vähävaraisten avun toimenpideohjelman 2014-2020 vuoden 2017 täytäntöönpanoraportista' ['Implementation report summary for the FEAD Action Program 2017–2020'], www.ruokavirasto.fi/globalassets/tietoa-meista/asiointi/oppaat-ja-lomakkeet/yhteisot/tuet-ja-kehittaminen/tiivistelma_taytantoonpanoraportti_2017_fead.pdf

McMahon, M. (2011) Personal correspondence, 16 October, Food Sovereignty versus Global Philanthropy Conference, University of British Columbia, Vancouver, 10 October.

Ministry of Economic Affairs and Employment (2019) 'The Fund for European Food Aid to the Most Deprived (FEAD) 2014–2020', https://tem.fi/en/the-fund-for-european-aid-to-the-most-deprived-fead-2014-2020

MSAH (Ministry of Social Affairs and Health) (2016) 'Yli miljoona euroa valtionapua erityisen tuen tarpeessa olevien auttamiseksi' ['Over €1 million in state aid to help those in need of special support'], Tiedote 165/2016, https://stm.fi/artikkeli/-/asset_publisher/yli-miljoona-euroa-valtionapua-erityisen-tuen-tarpeessa-olevien-auttamiseksi

MSAH (2017a) 'STM: Suomalaisten osallisuuteen vaikutetaan ruoka-apua tehokkaammin varmistamalla yhteiskunnan rakenteiden toimivuus' ['Social inclusion in Finland is more effectively advanced by ensuring functioning structures in society, not via food charity'], Tiedote 205/2017, https://stm.fi/artikkeli/-/asset_publisher/stm-suomalaisten-osallisuuteen-vaikutetaan-ruoka-apua-tehokkaammin-varmistamalla-yhteiskunnan-rakenteiden-toimivuus

MSAH (2017b) 'Sosiaali- ja terveysministeriö jakoi valtionavustuksia ruoka-apuun ja päihderiippuvaisten tukemiseen' ['Ministry of Social Affairs and Health granted state aid to food aid and to support for addicts'], Tiedote 139/2017, https://stm.fi/artikkeli/-/asset_publisher/sosiaali-ja-terveysministerio-jakoi-valtionavustuksia-ruoka-apuun-ja-paihderiippuvaisten-tukemiseen

MSAH (2019a) 'Valtionavustukset ruoka-apuun'] ['State grants to food charity'], https://stm.fi/rahoitus-ja-avustukset/ruoka-apu

MSAH (2019b) 'Activation model for unemployment security', https://stm.fi/en/unemployment/activation-model-for-unemployment-security

Official Statistics of Finland (2018) 'Income distribution statistics: income inequality international comparison 2016', www.stat.fi/til/tjt/2016/04/tjt_2016_04_2018-05-24_tie_001_en.html

Ohisalo, M. (2013) 'EU:n ruoka-apuohjelman vaikutus ruoka-avun vakiintumiseen Suomessa' ['The impact of the EU food aid programme on the entrenchment of food aid in Finland'], in M. Niemelä and J. Saari (eds) *Huono-osaisten hyvinvointi Suomessa* [*Welfare of the disadvantaged in Finland*], Helsinki: Kela, pp 146–72.

Ohisalo, M. (2014) 'Kuka tahansa meistä? Sosioekonominen asema ruoka-avussa' ['Anyone of us? Socio-economic status in food aid'], in M. Ohisalo and J. Saari (eds) *Kuka seisoo leipäjonossa? Ruoka-apu 2010-luvun Suomessa* [*Who stands in line? Food charity in 2010s' Finland*], Helsinki: KAKS – Kunnallisalan kehittämissäätiö, pp 27–41.

Ohisalo, M. (2017) *Murusia hyvinvointivaltion pohjalla: Leipäjonot, koettu hyvinvointi ja huono-osaisuus* [*Crumbs at the bottom of a welfare state. Charity food aid and subjective well-being of the disadvantaged*], Kuopio: Publications of the University of Eastern Finland.

Ohisalo, M. and Määttä, A. (2014) 'Viimeisen luukun jälkeen – ruoka-avussa käyvien paikka julkisessa palvelu- ja tulonsiirtoverkossa' ['After the final counter – positioning food-aid-goers in the network of public services and income transfers'], in M. Ohisalo and J. Saari (eds) *Kuka seisoo leipäjonossa? Ruoka-apu 2010-luvun Suomessa* [*Who stands in line? Food charity in 2010s' Finland*], Helsinki: KAKS – Kunnallisalan kehittämissäätiö, pp 42–58.

Ohisalo, M., Eskelinen, N., Laine, J., Kainulainen, S. and Saari, J. (2014) *Avun tilkkutäkki: suomalaisen ruoka-apukentän monimuotoisuus* [*Patchwork quilt of aid: The diversity of the field of Finnish food aid*], Avustustoiminnan julkaisuja, Helsinki: Raha-automaattiyhdistys.

Poppendieck, J. (1999) *Sweet charity? Emergency food and the end of entitlement*, New York, NY: Penguin Books.

Practical Action (2019) '6 R's', https://practicalaction.org/schools/6-rs/#resources

Prieto-Sandoval, V., Jaca, C. and Ormazabal, M. (2018) 'Towards a consensus on the circular economy', *Journal of Cleaner Production*, 179: 605–15.

Riches, G. and Silvasti, T. (2014) *First world hunger revisited: Food charity or the right to food?* (2nd edn), Basingstoke: Palgrave Macmillan.

Salonen, A. (2016) 'Food for the soul or the soul for food: users' perspectives on religiously affiliated food charity in a Finnish city', PhD dissertation, University of Helsinki.

Salonen, A.S. and Silvasti, T. (2019) 'Faith based organizations as actors in the charity economy: a case study of food assistance in Finland', in H. Gaisbauer, G. Schweiger and C. Sedmak (eds) *Absolute poverty in Europe: Interdisciplinary perspectives on a hidden phenomenon*, Bristol: Policy Press, pp 289–312.

Samaria (2018) 'Sosiaali- ja terveysministeriön myöntämän valtionavustuksen vaikutus järjestöjen ruoka-avustustyöhön 2016-2017 Samarian hakemissa avustuskokonaisuuksissa' ['Impact of the state grant issued by the Ministry of Social Affairs and Health on food aid activities in 2016–2017 in the grant units applied to by Samaria'], Arviointiraportti 1/2018, www.samaria.fi/documents/582388/716268/Ruoka-apu%2C+arviointiraportti+2018/39bbd0a0-533d-4b77-aa89-e85d08e52cee

Silvasti, T. (2015) 'Food aid – normalising the abnormal in Finland', *Social Policy and Society*, 14(3): 471–82.

Silvasti, T. and Karjalainen, J. (2014) 'Hunger in a Nordic welfare state: Finland', in G. Riches and T. Silvasti (eds) *First world hunger revisited: Food charity or the right to food?*, Basingstoke: Palgrave Macmillan, pp 72–86.

Sitra (2016) 'Leading the cycle – Finnish road map to a circular economy 2016–2025', https://media.sitra.fi/2017/02/24032659/Selvityksia121.pdf

Sitra (2019) 'Spreading the Shared Table model of community food assistance', www.sitra.fi/en/projects/spreading-shared-table-model-community-food-assistance/

Tanner, N. (2019) 'Töissä, mutta köyhä. Palkkatyököyhyys ja sen kustannukset ravintola- ja kiintoistöpalvelualoilla' ['Working poor: income poverty and its costs in the restaurant and real estate services sectors'], PAM 3/2019, www.pam.fi/media/1.-materiaalipankki-tiedostot-nakyvat-julkisessa-materiaalipankissa/tilastot-ja-tutkimukset/1342_palkkatyokoyhyys.pdf

THL (National Institute for Health and Welfare) (2019) 'Evaluation report on the adequacy of basic social security 2015–2019', www.julkari.fi/bitstream/handle/10024/137711/URN_ISBN_978-952-343-296-3.pdf?sequence=1&isAllowed=y

Tikka, V. (2019) 'Charitable food aid in Finland: from a social issue to an environmental solution', *Agriculture and Human Values*, 36(2): 341–52, https://doi.org/10.1007/s10460-019-09916-3

UNICEF (United Nations Children's Fund) Finland (2019) 'Kun UNICEF auttoi Suomea' ['When UNICEF aided Finland'], www.unicef.fi/unicef/historia/

Valtioneuvosto (2015) 'Finland, a land of solutions: strategic programme of Prime Minister Juha Sipilä's government', https://valtioneuvosto.fi/documents/10184/1427398/Ratkaisujen+Suomi_EN_YHDISTETTY_netti.pdf/8d2e1a66-e24a-4073-8303-ee3127fbfcac

Valtioneuvosto (2017) 'Finland, a land of solutions: mid-term review. Government action plan 2017–2019', https://valtioneuvosto.fi/documents/10184/321857/Government+action+plan+28092017+en.pdf

Yhteinen keittiö (Communal Kitchen) (2019) 'Home page', https://yhteinenkeittio.fi

Yhteinen pöytä (2016) 'Ruoka-avusta kansalaistoiminnaksi' ['From food charity to civil activity'], www.slideshare.net/Havikkiviikko/yhteinen-pyt-hankkeen-esitys-hvikkiruoan-hydyntmisest

Yhteinen pöytä (2019) 'Yhteinen Pöytä – Shared Table briefly in English', www.yhteinenpoyta.fi/en/

YLE (Yleisradio Oy) (1990) 'Pääministeri Holkeri kehotti suomalaisia syömään silakkaa' ['Prime Minister Holkeri advised citizens to eat herring'], https://yle.fi/aihe/artikkeli/2014/09/04/paaministeri-holkeri-kehotti-suomalaisia-syomaan-silakkaa?fbclid=IwAR20FnLyS_aW03wXDadTYnKRg9M40EEJmDDyqoegYtDqihavAVMi-JgsSyk

Zero Waste Europe (2019) 'Food systems: a recipe for food waste prevention. Policy briefing', https://zerowasteeurope.eu/downloads/food-systems-a-recipe-for-food-waste-prevention/

Ziegler, J., Golay, C., Mahon, G. and Way, S. (2011) *The fight for the right to food: Lessons learned*, Geneva: Palgrave Macmillan.

2

Social exclusion and food assistance in Germany

Fabian Kessl, Stephan Lorenz and Holger Schoneville

Introduction

While countries with widespread existential poverty need to fight hunger (for example, Rocha, 2014), this issue no longer seemed to be a problem for the German welfare state. As in other welfare regimes in the 20th century, issues of survival have ceased to determine the social policy agenda, being replaced by questions of social and cultural participation. Having enough to eat has been regarded as a self-evident precondition of social inclusion. It is widely understood that the welfare state has to enable or care for people through its programmes of welfare provision in such a way that hunger does not become an issue that would need an extraordinary social intervention. Therefore, the massive boom in food charities in European welfare states since the 1990s has been surprising, at least at first glance.

Food charity in the German context is mainly represented by organisations called '*Tafel*'. This can be literally translated as 'dinner table'. *Tafel* initiatives[1] currently dominate the debate about food charity in Germany, while other forms are discussed much less, both politically and in society in general. Other forms of food charity in Germany might include soup kitchens or food aid at social service institutions (for example, free meals for users). Beyond charity, we can also find self-organised initiatives (for example, food sharing organisations) and for-profit forms (for example, charity clothes shops). *Tafel* initiatives started collecting and distributing excess food in Germany in the early 1990s, particularly following the example of voluntary food assistance activities in the US. During the first decade of these activities, *Tafel* initiatives experienced moderate growth, which has been followed by rapid expansion since the middle of the first decade of the 21st century. This development correlates with fundamental social policy changes initiated during 2003–05 (when the so-called Hartz-Gesetze – a new law – attempted to implement the concept of a social investment state and workfare paradigm at the federal level). According to the official numbers published regularly by Tafel Deutschland eV, while the number of organisations has more recently stabilised, it has still shown a slight increase, to 934 member initiatives with more than 2,100 outlets in 2017 (more detailed numbers will be discussed later).

What is it that makes food charity such a 'success story' in an affluent society like Germany? This chapter will shed light on the phenomenon. In order to give context to the boom in food charity, the first section introduces the debates about inequality, poverty, social exclusion and social policy developments that have been taking place in Germany since the 1990s. As new forms of precarisation have sprung up and inequality has grown over recent decades, the country has also witnessed a transformation of welfare (state) arrangements that is leaving those in need with less material support, more obligations and an increasing reliance on civil society and private support.

The second section examines the development of *Tafel* initiatives in more detail. It discusses their aims, and the voluntary activities involved in collecting food waste and providing charitable assistance. It then draws attention to certain contradictions between the means and ends of such charities. Building on the debates about social exclusion, it argues that the example of food banks illustrates what exclusion means in a contemporary affluent society. Finally, it outlines typical conflicts at *Tafel* outlets, which are a result of the contradictions in the food bank conception.

Politicians, the media and research into food banks often focus on food bank activities and activists. However, to evaluate the effects of such charities, it is necessary to gain independent access to the people in need. Only by understanding their problems can others evaluate what is helpful and what is not. The third section is therefore dedicated to users' perspectives.

The fourth section broadens the focus beyond food banks, arguing that food banks and similar organisations can be classed as a part of a new 'charity economy'. Their activities are not merely an additional role for civil society; rather, they have become more and more interwoven with established institutions within the structure of welfare. The charity economy is both a symbol and an integral part of the transformation of the German welfare state.

The authors share the view that only social rights can reliably safeguard people's basic social security. However, the trend of social policy transformations producing a charity economy shows that this is not the current direction of travel.

Changes in social welfare, exclusion and the role of civil society

While debates in the social sciences about exclusion traditionally revolved around classes or strata, starting in the 1980s, there was a gradual shift to thinking more about different milieus, pluralistic lifestyles or even individualisation. As a consequence, cultural diversity seemed to become a more important factor in explaining social differences than socio-economic stratification. However, the 1990s brought a stronger focus back on inequality, with a discourse about new kinds of social marginalisation and precarity. During this time, the term 'social exclusion' started to become more important in the German debate. A specific German discourse, with 'system theory' as its starting point, had formerly stressed the non-hierarchical social order of a functionally differentiated society before discovering the phenomenon of exclusion (Luhmann, 1995; Leisering, 2008; Stichweh, 2010).

The French conceptions of social exclusion, based on Bourdieu (1998), Paugam (2008) and particularly Castel (2002), became more influential in the German debate from the early 2000s (see Vester et al, 2001; Kronauer, 2002). Castel offers a conception of social integration with respect to employment and welfare institutions. Work itself is important for social integration but it is even more so because social security institutions have been based on employment throughout the historical process of establishing welfare systems, especially in so-called conservative welfare regimes like Germany (Esping-Andersen, 1990). Castel distinguishes between three zones: a zone of social integration; followed by vulnerable positions; and a zone of marginalisation and disaffiliation. The vulnerabilities of the middle zone have been the subject of a great deal of research, with a focus on precarisation (Castel and Dörre, 2009). Such precarisation and the loss of an effective collective lobby in a pluralised society have been analysed as preconditions of the new phenomenon of disaffiliation, with a related debate about social exclusion (Bude and Willisch, 2008). A similar threefold distinction was conceptualised by Offe (1996). He observes the former situation of social conflicts between upper and lower classes as extending with a new line of distinction even to people outside these traditional conflicts, that is, without the opportunity to participate in the fight against inequality. While he follows the tradition of a work society perspective, his conception can plausibly be adapted to food bank analysis following a consumption and affluent society perspective (Lorenz, 2015). In such societies, choice has become the main value in conducting one's life. In choosing from the huge offers provided by the affluent economy, consumers leave the non-chosen surplus on the shelves. *Tafel* initiatives distribute such excess to poor people who cannot participate in the choices because their consumer status has become fragile. Thus, having no choice is the analytical criterion of social exclusion (for further discussion of social exclusion, see Barlösius and Ludwig-Mayerhofer, 2001; Lorey, 2012).

Processes of exclusion are linked to changes in social policy and new roles for the activities of civil society. In the early 1990s, *Tafel* initiatives were initially met with criticism from politicians and public opinion in Germany. The idea of distributing excess food to people in need did not fit with the country's general perception of itself as a developed welfare state (Molling, 2009). However, in the late 1990s, this changed completely. The debate was no longer about inappropriate means of solving social problems that should not exist in an established welfare system at all. Instead, most politicians and the media appreciated and applauded the commitment of civil society activists and their private sponsors. This shift from a problem-centred perspective to a helper-centred perspective appeared to be part of a political trend. Since that time, the state has been regarded as an over-regulating actor that should become less influential in society, and it is commonly thought that private and civil society commitments should be re-evaluated. As a consequence of political deregulation, welfare programmes have changed to become workfare policies, and state-based support has been reduced.

Welfare reforms and the transformation of the German welfare state

The German welfare state has been subject to major reforms over the last 20 years. The reforms themselves can be linked to a wider international shift in the policy and politics of welfare. Neoliberal ideas of deregulation, recommodification and private responsibility were particularly powerful throughout the 1990s and early 2000s. However, actual changes in German welfare policy were influenced by a specific mixture of these neoliberal ideas and a social-democratic policy background. Workfare policies, the idea of social investments and the activation paradigm have been particularly strong concepts underpinning these reforms. The reforms in Germany, brought forward by the coalition of Social Democrats and the Green Party under Chancellor Gerhard Schröder, were similar – and partly linked – to the workfare policies of the government led by Bill Clinton in the US and the 'Third Way' politics of the British Labour government under Tony Blair. While there are similarities and links between the ideas and debates – and even examples of policy papers that were jointly written (Blair and Schroeder, 1998) – the specific reforms and resulting changes need to be evaluated in their particular national contexts (Scherschel et al, 2012).

Within Germany's conservative welfare system, a particular mix of policies led to a 'neo-social', rather than 'neoliberal', reconfiguration of the welfare state (Lessenich, 2008). The transformation of the German welfare state could not be accurately described as a reduction in efforts made by the state; rather, it was a reconfiguration within the structure of the welfare state, its programmes, targets and institutions. While the employment-based social insurance system is still at the core of the German welfare system, the composition of the system as a whole and the ideas that strongly influence it have changed.

Against the backdrop of the ideas of social investment and the activation of women in the workforce, programmes for childcare and early education have seen particular expansion and intensified interest. At the same time, drastic changes have been made to social policy programmes relating to unemployment and efforts to fight poverty. Unemployment insurance guarantees individuals an income equivalent to 60 per cent of their former salary. The duration of these payments has been cut and is now restricted to a maximum period of one year. After this time, citizens who are unemployed can apply for means-tested unemployment benefits, which are designed to cover only the bare minimum of living expenses. Based on the activation paradigm, recipients of unemployment benefits are faced with a much stricter regime in order to get them back into work, even in cases where the current market makes it unlikely that they will find employment. These changes have led to the diagnosis of a post-welfare situation: a welfare arrangement where the state is still very active as an investor in social benefits, but where there is a different understanding of how to treat people who are regarded as not engaged enough in the employment market for their personal well-being (see Kessl, 2009; Schoneville, 2018).

Poverty and unemployment: the socio-economic background

One dominant narrative is that the German society, especially in comparison with other European countries, is not only stable, but also prosperous. To support this argument, figures for unemployment and employment are often used as a key benchmark to judge the state of society. The argument is that despite the effects suffered by a number of European states and their social fabrics stemming from the banking crisis of 2008 and the resulting turmoil in financial markets, Germany has seen a remarkable reduction in its unemployment rate. An examination of the figures seems to provide support for this argument: the number of people recorded as unemployed by official statistics went down. While the rate was between 9.4 per cent and 11.7 per cent during the period from 1995 to 2005, the statistics show that the unemployment rate in 2018 was 5.3 per cent – the lowest rate since 1995, as shown in Figure 2.1.

Figure 2.1: Unemployment rate in Germany, 1995–2018

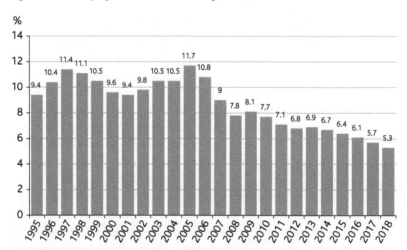

Note: Yearly averages (per cent) between 1995 and 2018.
Source: Figure compiled using data from Bundesagentur für Arbeit (2018: 60)

It is often argued that the reduction seen in the statistics is a direct outcome of the changes in social policy. The argument is that the shift to the social investment and workfare paradigm provided people with strong 'motivations' to apply for jobs (from a different perspective, this can be viewed as an initiative in which the state created an environment that 'forced' people into jobs). The general narrative focuses heavily on indices of economic growth and especially on the unemployment rate as a social benchmark. However, if the focus is widened and takes into account the development of incomes and the poverty rate, this appears to be much less of a success story. In the same years in which the unemployment rate fell from 11.7 per cent (in 2005) to 6.4 per cent (in 2015), the poverty rate rose from 13.9 per cent (in 2005) to 16.8 per cent (in 2015), as shown by Figure 2.2.

Figure 2.2: Poverty rate in Germany, 1995–2015

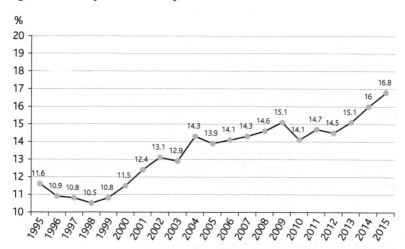

Notes: Poverty risk rate (<60 per cent of median income): yearly averages (in per cent).
Source: Figure compiled using data from German Federal Government (2017),
Socio-Economic Panel (SOEP) and German Institute for Economic Research (DIW)

The poverty rate shows that the proportion of people on very low incomes has increased over the years.[2] Despite the fact that there are fewer people registered as unemployed, the group living on less than 60 per cent of the median income has grown. Therefore, the poverty rate shows that the narrative of a success story – with the unemployment rate as its key indicator – does not hold up. The fact that fewer people are officially counted as unemployed does not translate to fewer people living below the relative poverty line. This phenomenon can mainly be explained by changes within the structure of the employment market, the growth in the number of people who can be classed as working poor and changes to welfare state programmes.

Despite the relatively low unemployment figure of 5.3 per cent shown in the statistics, it can be assumed that the group of people facing material difficulties within their everyday life is much larger than this. Government statistics show that 16.8 per cent of the German population was living below the relative poverty line in 2015. Other studies, which try to measure poverty in a more complex and multidimensional way, give even stronger results. A study by Groh-Samberg (2004, 2009) takes into account not only income, but also general living conditions (such as quality of housing, ability to make savings and effects of unemployment) to examine the impact of poverty and deprivation from a longitudinal perspective. In this way, the study was able to identify a group amounting to 8.4 per cent of the German population who faces severe hardship in multiple dimensions over a minimum period of four years. A further group representing 10.8 per cent is categorised as being in the zone of precarity and thus faces poverty and deprivation in at least one dimension over a minimum period of four years. One additional group equivalent to 5.7 per cent of the population is affected by poverty but for a period of less than four years. The study is therefore able to show that the bottom quarter of German society is confronted – in different ways and to different extents – with sometimes severe hardships in multiple dimensions of their lives. A large group – 19.2 per cent – is more or less permanently affected by poverty and precarity.

Food banks in Germany and the structural problems and conflicts of charitable food assistance

Food bank activities are mainly represented by *Tafel* initiatives in Germany. In contrast to food banks in other countries, they do not principally rely on a large infrastructure to support the collecting and storing of food for distribution to other charitable associations or institutions. Rather, collection and distribution activities are carried out by local *Tafel* initiatives themselves. However, this is more of a practical difference than a difference of principle. The next section introduces *Tafel* activities and discusses their structural ambivalences and misleading self-conceptions (Lorenz, 2012a), as well as resulting conflicts.

The development of Tafel initiatives, and public and scholarly debate around them

The development of *Tafel* started with the foundation of the first local initiative in Berlin in 1993. According to the story presented on the federal association of *Tafel* initiatives' own website, the foundation of the Berliner Tafel was based on the concept of the New York City Harvest (Tafel, no date). The Berliner Tafel is the biggest local initiative in Germany. It is reported that about 2,000 volunteers and 26 employees currently distribute 660 tons of food per month to 125,000 people (Berliner Tafel, 2018). At the federal level in 1995, a national association of *Tafel* initiatives was founded by 35 local initiatives. Tafel Deutschland eV (Tafel, 2017) provides various statistics. During the decade after the first food bank was founded – that is, between 1993 and 2003 – a moderate growth to 330 local *Tafel* initiatives took place. This was followed by a rapid increase resulting in 877 local initiatives running food banks by 2010. Thus, while the start of *Tafel* activities does not correlate with the previously mentioned social policy changes initiated between 2003 and 2005, the growth of *Tafel* activities does. Since around 2010, the number of local initiatives has stabilised, but there has still been some slight growth. In 2017, 934 member initiatives collected about 200,000 tons of food that was distributed via more than 2,100 outlets/pantries. A total of 60,000 people – mostly volunteers – are engaged in reaching about 1.5 million *Tafel* users. However, these numbers only include the activities of local initiatives that are members of Tafel Deutschland eV. As such, it is safe to assume that these numbers would be even higher if they took into account all the other channels for collecting food donations and distributing them to people in need for free or at a nominal price. These additional activities will be discussed in more detail later in the chapter.

As the example of Berlin shows, most *Tafel* activists are volunteers, but employees are involved in the organisation's operations too. Tafel Deutschland eV does not provide current data on its workforce. It normally refers to activists as volunteers, sometimes saying that 'most of them' are volunteers. In 2012, its website said that its 50,000 activists then included about 10 per cent working professionally in public relief roles (Tafel, 2012). For several years, people doing their *Bundesfreiwilligendienst* (publicly subsidised national voluntary service) have been able to complete their service with *Tafel* initiatives, with 740 active in 2016 (Bundesverband Deutsche Tafel, 2017).

An early study found that *Tafel* activists were mainly women and the elderly, who often had a religious affiliation, except in the eastern part of Germany where there was less religious commitment (Von Normann, 2003). Similarly, Selke (2008) reported that *Tafel* volunteers were often people at the end of their career or women who had previously been occupied with childcare. They were looking for new challenges and to find meaning in their life, or wanted to give something back after leading a busy working life. Selke and Maar (2011) also studied *Tafel* and similar social assistance activities carried out as part of the Caritas church initiative in one federal state. Women made up 80 per cent of volunteers, and the average age of voluntary activists was 63.

In accordance with the general conception of food banks, *Tafel* initiatives mainly focus on the collection of excess food and its distribution to poor people. Depending on local factors – such as the number of activists or sponsors available – food collection may take place on a weekly or daily basis and might also include specific food drives or charitable events. Distribution also varies between bigger and smaller local *Tafel* initiatives. For example, access may vary, with users being allowed to come once or twice a week, and being given prepared food parcels or having the opportunity to choose from the food available. However, Lorenz (2012b: 159–86) researched a variety of further activities using information available online from *Tafel* initiatives across Germany. Additional activities might include cooperation with supermarkets to receive monetary donations from bottle deposit schemes or distributing school equipment that is sponsored by businesses or private individuals. At the distribution end (which covers a range of very different forms of food distribution, food parcels and amounts of food), many *Tafel* initiatives offer further activities related to local opportunities, resources or ideas, sometimes in collaboration with other initiatives or associations. Clothes and cosmetics are often distributed too. Occasionally, furniture, household goods or medicine are made available. Some *Tafel* initiatives provide programmes for specific groups of people, for example, breakfast for schoolchildren or meal delivery services for the elderly. Also, leisure activities can be part of their range of offerings. Another field of activity is providing advice, for example, about how to handle disputes with landlords or other administrative problems. Finally, a range of educational courses can also be accessed, from cooking courses for children to language classes for migrants. Even so-called *Tafel* gardens have been started, where *Tafel* initiatives organise the growing of fruit and vegetables to then be distributed.

In 2015, Tafel Deutschland eV, the association on a national level, founded a *Tafel* academy to educate and train members, and to promote educational projects. Since 2004, the incumbent federal Minister of Family Affairs has acted as patron of the German *Tafel* initiatives. While there is no public sponsorship of the national association, such support can be found at local or federal state levels, for example, through the publicly funded jobs mentioned previously or financial support for the physical infrastructure of outlet facilities. Private sponsorship is differentiated by Tafel Deutschland eV into material donations, donated money and services (Bundesverband Deutsche Tafel, 2017: 30–6). The main sponsors are the big retailers MetroGroup, REWE and Lidl, as well the car manufacturer Mercedes-Benz.

A public and social science debate started after the large increase in this kind of charitable food assistance was highlighted (Selke, 2008, 2009, 2010; Lorenz, 2010). However, with the firm establishment of these charities, this discussion has abated over the years and may only come up on specific occasions or when scandals occur from time to time. Social science commentators have contributed critical views with regard to the decreased reliability of social policy support and about civil society food assistance as an inappropriate means to compensate for declining benefits. Some of the established charity organisations, particularly the church-based associations Caritas and Diakonie, have reinforced such criticisms by claiming professional standards for social assistance (Deutscher Caritasverband, 2008; Diakonie, 2010). Nevertheless, while *Tafel* initiatives started – and partly still act – as independent associations, they now more often (in 60 per cent of cases) work under the umbrella of long-established charity organisations, including Caritas and Diakonie (to be discussed later in this chapter). On the whole, a focus on the commitment of volunteers dominates the public debate, rather than the inappropriateness of such assistance for its users.

Structural ambivalences of food bank activities and the misunderstanding of hunger relief

In line with the general concept of food banks, the German *Tafel* initiatives aim to simultaneously tackle poverty and reduce food waste. They share these basic aims with other initiatives worldwide, and the European Federation of Food Banks (FEBA) encapsulated these several years ago in the slogan 'Fighting hunger and food waste'. Although social assistance is the more prominent aspect discussed in public debate, *Tafel* initiatives have also won awards for their commitment to the environment and sustainability. Delivering excess food to people in need appears to be an easy way to help them, and a win–win situation.

However, from an analytical point of view, one cannot just accept that these well-meaning activities are an appropriate means to address the situation (Lorenz, 2012a, 2012b). It is easy to see that there is a difference between aspiration and reality in the area of 'fighting food waste'. The reality is that *Tafel* activists typically complain about not receiving enough surplus food to distribute, rather than being happy that food waste has been reduced. This is the logical result of their contradictory conception of basing their social assistance efforts on a resource they want to fight against. Another contradiction follows from this: *Tafel* initiatives also collect saleable food from retailers' shelves – instead of discarded food – as part of sponsored events, for example, supported by their sponsor REWE, though this contradicts their basic guidelines.

The social assistance aspect is even more ambivalent. *Tafel* activists diagnose insufficient social rights as the motivation for their activities.

However, they cannot improve social rights through their charitable actions, but only relieve the pressure of poverty. The failure of its social assistance starts with the organisation's misunderstanding of 'fighting hunger' or food poverty. As mentioned previously, *Tafel* initiatives also often distribute items other than food but no one would talk about clothes poverty, cosmetics poverty, furniture poverty and so on. Empirical experience shows that the main problems in this area need to be addressed with a more comprehensive view of poverty and exclusion, though the phenomenon of food poverty or insecurity may well be part of this. People in need take whatever help they can get, whether that is in the form of food, clothes, cosmetics and so on, to compensate for deficits in any area of their everyday life, such as food, clothes, cosmetics and so on. Thus, there is no *specific* need for food, though receiving food cuts costs from the household budget and therefore helps them to get by. Talking about food poverty, or even hunger, obviously results from the main activities of food banking – collecting and distributing food. However, defining a want from the provided supply so that the need is only identified from the helpers' perspective is always problematic. It means missing the real underlying problems of users twice, that is, in their everyday life and also where social policy developments cause them problems. By referring to 'hunger', activists re-establish standards of social support from the 19th century in affluent contemporary Germany, instead of advocating for the higher standards of a developed welfare state or better conditions with regard to social inclusion.

The charitable food assistance of the *Tafel* initiatives highlights the problem of social exclusion as they practise at the dividing line between inclusion and exclusion but cannot overcome this problem through their own means. It is a one-way street of charitable supply and relief that cannot achieve social inclusion: it cannot give people a basic standard of living that would facilitate their participation in society. Adapting the social science conceptions of social exclusion introduced earlier in this chapter can illustrate what exclusion means in a contemporary affluent society. Users of *Tafel* initiatives, as well as users of other parts of the new 'charity economy' (see later) – soup kitchens or charity clothes shops – can be excluded in an existential way from the primary market and segregated into a secondary economic system. Castel (2002) and Offe (1996) differentiated categories of inclusion and exclusion. On the one hand, there are relations of inequality between positions of upper and lower social strata – or between more or less integrated or precarious positions – fighting for resources, rights and participation opportunities. On the other hand, we find positions of disaffiliation and exclusion. Social exclusion means positions and situations where people lack access to the basic needs for inclusion and do not even have a chance to take part in the struggle against the inequality of opportunity. This is what users of *Tafel* experience when they are no longer able to act as consumer-citizens in the dominant (capitalist) society.

However, while Castel and Offe describe exclusion from the perspective of a working society – with a focus on exclusion from waged labour and employment – the example of food banks highlights exclusion from the status of consumer in an affluent society. Lorenz (2015) lays out the pattern to be found in the case of food banks. While consumers choose from the huge offers provided by the affluent economy, they leave the non-chosen surplus on the shelves. *Tafel* initiatives distribute such excess to poor people who cannot participate in these choices because their consumer status has become fragile. This is not a question of unequal means of consumption, but an issue of exclusion from the very status of consumer. Having no choice but to take the leftovers of others' choices is what social exclusion and disaffiliation mean. In a society that makes choice a principal value in the conduct of one's life, being deprived of this consumer status is a massive loss. Charitable food assistance may relieve material pressure but it does not bring the excluded into a position of choice: it does nothing to help them achieve the normal consumer status enjoyed by everyone else in society. Instead, recipients are expected to be grateful and make the sponsors feel good for their help and reduction of food waste.

Tafel outlets as sites of social conflict

As the previous section makes clear, *Tafel* initiatives both represent and reproduce a social dividing line while working in an area of social tension. The pressure inherent in this situation mainly erupts in two specific ways at *Tafel* outlets. First, there are often conflicts between volunteers and recipients (Selke, 2008; Lorenz, 2012b). While recipients demand better treatment – for example, more opportunities to choose from the food that has been donated – volunteers reject what they call an 'entitlement mentality' on the part of users. Activists typically expect gratitude instead of demands, while some users want a form of consumer normality through being able to practise choice. This is a result and an expression of the underlying conflict. *Tafel* initiatives aim to support people who are in need at a very basic level. They often assess potential users' need – for example, by evaluating their indigence – on the basis of official documents that users have to present. They then provide what are called '*Tafel* passports': quasi-official documents enabling users to access help from *Tafel*. This can be enforced by administrative bodies that send people to *Tafel* initiatives for further help. This only takes place informally because administrative offices do not admit that state-based social support might be insufficient (Lorenz, 2012b: 220–37). However, as voluntary activists, *Tafel* volunteers cannot provide continual and reliable assistance. *Tafel* initiatives can only distribute what they have been able to collect, and they can only support people in need as long as volunteers are willing and able to give their time and effort. The largest numbers of volunteers do not consistently appear in the regions with the most recipients. Guaranteed provision of basic social benefits requires a legal basis and reliably functioning institutions.

Second, conflicts between migrant and non-migrant users are common at *Tafel* outlets. As *Tafel* users live in a situation of socio-economic marginalisation, some of them attempt to re-establish their social belonging at the expense of other excluded people (Lorenz, 2012b: 206–11), for example, by drawing a line between 'us' and 'them' using ethnic criteria. In early 2018, this situation escalated to the point where it became a public scandal in Germany. One local *Tafel* initiative decided not to allow new users to register without a German ID card. While representatives sought to justify the decision as a quasi-legal act – following the practice of issuing '*Tafel* passports' mentioned previously – it reinforced this line of conflict instead of de-escalating it. Such a decision quasi-officially confirmed that migrants are the problem – instead of the problem being a lack of functioning institutions providing government social assistance. Volunteers are overstressed from having to deal with the pressures and inherent tensions between social inclusion and exclusion. However, politicians' public indignation about this local decision proved to be hypocritical as it was not backed up with political efforts to ensure people's rights to basic social assistance and the infrastructure to deliver it.

Food bank users

While there is still insufficient empirical information on food bank users in Germany, especially concerning the quantitative dimensions and the socio-economic backgrounds of users, there has been an effort to conduct qualitative studies. These have provided knowledge regarding use practices, general living conditions and reasons and motivations behind the use of food banks, as well as their subjective relevance for individuals (Selke, 2008, 2013; Lorenz, 2012b; Schoneville, 2016). The most commonly used quantitative data regarding food bank users stem from the national association of German food banks.[3] The association claims that up to 1.5 million people use food banks regularly. While no detailed information about these 1.5 million users is available, some assumptions can be made regarding their socio-economic conditions. In most cases, local food banks only accept potential users if they can provide evidence that they are 'in need'. Organisationally, this is usually achieved by the provision of some form of official document. This means that most users are recipients of some kind of means-tested benefit provided by the German welfare state, for example, unemployment benefits, in-work benefits for people on very low salaries or subsidies for those on low pensions. This allows certain conclusions regarding their socio-economic living conditions to be drawn. People who qualify for such means-tested benefits live in economic situations below the relative poverty line in Germany. It can therefore be assumed – and the data from qualitative studies back this up – that food bank users in Germany live in relative poverty.

In a biographical study,[4] food bank users were asked to tell their life stories and give details of what led them to use a food bank. It showed that users themselves state that their food bank usage is a result of them living in poverty. Within the narrative constructions in the interviews, their economic situation is presented as a structural force driving their use of food banks. Their living situation is described as being characterised by continual shortage. Such shortage means that they are faced with exclusion from social and cultural participation. Activities like visits to the cinema and theatre, as well as holidays and short trips, are not possible. Similarly, providing school trips for their children and materials for school at the beginning of an academic year is financially challenging. Users also report that shopping for new clothes is a problem and can only be done during sales and if other costs are avoided. They describe the cost of food as a real burden within a tight financial household budget, especially groceries that they view as good and nutritious. In a few of the interviews, food bank users report that they have experienced situations where they were not able to provide food for themselves and their families, or its provision was only possible with severe restrictions regarding the quality and quantity of the food. The living conditions of food bank users can therefore be described as being dominated by shortage and a lack of basic goods and resources, as well as by the effects and processes of exclusion from certain forms of social and cultural participation, including their status as consumers.

Even with these motivations, it is quite often stated within the interviews that the process leading to the decision to use a food bank was neither easy nor purely rational and economic. Instead, the interviewees point out that the considerations were emotionally difficult and they had doubts for a long time. Some report that they tried to avoid using a food bank for as long as they were able. Within their narratives, the use of food banks goes hand in hand with negative classifications and stigmatisation (Neckel and Sutterlüty, 2005, 2008). Some potential users try to avoid these issues by not using food banks (Kunhenn, 2014; Schoneville, 2016). They often report that they were faced with an occasion when the worsening of their economic resources intensified to such a degree that they saw no alternative but to act despite their doubts. Therefore, the complex and emotionally difficult decision about food bank usage is itself situated within a context of everyday life that is shaped by exclusion from social and cultural participation, as well as the shortage of basic goods. These descriptions of living circumstances, reasons to use food banks and doubts about doing so can be understood as accounts of the 'silent force of deprivation' (Schoneville, 2016).

Within these narratives, food banks are thematised as not part of the 'normal' options that their users would usually consider. Users' descriptions make it clear that the offers of food banks are outside social norms, and they can therefore be read as accounts of exclusion from food provision within the market sphere (supermarkets and so on). Beyond that, food banks are identified by users as occupying a social position 'at the bottom' of society. This social inequality is also reflected in the products available, with the groceries offered seen as a symbolic representation of inequality. Interviewees express this by pointing out that the groceries in food banks are goods that customers in supermarkets did not want and left there (Schoneville, 2013). The users of food banks see themselves as being forced to consume food that was left over by those who have the financial resources to choose whether they want to buy something or not, while the food bank users themselves do not have the opportunity to choose. The deviation from social norms and the abnormality and negative classification that go hand in hand with food bank usage are all part of this social reality.

In theoretical terms, it would not be satisfactory to describe the relationship between food bank users and society as complete social exclusion. Rather, users experience simultaneous social exclusion and inclusion. The support that food banks provide can be understood as a form of 'secondary integration' (Land and Willisch, 2006). However, this type of inclusion is realised under conditions of exclusion from central forms of social participation. Food banks themselves are part of society but, at the same time, provide their services under conditions closely associated with forms of social exclusion. Simultaneous inclusion and exclusion is also noticeable in the identification of users with social norms and values. Contrary to the thesis of a 'culture of poverty', it can be observed that users identify strongly with social norms. However, they are faced with a reality of living conditions that do not allow these norms to be fulfilled, or at least endanger their fulfilment. Within the biographical interviews, food bank users emphasise again and again the relevance of work and employment to their lives. These narratives can be understood as a sign that the norms of working society are at the centre of food bank users' identities – despite the fact that the interviewees were unemployed at the time of their interviews. Similar forms can be found in relation to normative expectations of 'good parenting'. While parents who are faced with poverty address themselves with normative expectations of being good parents, they are simultaneously confronted with material difficulties that massively restrict the fulfilment of these normative self-expectations. They are therefore in a situation where their own idea of good parenting is constantly challenged (Schoneville, 2019). The lack of economic resources and the lack of opportunities to realise their own expectations shape the contradiction in the everyday lives of food bank users between their normative self-expectations and the structural possibilities to fulfil these norms.

This contradiction is a crucial factor in users' experience of shame. Shame, as the emotional reaction to a negative deviation from social norms, is embedded in the structure of social inequality (Neckel, 1992). The link between feelings of shame and poverty in general has been pointed out in a number of studies. Research projects that concentrate on the use of food banks in Germany (Lorenz, 2012b; Schoneville, 2013, 2016; Selke, 2013) and other European countries (Van der Horst et al, 2014; Garthwite, 2015) recognise that the general living situation of food bank users and the usage of food banks are entwined with feelings of shame. Empirical analysis shows that there are various interlinked reasons and occasions for shame impacting on food bank users. Their recognition that they are poor compared to the vast majority of society is one of the central reasons why people feel ashamed. Another reason for shame is being unemployed in a society where employment is regarded and enforced as a central norm of social integration. Distinguished from this first group, we can identify a second group of reasons for shame that stem from food banks being socially embedded in society. Food bank users express this in different ways but affiliation – and more specifically public affiliation – with a food bank (as a social place within society) becomes a reason for shame; therefore, visiting the food bank is an occasion for feelings of shame to occur. This is linked to the previously discussed more general form in which poverty is a reason for shame. A food bank is a social place that is socially designed for people 'in need'. It therefore becomes a place where users are visible as poor people and are confronted with this identification as being poor. Within the interviews, users quite often report that queuing in front of a food bank is an occasion when they feel ashamed because they can be seen by others as needing to use the food bank (Schoneville, 2016). The powerful eye of others confirms them publicly as people who use a food bank – a facility for people 'in need' – which definitively makes a user into someone who is poor. In similar ways, this is represented in the narratives heard when users talk about the food itself.

A third group of reasons is the specific interactions within food banks: organisational routines; things users think they have to do and ways they think they have to behave in order to receive goods; things that are said; and gestures by the volunteers. Within these interactions, users realise their own inferiority to the volunteers. They feel that they have to behave like someone who is 'in need' and must ask for basic forms of support. For food bank users, these interactions confirm the reality that the usage of food banks is based on a relationship of (personal) dependency.

While food banks in Germany are not officially part of welfare state institutions, links can be identified within the practices of usage that transcend a clear distinction between the welfare state, on the one hand, and civil society organisations, on the other.[5] Within the interviews, users confirm that representatives of state employment agencies explicitly point to local food banks as a possible source of additional support. Furthermore, other social work institutions support initial contact (Schoneville, 2016). The links are also reflected linguistically in the accounts of the users. For example, they report that they were 'referred' by an employee of a state employment agency. In another case, employees of a state shelter for male drug addicts 'helped' a user to go to a food bank. The linguistic codes show that the distinction between food banks and welfare institutions is more blurred than a formal analytical analysis might suggest.

The results of research with food bank users point to the contradictions in which food bank users find themselves. The food banks are part of these contradictions, offering a certain form of support, which is why users turn to them. However, food banks do not tackle poverty. They are neither able nor designed to overcome poverty; they are only capable of softening the harsh reality of poverty. However, in their form of individual emergency aid, food banks inevitably bring stigmatisation and social exclusion.

Charity economy

A perspective focusing only on food charity and one national association as the dominant actor is in danger of obstructing our general view regarding the transformation of welfare provision. The boom of *Tafel* initiatives in Germany or similar activities in other Organisation for Economic Co-operation and Development (OECD) countries (as examined in other chapters of this book) is a symbol of that transformation but it is necessary to pay attention to much more than just food charity and reflect on the current transformation of the welfare state. First of all, the reification of the dominant rationale has to be avoided. Why is that so? The return of the struggle for food security to a central position in a developed welfare state indicates a real shift in the organisation of social security. Current developments must be understood as a shift in the existing modes of social exclusion, as has been argued previously in this chapter. However, they also have to be understood as a shift from public forms and practices of *poverty reduction* to a mix of private and public *poverty relief*. If a member of society suffering poverty cannot be certain that social support from the state will be guaranteed, but instead finds themselves dependent on the donations of those who have surplus, then we are witnessing the undermining of the fundamental promise of welfare: to organise 'solidarity among strangers' (Brunkhorst, 2005: 76). Social scientists and activists in the fields of social policy and social work have to be aware that current developments can be accelerated or even just legitimised by the acceptance of this shift from (publicly guaranteed) poverty reduction to (no longer publicly ensured) poverty relief if the analysis in this area focuses only on food security and food aid.

Second, inclusion in 'welfare societies' was publicly organised to establish systems of social support in order to free people from the dependency and contingency of private loyalty. Even existing welfare states have never successfully established such a system of solidarity among strangers to include all. They have been accused of neglecting the universal promise of 'welfarism' in many cases – not least in social movements' critiques of the welfare provision in developed welfare states. However, this criticism clearly showed that this promise was nevertheless on the agenda in the 20th century.

Ideally, welfare should bring an end to people's everyday struggle for individual survival (for example, eradicating hunger and ensuring a basic minimum of hygiene) as a product of the progress of civilisation. This is fundamentally relevant for democracies because people cannot be full citizens – cannot participate politically – as long as they have to put all their energy and resources into pure survival on a daily basis. Berthold Brecht was right when he stated that 'food comes first, then morals'. Consequently, to reduce the question of welfare to a matter of food charity overlooks this essential relationship between welfare and democracy. However, that is exactly what has happened over the last 20 years or so in a number of European states and beyond. Existing welfare states as public systems of poverty reduction are being complemented by a private–public system of poverty relief, which has been established in the shadow of formal state institutional arrangements. This system incorporates food charity as a major component but it is still only one of several components.

Therefore, it seems necessary to broaden the analytical perspective in order to capture this transformation of welfare adequately. Following a number of social theorists, this section discusses the emergence of a new 'charity economy' (Kessl, 2009, 2015) to categorise the current developments. The term 'charity economy' (see Kessl, 2019; Kessl et al, 2019) describes a distribution system in which basic goods – often goods considered to be surplus – are distributed or sold at discount prices to 'the poor' or 'the needy' by voluntary workers.[6] This system is based on the provision of everyday consumer goods for any one of the following reasons: they are provided directly as a result of industrial overproduction (Lorenz, 2012b); they can no longer be offered for sale due to statutory standardisation specifications or marketing objectives; or they are no longer needed by private households.

The new charity economy targets groups of people who do not have sufficient resources at their disposal to enable them to participate in the primary capitalist system of goods distribution in a manner that secures their standard of living. Given that the goods to be distributed within the new charity economy are primarily basic goods for day-to-day living, this distribution system affects the forms and concepts of subsistence or livelihood support that, up till now, had been virtually the exclusive responsibility of agencies of the welfare state. Material supply gaps based on legal claims have primarily been buffered through cash benefits in the social security system of the welfare state.[7] The establishment of the new charity economy places non-monetary benefits as a subsidy for 'the needy', alongside statutory social insurance, supply or welfare structures. In some cases, it replaces these altogether.

In the case of replacement, users are referred to the new donation-based livelihood support services where availability is not based on 'having an entitlement, but on receiving charitable gifts' (Schoneville, 2013: 25, own translation). This explicit dimension of charity also distinguishes these non-monetary benefits from non-monetary benefits in other areas, for example, aid for refugees or people without formal residency status. Surprisingly, against this background, the new charity economy has turned out to be a system of poverty relief that is deeply connected on the organisational side with institutionalised welfare services. Around 90 per cent of all German organisations in the field of the new charity economy are directly related to social services (state/municipal social services or quasi-state organisations). In the main, they are part of a social service organisation or connected to one through offering users a combination of professional services and the charity service. Also, almost three in four German organisations (71 per cent) in the new charity economy are able to refer users to professionals, for example, as coordinators of a *Tafel* initiative or in a connected part of the same organisation. Furthermore, 42 per cent of these organisations receive some kind of public funding (Oechler and Schröder, 2015).

However, not only is the connection to state social services – as a central part of the existing welfare state – much stronger than could have been predicted, but so is the connection between the predominant capitalist commodity economy and the secondary market of the charity economy (Kessl and Wagner, 2011). Closely interconnected with the primary market, the charity economy facilitates the transfer of surplus goods from the primary economy to a secondary system. This transfer also provides an economic benefit to those who donate the primary goods because they receive an equivalent profit from their donations. Food discounters, for instance, are still able to make a profit from donated goods because donation reduces their disposal costs and allows some possible tax savings, and companies that are official contributors or sponsors can benefit from enhancing their public image through donations as a form of corporate social responsibility. Nevertheless, the charity economy cannot be subordinated to the capitalist economy altogether. It is a specific segment that is linked to the predominant market economy while featuring an area that goes beyond the logic of the predominant capitalist commodity economy because the charity economy is also arranged in accordance with the concepts of alms and gift economics. This and other findings indicate that the exchange cycle that results from the inclusion of alternative forms of poverty assistance cuts across the classic sectors of civil society, economy and the state; it cannot be clearly situated in any one of these sectors (Kessl et al, 2019) and is not sufficiently explained in popular descriptions of the changes regarding the welfare state arrangement (Schoneville, 2018).

Conclusions

Tafel and similar initiatives have established a new kind of social assistance in Germany. Over the last 25 years, they have seen an astonishing growth and expansion of their activities. As policies of social support have become more restrictive, there has been increased demand for support from charities. The charity economy as a whole is focused on alleviating the immediate effects of life in poverty but the support is neither able nor designed to overcome poverty.

At the same time, the social support provided by food banks and similar organisations is highly contradictory. These contradictions can be found at the level between the self-description of the German welfare state, which can be found in legal documents as well as in policy declarations, and the existence of food banks and the charity economy as a whole. While the arrangement of the welfare state addresses itself as an entity that fights poverty, the existence of food banks can be understood as a symbol that this goal has not been achieved (Schoneville, 2018).

Contradictions can also be found at the organisational level. While food banks seek to help people in poverty, they cannot provide any form of support that enables people to overcome poverty. They provide a specific type of basic support under conditions of social exclusion. They are an institutional answer to a process of social exclusion but they also establish a new form of exclusion themselves by including users in a secondary system of consumption and aid.

In addition, accounts from food bank users highlight such contradictions. These accounts demonstrate that users are forced to rely on some form of support because they have insufficient financial resources. At the same time, they report experiences of stigmatisation and feelings of shame connected to their living situation and use of food banks. These contradictions are the result of the form in which food banks are socially embedded within society, as well as the organisational form in which they provide support.

Tafel initiatives, food banks and similar associations cannot change government social policy on their own, but they are playing a part in problematic developments. First of all, they have been active in establishing charitable food assistance but hardly in advocating political support for the excluded. Second, with the establishment of this new kind of social assistance, food charity and hunger relief have become publicly acceptable methods of providing social support. They mostly receive good press, and politicians have typically applauded such voluntary services since the mid-1990s. This has contributed to standards of social support in a rich welfare state being reduced to the level of securing survival, rather than opening up participation in society. Existing theories of welfare state transformation – as well as of current logics and structures of social exclusion (and inclusion) – still do not adequately reflect these dynamics, not least in their perspectives on labour and employment.

The growth of *Tafel* is part of a fundamental change in the German welfare system, which the authors would not be alone in calling the establishment of a new charity economy. On closer inspection, this new approach to poverty appears to be part of a process of wide-reaching change, leading to a new welfare arrangement.

What conclusions can be drawn and what areas are important topics for further debate and research? This chapter has shown that the German welfare system has provided some continuity but has ironically failed to assist the most vulnerable, and has arguably even worsened their situation. This has been true even during times of economic prosperity. However, the trend of restricting social rights and promoting charitable assistance is what the development of food charity in Germany shares with other 'Western' welfare countries (Riches, 2018). The interplay of such transnational trends with the particularities of the German welfare system needs more evaluation (Schoneville, 2018). One feature of this transnational trend is a change in the controversial role of civil society. While the promotion of an active civil society was part of progressive ideas in the 1990s, that was intended as a means to overcome paternalistic patterns of the state and administration. Now, other conceptions of civil society have obviously become more successful, at least in the realm of social assistance. The establishment of food banks makes the fact that civil society has its limits clear: voluntary commitment is no substitute for basic social security. This should spark a debate about what role civil society can play in democratic welfare countries.

Notes

[1] In Germany, everyone uses the term '*Tafeln*', which is the plural form of '*Tafel*'. As no one would understand this in English but using an English plural ('*Tafels*') would be inappropriate, we have chosen '*Tafel* initiatives' as a compromise. The organisation of *Tafel* initiatives at a national level has been called Tafel

Deutschland eV since June 2017. Previously, it was known as Bundesverband Deutsche Tafel eV. Both terms appear in the article depending on the references. The organisation itself uses the English term 'National Association of German Tafel'.

[2] It is not only income distribution that has become more unequal. The distribution of wealth in Germany, as in all Organisation for Economic Co-operation and Development (OECD) countries, is also markedly unequal and has become even more so over recent decades (DIW, 2016, 2017, 2018).

[3] This is not without problems. Not only do the data only represent food banks that are part of the national association – while there are no data about other initiatives – but it is also unclear where these data really come from and how they are collected. In particular, the figure of 1.5 million food bank users seems to be at least questionable and could equally be higher or lower. The association's decentralised, locally based structure means that the data have to be collected from local organisations. While some local food banks work in a highly professional way using bespoke software and 'customer systems', others remain much more like grass-roots initiatives, which are not – and do not want to be – professionally managed. It is very likely that for the second group, the information gathered is closer to educated guesses than factual data.

[4] The research results presented here are from an empirical study of food banks (Schoneville, 2016). Within the study, biographical interviews with food bank users were treated as narrative constructions of identity. The analysis focused on the question of how people who live in poverty and use food banks tell their life stories. The pathways of their lives, the ways in which they narratively construct the reasons for using a food bank and the impact on their self-concepts were at the core of the project.

[5] This division becomes even less clear once the organisational structure of food banks is analysed, as discussed in this chapter.

[6] At the phenomenological level, this definition has fuzzy edges, for example, food pantries may purchase some of their food with monetary donations to top up their stock levels. In such cases, no donated elementary goods are distributed. Nevertheless, the fundamental principle remains intact so the definition requires no change.

[7] The distribution of non-monetary benefits, as well as the distribution of food vouchers, in the context of social security or asylum seeker support is rejected and often criticised as patronising those in need. In recent times, a social and political debate has followed on from this about the so-called 'education and participation package'.

References

Barlösius, E. and Ludwig-Mayerhofer, W. (2001) *Die Armut der Gesellschaft* [*Poverty of Society*], Opladen: Leske + Budrich.

Berliner Tafel (2018) 'Die Berliner Tafel wird 25' ['Berlin Tafel becomes 25 years old'], www.berliner-tafel.de/nc/berliner-tafel/aktuelles/meldung

Blair, T. and Schroeder, G. (1998) 'Europe: the third way/die neue mitte', http://library.fes.de/pdf-files/bueros/suedafrika/02828.pdf

Bourdieu, P. (1998) 'Prekarität ist überall' ['Precarity is everywhere'], in P. Bourdieu (ed) *Gegenfeuer. Wortmeldungen im Dienste des Widerstands gegen die neoliberale Invasion* [*Backfire. Statements against the neoliberal invasion*], Konstanz: UVK, pp 96–102.

Brunkhorst, H. (2005) *Solidarity: From civic friendship to a global legal community*, Cambridge, MA, and London: MIT Press.

Bude, H. and Willisch, A. (eds) (2008) *Exklusion. Die Debatte über die 'Überflüssigen'* [*Exclusion. The debate about the 'superfluous' people*], Frankfurt aM: Suhrkamp.

Bundesagentur für Arbeit (2018) 'Berichte: Blickpunkt Arbeitsmarkt–Monatsbericht zum Arbeits- und Ausbildungsmarkt, August 2018' ['Reports: focus on labor market monthly report on the employment and training market, August 2018'], Nürnberg, https://statistik.arbeitsagentur.de/Statistikdaten/Detail/201808/arbeitsmarktberichte/monatsbericht-monatsbericht/monatsbericht-d-0-201808-pdf.pdf

Bundesverband Deutsche Tafel (2017) 'Jahresbericht 2016' ['Annual report 2016'], www.tafel.de/fileadmin/media/Publikationen/Jahresberichte/PDF/Tafel_JB16_PDF_Online.pdf

Castel, R. (2002) *From manual workers to wage laborers: Transformation of the social question*, Piscataway, NJ: Transaction Publishers.

Castel, R. and Dörre, K. (eds) (2009) *Prekarität, Abstieg, Ausgrenzung. Die soziale Frage am Beginn des 21. Jahrhunderts* [*Precarity, social decline, exclusion. The social question in the early 21st century*], Frankfurt aM and New York, NY: Campus.

Deutscher Caritasverband (2008) 'Eckpunkte des Deutschen Caritasverbandes zur Beteiligung an existenzunterstützenden Dienstleistungen in Form von Lebensmittelläden' ['Key points of the Caritas about its participation on basic social assistance through food pantries'], www.caritas.de/cms/contents/caritasde/medien/0112200 8eckpunkteleb2/241114_081201_eckpunkte_lebensmittellaeden.pdf

Diakonie (2010) '"Es sollte überhaupt kein Armer unter Euch sein". "Tafeln" im Kontext sozialer Gerechtigkeit' ['Tafeln in the context of social justice'], www.diakonie.de/fileadmin/user_upload/Diakonie_Text-2010-03-Tafeln.pdf

DIW (German Institute for Economic Research) (2016) 'Development of top incomes in Germany since 2001', www.diw.de/documents/publikationen/73/diw_01.c.524282.de/diw_econ_bull_2016-01-1.pdf

DIW (2017) 'Wie steigende Einkommensungleichheit das Wirtschaftswachstum in Deutschland beeinflusst' ['How increasing income inequality impacts economic growth'], www.diw.de/documents/publikationen/73/diw_01.c.554080.de/17-10-1.pdf

DIW (2018) 'Inequality in Germany: decrease in gap for gross hourly wages since 2014, but monthly and annual wages remain on plateau', www.diw.de/documents/publikationen/73/diw_01.c.579137.de/dwr-18-09-1.pdf

Esping-Andersen, G. (1990) *The three worlds of welfare capitalism*, Cambridge: Polity Press.

Garthwite, K. (2015) *Hunger pains: Life inside foodbank Britain*, Bristol: Policy Press.

German Federal Government (2017) *The German Federal Government's 5th report on poverty and wealth*, Berlin: Federal Ministry of Labour and Social Affairs, www.bmas.de/SharedDocs/Downloads/EN/PDF-Publikationen/a306e-the-german-federal-governments-5th-report-on-poverty-and-wealth.pdf?__blob=publicationFile&v=1

Groh-Samberg, O. (2004) 'Armut und Klassenstruktur' ['Poverty and class structure'], *KZfSS Kölner Zeitschrift für Soziologie und Sozialpsychologie*, 56(4): 653–82.

Groh-Samberg, O. (2009) *Armut, soziale Ausgrenzung und Klassenstruktur. Zur Integration multidimensionaler und längsschnittlicher Perspektiven* [*Poverty, social exclusion, and class structure. On the integration of multidimensional and longitudinal perspectives*], Wiesbaden: Springer VS.

Kessl, F. (2009) 'Marked silence, neo-feudalistic reactions and the stabilized moral regime – the current de- and reformation of "the social"', *Social Work & Society*, 7(1): urn:nbn:de:0009-11-20375.

Kessl, F. (2015) 'Charity economy – a symbol of a fundamental shift in Europe', *Tiddskrift for Socialpedagogik*, 18(1): 147–52.

Kessl, F. (2019) '"Charity economy": in the shadow of the welfare state', *Global Dialogue*, 8(3), http://globaldialogue.isa-sociology.org/charity-economy-in-the-shadow-of-the-welfare-state/

Kessl, F. and Wagner, T. (2011) '"Was vom Tisch der Reichen fällt …": Zur neuen politischen Ökonomie des Mitleids' ['On the new political economy of charity'], *Widersprüche*, 31(119/20): 55–76.

Kessl, F., Oechler, M. and Schröder, T. (2019) 'Charity economy and social work', in F. Kessl, W. Lorenz, H.-U. Otto and S. White (eds) *European social work – A compendium*, Leverkusen and Farmington Hills: Barbara Budrich Publishers, pp 365–81.

Kronauer, M. (2002) *Exklusion. Die Gefährdung des Sozialen im hoch entwickelten Kapitalismus* [*Exclusion. Endangering the social in high developed capitalism*], Frankfurt aM and New York, NY: Campus.

Kunhenn, J. (2014) 'Aversive Nutzung und Nicht-Nutzung der Tafeln als Formen der Armutsbewältigung' ['Aversive use and non-use of food banks as forms of poverty reduction'], unpublished master's thesis, Bergische Universität Wuppertal.

Land, R. and Willisch, A. (2006) 'Die Probleme mit der Integration. Das Konzept des "sekundären Integrationsmodus"' ['Problems of integration. The concept of "secondary integration modes"'], in H. Bude and A. Willisch (eds) *Das Problem der Exklusion. Ausgegrenzte, Entbehrliche, Überflüssige*, Hamburg: Hamburger Edition, pp 70–93.

Leisering, L. (2008) 'Dynamik von Armut' ['Dynamic of poverty'], in E.-U. Huster, J. Boeckh and H. Mogge-Grotjahn (eds) *Handbuch Armut und Soziale Ausgrenzung* [*Handbook poverty and exclusion*], Wiesbaden: VS Verlag für Sozialwissenschaften, pp 118–32.

Lessenich, S. (2008) *Die Neuerfindung des Sozialen. Der Sozialstaat im flexiblen Kapitalismus* [*New invention of the social. The welfare state in flexible capitalism*], Bielefeld: Transcript.

Lorenz, S. (ed) (2010) *TafelGesellschaft. Zum neuen Umgang mit Überfluss und Ausgrenzung* [*Tafel-Society. About new ways of dealing with abundance and exclusion*], Bielefeld: Transcript.

Lorenz, S. (2012a) 'Socio-ecological ambivalences of charitable food assistance in the affluent society – the German "Tafel"', *International Journal of Sociology and Social Policy*, 32(7/8): 386–400.

Lorenz, S. (2012b) *Tafeln im flexiblen Überfluss. Ambivalenzen sozialen und ökologischen Engagements* [*'Tafel' in flexible affluence. Ambivalences of social and ecological commitment*], Bielefeld: Transcript.

Lorenz, S. (2015) 'Having no choice: social exclusion in the affluent society', *Journal of Exclusion Studies*, 5(1): 1–17.

Lorey, I. (2012) *Die Regierung der Prekären* [*Governing Precarity*], Vienna: Turia + Kant.

Luhmann, N. (1995) 'Kausalität im Süden' ['Causality in the South'], *Soziale Systeme. Zeitschrift für Soziologische Theorie*, 1(1): 7–28.

Molling, L. (2009) 'Die "Berliner Tafel" zwischen Sozialstaatsabbau und neuer Armenfürsorge' ['Berlin Tafel between welfare cutbacks and new poor relief'], in S. Selke (ed) *Tafeln in Deutschland. Aspekte einer sozialen Bewegung zwischen Nahrungsmittelumverteilung und Armutsintervention* [*Tafel initiatives in Germany. Aspects of a social movement between redistribution of food and fighting poverty*], Wiesbaden: Springer VS, pp 175–96.

Neckel, S. (1992) *Status und Scham. Zur symbolischen Reproduktion sozialer Ungleichheit* [*Status and shame. For the symbolic reproduction of social inequality*], Frankfurt aM and New York, NY: Campus.

Neckel, S. and Sutterlüty, F. (2005) 'Negative Klassifikationen. Konflikte um die symbolische Ordnung sozialer Ungleichheit' ['Negative classifications. Conflicts on the symbolic order of inequality'], in W. Heitmeyer and P. Imbusch (eds) *Integrationspotenziale einer modernen Gesellschaft*, Wiesbaden: Springer VS, pp 409–28.

Neckel, S. and Sutterlüty, F. (2008) 'Negative Klassifikationen und die symbolische Ordnung sozialer Ungleichheit' ['Negative classifications. Conflicts on the symbolic order of inequality'], in S. Neckel and F. Sutterlüty (eds) *Mittendrin im Abseits*, Wiesbaden: Springer VS, pp 15–25.

Oechler, M. and Schröder, T. (2015) 'Die neue Mitleidsökonomie – Armutsbekämpfung jenseits des Sozialstaates? Befunde zu Organisations- und Nutzungsstrukturen spendenbasierter Angebote' ['New charity economy – fighting against poverty beyond the welfare state?'], *Neue Praxis*, 45(6): 572–92.

Offe, C. (1996) 'Moderne "Barbarei". Der Naturzustand im Kleinformat?' ['Modern barbarism. The small-scale natural state?'], in M. Miller and H.-G. Soeffner (eds) *Modernität und Barbarei. Soziologische Zeitdiagnose am Ende des 20. Jahrhunderts* [*Modernity and barbarism. Sociological diagnoses at the end of the 20th century*], Frankfurt aM: Suhrkamp Taschenbuch, pp 258–89.

Paugam, S. (2008) *Die elementaren Formen der Armut* [*The basic forms of poverty*], Hamburg: Hamburger Edition.

Riches, G. (2018) *Poverty, corporate charity and the right to food*, New York, NY: Routledge.

Rocha, C. (2014) 'A right to food approach: public food banks in Brazil', in G. Riches and T. Silvasti (eds) *First world hunger revisited: Food charity or the right to food?* (2nd edn), Basingstoke: Palgrave Macmillan, pp 29–41.

Scherschel, K., Streckeisen, P. and Krenn, M. (eds) (2012) *Neue Prekarität. Die Folgen aktivierender Arbeitsmarktpolitik – europäische Länder im Vergleich*, [*The new precarity. The consequences of activating labour market policies – a comparison of European countries*], Frankfurt aM and New York, NY: Campus.

Schoneville, H. (2013) 'Armut und Ausgrenzung als Beschämung und Missachtung. Hilfe im Kontext der Lebensmittelausgaben "Die Tafeln" und ihre Konsequenzen' [Poverty and social exclusion as shame and disrespect – support within the context of food banks and its consequences'], *Soziale Passagen*, 5(1): 17–35.

Schoneville, H. (2016) 'Armut, soziale Ausgrenzung und die Neugestaltung des Sozialen. Die Lebensmittelausgaben "Die Tafeln" in Deutschland' ['Poverty, social exclusion and the reconfiguration of the social. Food banks in Germany'], unpublished dissertation, University of Kassel.

Schoneville, H. (2018) 'Poverty and the transformation of the welfare (state) arrangement: food banks and the charity economy in Germany', *Social Work & Society*, 16(2), https://socwork.net/sws/article/view/570/1117

Schoneville, H. (2019) 'Familien in Armut. Erziehung im Widerspruch von Armut' ['Families in poverty. Parenting in the contradiction of poverty'], *Grundschulzeitschrift*, 314: 28–31.

Selke, S. (2008) *Fast ganz unten. Wie man in Deutschland durch die Hilfe von Lebensmitteltafeln satt wird* [*Almost hit rock bottom. How people get fed through food banks in Germany*], Münster: Westfälisches Dampfboot.

Selke, S. (ed) (2009) *Tafeln in Deutschland. Aspekte einer sozialen Bewegung zwischen Nahrungsmittelumverteilung und Armutsintervention* [*Tafel initiatives in Germany. Aspects of a social movement between redistribution of food and fighting poverty*], Wiesbaden: Springer VS.

Selke, S. (ed) (2010) *Kritik der Tafeln in Deutschland. Standortbestimmungen zu einem ambivalenten sozialen Phänomen* [*Tafel criticism in Germany. Positions on an ambivalent social phenomenon*], Wiesbaden: Springer VS.

Selke, S. (2013) *Schamland: Die Armut mitten unter uns* [*Poverty in between us all*], Berlin: Econ.

Selke, S. and Maar, K. (2011) 'Grenzen der guten Tat. Ergebnisse der Studie "Evaluation existenzunterstützender Angebote in Trägerschaft von katholischen und caritativen Anbietern in Nordrhein-Westfalen"' ['Limits of the good deed. Findings of the study "Evaluation of basic social assistance through Catholic and charitable institutions in North Rhine-Westphalia"'], in Caritas in NRW (ed) *Brauchen wir Tafeln, Suppenküchen und Kleiderkammern? Hilfen zwischen Sozialstaat und Barmherzigkeit* [*Do we need food banks, soup kitchens and clothes charities? Social assistance between welfare state and mercy*], Freiburg: Lambertus, pp 15–91.

Stichweh, R. (2010) 'Inklusion/Exklusion, funktionale Differenzierung und die Theorie der Weltgesellschaft' ['Inclusion/exclusion, functional differentiation and the theory of the world society'] in U. Beck and A. Poferl (eds) *Große Armut, großer Reichtum. Zur Transnationalisierung sozialer Ungleichheit* [*Huge poverty, great wealth. About the transnationalisation of social inequality*], Berlin: Suhrkamp, pp 240–60.

Tafel (no date) 'Geschichte' ['History'], www.tafel.de/ueber-uns/die-tafeln/geschichte/

Tafel (2012) 'Zahlen & Fakten' ['Figures and facts'], www.tafel.de/die-tafel/zahlen-fakten.html

Tafel (2017) 'Zahlen & Fakten' ['Figures and facts'], www.tafel.de/ueber-uns/die-tafeln/zahlen-fakten

Van der Horst, H., Pascucci, S. and Bol, W. (2014) 'The "dark side" of food banks? Exploring emotional responses of food bank receivers in the Netherlands', *British Food Journal*, 116(9): 1506–20.

Vester, M., Von Oertzen, P., Geiling, H., Hermann, T. and Müller, D. (2001) *Soziale Milieus im gesellschaftlichen Strukturwandel: Zwischen Integration und Ausgrenzung* [*Social milieus in structural changes: In between integration and exclusion*], Frankfurt aM: Suhrkamp.

Von Normann, K. (2003) *Evolution der Deutschen Tafeln. Eine Studie über die Entwicklung caritativer Nonprofit-Organisationen zur Verminderung von Ernährungsarmut in Deutschland* [*The evolution of the German Tafel. A study on the development of charity NGOs relieving food poverty*], Bad Neuenahr: Wehle.

3

The role of food charity in Italy

Sabrina Arcuri, Gianluca Brunori and Francesca Galli

Introduction

Food poverty is not perceived as a policy priority in Italy, and scholars have only recently started to analyse the relationship between poverty and food charity using various approaches (Santini and Cavicchi, 2014; Baglioni et al, 2017; Arcuri, 2019; Galli et al, 2019). This chapter's starting point in framing the relationship is based on the traditional scarcity of resources and fragmentation of the Italian social assistance sector, which has been instrumental in the institutionalisation of charitable assistance. Charitable assistance has traditionally played a crucial role in the provision of basic services to the most vulnerable people in Italy, including through food aid (Madama et al, 2013), often carried out through a regime of 'mutual accommodation' (Ranci, 1999). This entailed very little cooperation between the state and the third sector in setting goals and planning long-term strategies for the supply of services; however, in functional terms, there was strong interdependence (Ranci et al, 2005).

During the years 2011–13, a rise in the use of charitable food aid was recorded, providing a clear signal that thousands of people were experiencing financial hardship. A record high was reached in January 2013, when 4,068,250 individuals were receiving European food aid – a 47 per cent increase from the 2,763,379 individuals in 2010 (AGEA, 2013). On the front line of providing an immediate response to what was called a 'food emergency' (Secondo Welfare, 2013; FBAO, 2014), both faith-based and secular charitable organisations across Italy deployed traditional instruments to fight food poverty: soup kitchens and food parcels. These 'low-threshold services' (Tomei and Caterino, 2013), mostly run by volunteers, are commonly used by marginalised individuals and households in exceptional circumstances, who are given help in the form of a prepared meal or a non-perishable food parcel. However, over the past few years, in the wake of the economic crisis – besides worsening conditions for those who were already experiencing some form of destitution – many additional households have fallen into poverty. Simultaneously, public services and resources have been further reduced as a result of government austerity measures (Caritas Europe, 2015; Caselli, 2015; Gori et al, 2016).

At a time of great difficulty for food aid – when charitable operators faced increasing requests but were struggling on the supply side due to unpredictable food waste recovery and a temporary interruption of European food aid – 35 organisations took a stand and pooled their efforts by establishing the Alleanza contro la povertà (Alliance against Poverty) (REIS, no date). For instance, Caritas – one of the key actors in charitable food assistance in Italy and a founding member of the alliance – has begun to act on two fronts. On the one hand, it continues to provide basic material assistance to poor people, primarily through food distribution programmes but also by attempting to adjust its services to meet emergent needs, as with the new 'Emporia of Solidarity' (Caritas Italiana, 2014). On the other hand, it has started to publicly raise the issue of the inadequacy of social policy tackling poverty (REIS, no date; Caritas Italiana, 2015b, 2016, 2017b). This is something of a novelty in Italy, where food poverty has always been dealt with using an emergency approach, with solutions mostly tending towards the creation of a donation-friendly environment rather than seeking to address the root causes of deprivation (Baglioni et al, 2017; Arcuri, 2019). In 2016, for instance, a new law on food waste recovery (ln [Law nr.] 166/2016) was adopted, amending former so-called 'Good Samaritan' legislation.

The inadequacy of the traditionally patchy and incomplete Italian model of welfare has become even more evident since the late 2000s, with the Great Recession making policy intervention of the utmost urgency (Natili, 2018). In other countries, austerity measures seem to have weakened the social safety nets that were formerly available, and charities are increasingly filling the gap by providing resources to those in need. Contrary to this, in Italy, charitable organisations have always had a crucial role in social assistance services. Recently, they have committed themselves to building on this prominent role in order to emphasise the need for state-based social policies and move the public debate forward. It is certainly too early to say that there has been a reversal in the Italian system of social protection. Suffice it to say that in 2016, the most recent European Union (EU) Social Justice Index data did not give cause for hope that the worst is over. In 25th position, Italy showed no signs of recovery to pre-crisis levels, remaining at the lower end of the spectrum for almost all the dimensions considered to be relevant for measuring social justice (Schraad-Tischer et al, 2017).[1]

This chapter explores how the role of food charity has evolved in the Italian context over the last decade or so as a consequence of rising levels of (food) poverty, which were further exacerbated by the economic crisis and austerity measures. To this end, this chapter provides an overview of the key features of the Italian welfare system, traditionally lacking in terms of social provision and reliant on charitable organisations, and how this has resulted in rising need for food charity. It then analyses how the key actors involved in food assistance have developed their role and how this role is being reshaped. Finally, it looks at recent shifts in social policy and examines the uncertain future scenarios, also encompassing the development of a global food policy movement that has lately been having some effect in Italy.

For the purposes of this chapter, the authors have decided to avoid the term 'food insecurity'. In Italian, '*sicurezza alimentare*' has the double meaning of 'food security' and 'food safety', and the term is rarely employed in public discourse in relation to poverty in rich countries. This chapter will therefore refer to the concept of 'food poverty', borrowing from Dowler (2002) and Riches (1997). They recognise that the experience of food poverty is directly related to the society in which people live and can thus be defined as 'the inability to acquire or consume an adequate quality or sufficient quantity of food in socially acceptable ways, or the uncertainty that one will be able to do so' (Dowler, 2002: 709). 'Food poverty' ('*povertà alimentare*') has become a widespread term in Italian public discourse and is employed by researchers (Maino et al, 2016; Arcuri, 2019; Galli et al, 2019), policymakers (MIPAAF, 2013) and undoubtedly charitable organisations working towards its alleviation, above all Caritas and the Food Bank Foundation (FBAO).[2]

Together, the FBAO and Caritas provide nearly 70 per cent of all food aid in Italy (Caritas Italiana and FBAO, 2015: 1), though their organisational arrangements and roles take different forms. The FBAO has represented Italy in the European Federation of Food Banks since 1989 and is a second-tier organisation that coordinates a network of 21 regional agencies operating at the local level. Its main aim is to recover surplus food donations from firms and companies, and to redistribute these to front-line agencies. For this purpose, the FBAO relies on consolidated knowledge and logistics infrastructures, as well as highly hierarchical and centralised management, ensuring the standardisation of procedures at a national level (FBAO, no date; Baglioni et al, 2017).

Caritas – the Latin word for 'charity' – is a church-based organisation that has been operating at international, national and local levels since

1971. In Italy, it is the organisation of the Italian Bishops Conference and aims to support the most vulnerable people through its day-to-day activities, using volunteers to target problems related to new and old forms of poverty, immigration, homelessness, mental ill health and issues of peace and justice (Caritas Europe, 2017). Caritas's widespread presence through its branches across Italy mirrors the organisational structure of the Catholic Church, amounting to 218 dioceses nationwide, each, in turn, divided into several parishes.

Changing poverty and food poverty in Italy

The recent rise in demand for food aid has proved decisive in terms of its contribution to highlighting the changes occurring in the prevalence and composition of poverty. The 'Italian model of poverty', as defined by Morlicchio (2012), had remained relatively constant – fluctuating slightly around a 3 per cent incidence of individuals in absolute poverty[3] – until the economic downturn of the late 2000s (Caselli, 2015). The complex legacy of the 2007/08 crisis appears to be a substantial 'normalisation of poverty' (Gori et al, 2016), initially manifesting as a large increase in the incidence of (absolute) poverty – from 4.1 per cent in 2007 to 9.9 per cent in 2013 (I.Stat Database, no date). Although this figure has declined somewhat since the peak in 2013, it still remains higher than pre-crisis levels and is rising again. In 2017, 5,058,000 people – equal to 8.4 per cent of the population and 6.9 per cent of households – were living in absolute poverty in Italy (I.Stat, 2018a), compared to 7.9 per cent of individuals and 6.3 per cent of households in 2016 (I.Stat, 2017). Segments where the incidence of absolute poverty is still notably on the rise include households living in the South and Islands area (from 8.5 per cent in 2016 to 10.3 per cent in 2017), households with one child (from 7.2 per cent in 2016 to 9.5 per cent in 2017) (I.Stat, 2018a) and households exclusively composed of non-nationals, which are being seriously hit (rising to 29.2 per cent).

Employment status is also crucial with regard to poverty. Poverty incidence is on the increase in households where the reference person is unemployed (from 6.1 per cent up to 7.7 per cent in 2017), but if the reference person is of working age, absolute poverty is almost three times as high (11.8 per cent) as in households where the reference person is retired (4.2 per cent) (I.Stat, 2018a). A further element of concern that is linked to the normalisation phenomenon is the increase in the number of working poor and the consequent implications for the previously protective function of work, as highlighted by sociologist Chiara Saraceno (2018a). She observes that for 11.7 per cent of working people, having a job is not enough to keep their families out of poverty (an increase of 2.2 per cent compared to 2010), with even worse levels for people on fixed-term contracts (16.2 per cent) and part-time contracts (15.8 per cent) (Saraceno, 2018a). Similarly, Caritas has highlighted how poverty in Italy is inversely proportional to age: almost half (48.7 per cent) of the total number of individuals in absolute poverty in 2016 were younger than 34 years old (Caritas Italiana, 2017a). Relative poverty[4] is rising as well, both in terms of the proportions of households (12.3 per cent in 2017, up from 10.6 per cent in 2016) and individuals (15.6 per cent in 2017, up from 14.0 per cent in 2016) (I.Stat, 2018a).

In 2016, more than 18 million Italians were at risk of poverty and social exclusion – a Eurostat indicator that corresponds to the total number of people at risk of poverty, severely materially deprived or living in households with very low work intensity. This was equal to 30 per cent of the population and represented a 4.5 per cent increase compared to 2008 (Eurostat Database, no date).

The year 2013 was also particularly bad in terms of households' spending capacity, which reached its lowest level after a 2.5 per cent decrease on the previous year (I.Stat, 2014). Families had to put in place various coping strategies, starting by cutting expenditure on recreation and culture, clothing, household goods, and services. For instance, although food expenditure remained stable, in 2013, an increase was observed in the proportion of households that had to reduce either the quality (from 7.7 per cent in 2012 to 8.2 per cent) or the quantity (from 39.5 per cent in 2012 to 40.6 per cent) of food purchased, or both (from 15.4 per cent in 2012 to 16.2 per cent). The proportion of families using hard discount stores also rose from 12.3 per cent to 14.4 per cent (I.Stat, 2014). Despite these measures, the share of households reporting not having enough money to buy food at certain times of the year rose from 5.3 per cent in 2007 to 8.5 per cent in 2013 (Caritas Italiana, 2015a).

Although household food expenditure has not yet recovered to pre-crisis levels, a 3.8 per cent increase on the 2013 figures shows that households' expenditure on food is slowly returning to normal (I.Stat, 2018b). However, confirming Engel's law – that as incomes rise, the proportion spent on food decreases – the spending of Italian households reveals geographical differences in the share taken up by food expenditure. In 2017, it reached its highest share in the Southern regions (22.5 per cent), with the lowest in the North-East (15.7 per cent), and with a national average of 17.8 per cent (I.Stat, 2018b).

Apart from what can be derived from data on household spending, food poverty has no presence in Italy's official statistics. The only exception is the food component of the European Union Statistics on Income and Living Conditions (EU-SILC) set of indicators on material deprivation, which remains, to date, the only available measure of food poverty in most European countries. It is measured as the percentage of individuals who cannot afford a protein-based meal every second day. In Italy, this figure rose from 7.6 per cent in 2008 to 14.3 per cent in 2016, with a record high of 17 per cent in 2012 (Eurostat Database, no date).

Caritas works on the assumption that people who cannot afford to buy food do not have sufficient income to ensure an adequate standard of living for themselves and their families (Caritas Italiana, 2015a). Therefore, even if the largest share of services that Caritas provides entail food distribution, it points out that food poverty is not a specific target to be addressed and should rather be part of a broader definition of poverty. Moreover, what has been called a 'food emergency' has little to do with a reduction in the amount of food available to people, but is a result of economic hardship (Caritas Italiana, 2014, 2015a). Increases in the share of so-called 'new poor' among recipients of charitable food aid have consistently been observed, including Italian users and social groups not usually associated with extreme marginalities (Caritas Italiana, 2014, 2015a). Empirical evidence collected by 1,982 Caritas counselling centres[5] shows that even in 2017, insufficient or no income was the main financial problem affecting Caritas service users (78.4 per cent of users), followed by unemployment (54 per cent), housing problems (26.7 per cent), health conditions (12.8 per cent), family issues (14.2 per cent) and difficulties related to refugee or asylum status (12.5 per cent) (De Lauso, 2018: 55).

Economic crisis, austerity and Italy's welfare state

During the years 1951–53, a 'parliamentary inquiry on misery' was carried out in Italy with the aim of investigating extreme poverty[6] and identifying the most appropriate instruments to address it. The inquiry revealed that, at that time, 11.8 per cent of Italian families were living in extreme poverty and a further 11.6 per cent in destitution, mostly in the Southern regions, the depressed areas of Central Italy and the suburbs of the biggest cities (Inaudi, 2015). The inquiry found that poor nutrition affected households living in poverty. Their low-cost diet, based on starchy foods and with a poor intake of animal proteins, resulted in serious health conditions, especially for children (Inaudi, 2015).

The results of the inquiry have largely remained a dead letter but the inquiry itself was nevertheless crucial in that it revealed the coexistence of 'two Italies' (Ferrera, 1996), which experienced only a partial rebalancing later in the 1950s through the wealth redistribution of the economic expansion known as 'the Italian miracle'. However, not only has the Italian welfare state been unable to iron out regional disparities, but the pronounced differences between richer and poorer areas of the country and the geographical variation in welfare performance have led to the Italian system being described as 'two (separate) welfare states' (Pavolini, 2015, cited in Del Pino and Pavolini, 2015).

Italy's welfare state has been classified as a specific type of the Southern European welfare model (Ferrera, 1996), according to the addition made to Esping-Andersen's (1990) original classification. Several distinctive features have been identified as characterising such a model: fragmented and underdeveloped social services (Madama et al, 2014); a hypertrophic old-age pension system (Ferrera et al, 2012) and a traditional link between social rights and working status (Saraceno, 1994); and heavy reliance on the family – and, within this, on the crucial role of women as care providers – but with a scarcity of transfers and alternative services assigned to families (Saraceno, 1994).

In addition, until very recently, the long-time absence of a national strategy to tackle poverty and, specifically, of a minimum income scheme (MIS) for working-age individuals[7] has been one of the distinguishing features of the Italian welfare state (Madama et al, 2014; Pavolini et al, 2015). There had been several attempts to design and implement some form of national MIS, which mostly ended up as a range of pilot programmes that never turned into a stable measure (Madama et al, 2014). In the best cases, some regional and local schemes were introduced over the last two decades. However, besides being discretionary, uncertain in their delivery and heavily affected by budget constraints (Natili et al, 2018), they have contributed to further geographical fragmentation of social assistance provision, causing both gaps and overlaps in coverage (Madama et al, 2014; Natili, 2016). At the same time, a gradual decentralisation of public services and competences has occurred in Italy over the last 40 years, with sub-national units – regional, municipal and inter-municipal – acquiring a larger share of responsibilities through this rescaling (Del Pino and Pavolini, 2015).

However, with regard to social policies, it is worth pointing out the substantial lack of regulatory clarity. Although competences were assigned to the regions in 1977, in the absence of a law establishing a national framework (which was planned), most policies and social services have been designed in an institutional vacuum. This has contributed to making access to what should be social rights discretionary and highly variable across the nation (Jessoula et al, 2014). The long-awaited framework law[8] (ln 328/2000) introduced several new provisions and was, above all, an attempt to rebalance variability by involving different administrative levels and stakeholders – including the third sector – in the design and implementation of policy (Kazepov, 2008). However, most of these changes were neutralised by a constitutional reform one year later (ln 3/2001), whereby regional governments were assigned a large share of competences, including for social policies, exercised in collaboration with municipalities according to the principle of subsidiarity (Kazepov, 2008; Jessoula et al, 2014; Vampa, 2017).

Apart from such rescaling, at the onset of the economic crisis, the Italian welfare state was 'almost a totally frozen landscape' (Pavolini et al, 2015: 61), with per capita public expenditure on families and social exclusion equal to, respectively, 57 per cent and 13 per cent of the EU-15 average in 2007 (Pavolini et al, 2015). Contrary to what happened in the cases of pensions and the labour market, which were affected by specific reforms urged by the EU (Pavolini et al, 2015; Natili et al, 2018), austerity measures have mostly taken the form of severe cuts to public expenditure in a national context already shaped by low levels of social expenditure. Fiscal consolidation and the strict control of public spending have been the main drivers of what is considered to be a 'hidden retrenchment' (Streeck and Thelen, 2005, cited in Pavolini et al, 2015) of the welfare state. Rather than explicit reforms reducing universal coverage – in the form of Italian health care and education – budget cuts, freezes in salaries and recruitment, and tax increases were undertaken from 2009 onwards (Culpepper, 2014; Del Pino and Pavolini, 2015). Between 2008 and 2012, for instance, the state financing of the National Fund for Social Policies was cut by 91 per cent (Gori, 2012; Madama et al, 2014; Pavolini et al, 2015). Budget cuts have particularly affected the sub-national level, where the largest part of expenditure is devoted to welfare policies (Del Pino and Pavolini, 2015; Natili et al, 2018). However, even after the most difficult period of the economic crisis, expenditure on social and health services has remained among the lowest in Europe (I.Stat, 2019). Taking a closer look at social spending, Italy allocated 29.7 per cent of national gross domestic product (GDP) to social protection in 2016, in line with the European average (27 per cent), but almost half (48.7 per cent) of this was devoted to old-age pensions and 23 per cent was dedicated to sickness and health care, with the remainder covering all other functions, from disability to unemployment, families and social exclusion (I.Stat, 2019).

At the sub-national level, municipal governments' total expenditure in 2016 on social assistance provision (excluding health care and pensions) amounted to over €7 billion for social services (0.4 per cent of national GDP) (I.Stat, 2019). In terms of per capita expenditure, municipalities spent on average €116 for each resident in 2016 (up from €114 in 2015), but with large regional disparities. Values range from the highest in the Autonomous Province of Bolzano (€517 per capita) to the lowest in Calabria in Southern Italy (€22 per capita) (I.Stat, 2019). Southern regions benefited from 10 per cent of these resources, although they represent 23 per cent of the national population (I.Stat, 2019). These figures clearly portray the geographical variation in social assistance services in Italy, with fewer resources available in areas with higher levels of poverty and vulnerability. In terms of sources of funding, 61.8 per cent came from municipal resources (single municipalities or municipal unions) and 17.8 per cent from regional social policy funds; 16.4 per cent was financed by the Italian state or EU funds, with only 9 per cent provided by the National Fund for Social Policies (I.Stat, 2019). In this context of scarcity of resources and austerity cuts, the Italian welfare state's traditional reliance on family solidarity and charitable organisations could only increase (Saraceno, 1994; Ranci, 1999; Madama et al, 2013).

Supply-side issues in the story of Italian food charity

Italy has a history of food programmes based on surplus. After the Second World War, a special national authority (the Administration of International Aid [AAI][9]) was expressly appointed to manage food aid from the US. A first round of food aid was part of the Marshall Plan, and was therefore intended as a symbol of international social solidarity, particularly addressing children and women affected by the war (Inaudi, 2015). In contrast, a second round (1955–64) of food and nutrition assistance programmes was primarily led by a necessity for the US government to dispose of agricultural surplus while simultaneously attempting to exert political influence over Italian voters (Inaudi, 2015).

Later, surplus food from the European Common Agricultural Policy (CAP) was the basis for the European Food Distribution Programme for the Most Deprived Persons of the Community (MDP),[10] which, for 26 years, sustained many charitable organisations working towards the alleviation of food poverty in Italy. The programme, conceived as an economic measure to stabilise prices and support European farmers, was intended to redistribute food from intervention stocks through the voluntary activities of charitable agencies (Caraher, 2015). From the outset of the MDP, charities had a primary role in running operations. They were, in fact, considered to be best suited to reaching the most deprived and marginalised individuals because they already had the necessary infrastructures and distribution channels in place (Caraher, 2015). Over the years, several charities specialised in this field and organised themselves in a complex network. In Italy, this involved the Ministry of Agriculture and the Agency for Payments in Agriculture (AGEA) managing the programme and coordinating the operations of seven charitable organisations that acted as partners. These were the FBAO, Caritas Italy, Red Cross Italy, Community of Sant'Egidio, Organisation 'Banco delle opere di Carità', Food Bank Association Rome and Association 'Sempre Insieme per la Pace' (Metis and Fondazione Giacomo Brodolini, 2018). The budget allocated to the MDP grew year on year, rising from €100 million in 1987 to €500 million from 2009 until the programme's termination in 2013. For this reason, during the years 2011–13 – before the replacement of the MDP with a new fund – several non-governmental organisations, charities and EU member states (including Italy) lobbied to raise awareness of the possible consequences of discontinuing food aid (Caritas Italiana, 2014). The Italian Ministry of Agriculture launched a special National Fund for Food for the Most Deprived in 2012 to address the temporary lack of food resources supplied to charities during the transition period. In 2014, the Fund for European Aid to the Most Deprived (FEAD) was established, moving food aid from the CAP to the realm of European social policies (Frigo and Tola, 2017). The FEAD aims to strengthen 'social cohesion by contributing to the reduction of poverty, and ultimately the eradication of the worst forms of poverty in the Union, by supporting national schemes that provide non-financial assistance to alleviate food and severe material deprivation and/or contribute to the social inclusion of the most deprived persons' (Article 7, EU Regulation Number 223/2014). Its significance for the Italian system of food assistance can be seen in the fund's allocations. From a total budget of €3.8 billion across the EU-28 countries for the period 2014–20, Italy receives €670 million, complemented by €118 million from national resources (Metis and Fondazione Giacomo Brodolini, 2018). A 60 per cent share of the total (equivalent to €480 million) goes to food aid purchasing and distribution, with the remainder divided between supporting children in deprived families with school materials and equipment, and helping homeless people (Ministero del Lavoro e delle Politiche Sociali, 2015; Frigo and Tola, 2017). Among the new features introduced by the FEAD are obligations on organisations applying for resources to select beneficiaries according to strict eligibility criteria, and to provide supplementary measures to complement food aid, according to the capacities and resources of partner organisations (Metis and Fondazione Giacomo Brodolini, 2018).[11] Recipients qualify for regular food support after an assessment of their economic and social conditions, for which they need to prove a state of deprivation (Ministero del Lavoro e delle Politiche Sociali, 2015).[12]

The FEAD inherited most of its organisational arrangements from the former MDP programme. The AGEA manages the procurement of food stocks, which are delivered to the 219 premises and warehouses of the seven main partner organisations. Their representatives, together with the Ministry of Labour and Social Policies, constitute the coordinating group. The food is ultimately distributed by 11,554 front-line agencies operating locally. In 2015, these provided 2,809,131 recipients with 87,517 tons of food (Ministero del Lavoro e delle Politiche Sociali, 2015; Metis and Fondazione Giacomo Brodolini, 2018).

As intervention stocks currently represent only a marginal share of the total food distributed through the programme, the AGEA purchases most of the food through public auctions, with the quantity and type determined by reported needs and the available budget (Frigo and Tola, 2017; Metis and Fondazione Giacomo Brodolini, 2018). However, the FEAD maintains a connection to surplus food reduction by financing, among other things, the storage and transport infrastructure for donated food with a view to diversifying and expanding the supply of food and reducing food waste (Article 4, c1, EU Regulation Number 223/2014).

Italy is not unprepared in the area of food recovery. Since 2003, it has been the only European country with Good Samaritan legislation in place (ln [Law nr.] 155/2003), which was recently recognised as being among the best practices to encourage food donations (O'Connor et al, 2014). Basically, Good Samaritan legislation gives non-profit organisations, such as food banks, the status of final consumers. The aim is to reduce companies' reluctance to donate food by lowering their liability for any misuse of their donations, thus increasing donations of surplus food from firms (O'Connor et al, 2014). After the introduction of this Good Samaritan legislation, pioneering initiatives have included Siticibo – the FBAO initiative recovering prepared meals from food services and school canteens (FBAO, no date) – and

Buon Fine – a project by the large retailer Coop for the recovery and redistribution of unsold food (Coop, no date). Although much of this activity was already under way, these initiatives have fostered a public debate that connects increasing levels of food poverty and the five million tons of food going to waste every year along the Italian food supply chain (Garrone et al, 2015). Consequently, a large number of operators have called for the further simplification of procedures (FBAO, 2015), particularly during the Universal Exposition 'EXPO 2015 – Feeding the planet, energy for life' hosted in Milan (MIPAAF, 2015). In the wake of this high-profile debate, a new law on food waste recovery – known as the 'Gadda law'[13] – was eventually passed in 2016. Regulating 'donations and distribution of food products and pharmaceuticals for the purposes of social solidarity and food waste limitation' (authors' own translation), the Gadda law basically aims to streamline existing heterogeneous procedures for food donations (Azzurro, 2015; Arcuri, 2019). The impact of the law on food waste reduction may possibly be limited by the lack of national targets and monitoring systems (Segrè and Azzurro, 2016). Nonetheless, it has made some impact by harmonising previously disparate hygiene and fiscal regulations.

The Gadda law and FEAD food provision do complement each other. Over the years, using the experience and knowledge of a large network of private and public operators, the FEAD has built a distribution system that is now well established. The law has now become part of this system and will help to sustain it in turn. In addition, both contribute to filling the social protection gaps in the Italian welfare system.

Reasons why such aid is based on the provision of food can be found both in the deeply rooted ethics – not only religious – of feeding the poor as well as the symbolic meaning of sharing a meal (Bane et al, 2000), and in the institutionalised supply system underpinning charitable food provision in Italy. European food aid, for instance, serves as an important base of material resources that allows operators to ensure the continuity of their activities while putting their main efforts into meeting the other needs of recipients. The majority (80 per cent) of charitable aid providers distribute food from different sources, but, as Caritas observes, FEAD food still accounts for about 70 per cent of the total amount distributed (De Lauso, 2018: 71). This gives an indication of the pressure on food charities during the transition from the MDP to the FEAD, when the temporary lack of resources at the EU level contributed to creating the so-called 'food emergency' (Caritas Italiana, 2014; FBAO, 2014). If material hardship constitutes the main driver on the demand side, basic material assistance is, indeed, the response most frequently provided from the supply side (63 per cent), especially in the form of food provision (48 per cent). Caritas also provides cash donations (21 per cent), used especially by Italian recipients for paying bills and taxes, whereas foreign users tend to make more use of counselling, health-care and housing services (Caritas Italiana, 2017a; De Lauso, 2018). However, as Caritas observes, the feeling is that people tend to ask for what they expect to be provided (De Lauso, 2018) – a factor that might possibly have affected the demand for food assistance as this is both the most common method and easiest way of helping people in need, allowing them to save money for other, less flexible expenses.

Changes in the practices of food provision

A 2015 mapping initiative by Caritas revealed a total of 353 soup kitchens and 3,816 food distribution centres operating in Italy,[14] with the soup kitchens serving 6,273,314 meals to over 190,000 recipients (Caritas Italiana, 2015a). However, there is a whole plethora of informal, voluntary initiatives and independent local projects that are particularly difficult to document (Tomei and Caterino, 2013; Caritas Italiana, 2015a) so this is only a partial picture of the magnitude of the most traditional forms of food aid.

In order to better target and address recipients' needs, the focus of Caritas's activities is its 3,366 *Centri d'Ascolto* (counselling centres). These act as a first point of access where individuals are provided with a 'listening ear' and are then registered and directed to specific services according to their needs. Services range from food aid to family budgeting, job counselling and microloans (Caritas Europe, 2015; Caritas Italiana, 2015a; Maino et al, 2016).

In light of their front-line role and first-hand knowledge of the increasingly complex needs of their users, in 2012, Caritas's counselling centres committed themselves to making a collective effort towards the national harmonisation of data in order to enhance the understanding and monitoring of social phenomena connected to poverty (Caritas Italiana, 2012, 2015a; De Lauso, 2018). It is worth noting that the former national Commission on Poverty and Social Exclusion – which had provided official recognition and understanding of poverty issues since 1984 – was wound up in 2012 due to austerity cuts in public spending (CIES, no date). This epitomises the low priority given to and limited public engagement with increasing levels of poverty during the early stages of the economic crisis.

In addition to monitoring demand, many of Caritas's leading operators have been appraising the adequacy and helpfulness of their provision, aware that traditional forms of food assistance may need to be redesigned according to households' composition, nutrition requirements and causes of need, as well as the social acceptability of their response. They have therefore started to reflect on how to improve food provision – as an emergency response that is still necessary – and also on how to manage their sources of supply to cope with unpredictable resources.

Emporia of Solidarity[15] are a new, enhanced form of food assistance provision that has arisen out of a specific intent to overcome the issues related to traditional forms of emergency food provision (Maino et al, 2016). Conceived as a special model of social supermarkets, emporia mainly target households outside the usual areas of marginality that temporarily fall into a state of need (Caritas Italiana, 2015a; Maino et al, 2016). The process of determining eligibility is carried out by a counselling centre in collaboration with social services, through an official system of referral or simply through informal signposting by social services (Tomei and Caterino, 2013; Maino et al, 2016). Recipients are selected according to eligibility criteria that require proof of a low income as measured by a composite indicator of economic conditions (ISEE) and proof of residence, with household composition, unemployment and health conditions positively evaluated in the assessment.

The most obvious new aspect of this model is in its physical set-up: each emporium is organised like a small shop, where users push trolleys around the shelves and choose what they need most from the available products.[16] All items in the emporium have a price in 'points', depending on their availability and expiry date, and users 'pay' by means of a specific e-card, to which a certain amount of points is assigned according to a previous assessment of their needs. The underpinning idea is to preserve the role of customers/consumers as much as possible for users, and thus reduce the stigma attached to food assistance (Caritas Italiana, 2015a; Maino et al, 2016). The emporium also provides opportunities for recipients to access broader support beyond food aid (Caritas Italiana, 2015a; Maino et al, 2016). This might include cooking classes and food education, family budgeting, job and legal counselling, language classes, and babysitting services, according to the resources available (Caritas Italiana, 2015a; Emporio della Solidarietà di Prato, 2015; Maino et al, 2016). In turn, resources depend on the network of actors involved in any specific initiative. Although many have been started by Caritas and other voluntary – often faith-based –

organisations, emporia are generally established through partnerships between municipalities and other local authorities (53.3 per cent) and bank foundations and other private actors (Caritas Italiana, 2015a). It is worth noting that none of these actors could have run a similar project by relying solely on its own resources (Maino et al, 2016).

Food provision is also closer to the model of a shop. The variety of products tends to be greater, especially compared to food parcels. This is a result of the diversification of supply sources, which are more anchored in local networks based on direct relationships with companies and other donors. Most emporia involve local supermarkets and retailers in their supply (76.7 per cent of emporia), as well as private donations (76.7 per cent), followed by FEAD/AGEA (55.8 per cent) and the FBAO (53.5 per cent) (Caritas Italiana, 2015a). Such diversification and increased reliance on local, direct arrangements with suppliers has been decisive in reducing dependency on European food aid, and was crucial in ensuring the continuity of activities during the transition from the MDP to the FEAD (Emporio della Solidarietà di Prato, 2015). In addition, common sources of supply include food drives and, when necessary, direct purchase in the market. However, it is worth highlighting the proportion of emporia that have also been supplied in recent years through social agriculture projects (11.6 per cent). Increasingly, these community growing initiatives are run by Caritas (23.8 per cent of dioceses) to promote social inclusion and provide opportunities for vulnerable individuals to make social connections (Caritas Italiana, 2015a).

Emporia have become the third most common form of charitable food provision in Italy, behind food parcels and soup kitchens (De Lauso, 2018). Rather than being a replacement for traditional forms of aid, emporia seem to have the potential to fill a gap in the charitable food system (Maino et al, 2016), positioned at the intersection between food poverty and food waste goals, and often between charitable and social operators.

However, in contrast to traditional forms of aid that are easily provided by almost any organisation – food parcels being the prime example – running an emporium requires the operators to complete an array of more complex tasks and activities, ranging from logistics and supply management to front-line services. Therefore, specific competences and expertise are needed, requiring devoted and/or paid staff, as well as financial resources and partners. Such support might not be available to many charitable organisations, especially considering the uneven development and distribution of resources between the most wealthy and deprived areas of Italy.

In addition, as Lorenz (2012) points out, there is a tension between ordinary daily operations and the importance of the witness function of charity, implying that the increasing complexity of the former necessarily reduces time and energy devoted to the latter. Over the past few years, a further reaction to rising poverty and demand for food aid has been that Caritas, among others, has decided to look beyond food assistance and reinforce its witness role by overtly advocating for the poor.

A new role for food charity?

Olivier De Schutter (2013), former United Nations (UN) Special Rapporteur for the Right to Food, has often pointed out that food banks should not be seen as a 'normal' part of national safety nets; however, they might be able to signal where and why our social protection systems are failing to prevent people from falling into poverty. In 2017, Caritas reported a 9 per cent decrease in the number of people visiting its counselling centres, and observed that rather than signalling a decrease in need, this is more likely to indicate a saturation effect on the organisation's capacity to take on responsibility for new users (Caritas Italiana, 2017a). This seems likely when considering that users' needs have become more complex and multidimensional in recent years, requiring longer and more active commitment – the average number of intervention requests per user has increased from eight times per year in 2004 to 18 in 2016 (Caritas Italiana, 2017a: 38).

Overall, these figures highlight the magnitude of the effort and responsiveness of charitable support in a moment of great need. Bearing in mind that in the absence of anti-poverty measures, the repercussions of the crisis could have resulted in the 'obligatory replacement' of the state's commitment to fight poverty (Caritas Italiana, 2015a: 70, authors' translation), it is important that Caritas has reaffirmed its witness function. This has meant observing and providing empirical evidence of existent 'poverties', primarily stressing the necessity to consider the multifaceted nature of deprivation, at a time when a great deal of public attention was focused on the food emergency. For instance, in addition to its traditional annual report on poverty and social exclusion, Caritas has fulfilled this role by drawing up an extra document in which academic experts and charitable operators have contributed to the debate on social policies. The document has two objectives: first, it aims to inform a broader audience, raising awareness of the issues; and, second, it is designed to hold decision-makers to greater account for the consequences of their actions, providing empirical evidence about the results of the choices that they have made (Gori and Marsico, 2015: 12). In Caritas's view, the policies implemented in recent years have been ineffective in tackling poverty and social exclusion (Caritas Italiana, 2014, 2015b, 2017a, 2017b). In particular, the lack of a comprehensive government strategy to tackle poverty and the experimental approach to the implementation of certain measures have stood in the way of delivering positive effects, as in the case of Sostegno per l'Inclusione Attiva (Active Inclusion Support [SIA][17]) (Caritas Italiana, 2017b).

The Alliance against Poverty arose from the need to engage in concrete action to tackle poverty in Italy. The alliance is an advocacy coalition of 35 organisations that have joined together with the aim of raising awareness and advocating for the implementation of adequate public policies against poverty (REIS, no date).[18] The first novel element is the composition of the alliance: it is the first organisation in Italy to bring together faith-based and third sector organisations, trade unions, and municipality unions (Gori and Lusignoli, 2017). In Italy's welfare state, well-established interest groups have traditionally mediated citizens' interests. In this context, faith-based organisations and trade unions had previously been opposed to the introduction of any MIS (Madama and Jessoula, 2015). The alliance's explicit purpose of giving voice to the interests of the poor is also new. This segment of the population is so diverse and fragmented in terms of social composition that it has traditionally lacked political representation (Madama and Jessoula, 2015).

Consequently, besides raising criticisms about policy measures implemented under recent governments, the Alliance against Poverty has put forward a concrete policy proposal according to its guiding principle that all citizens should be assured of an adequate standard of living (Soddu, 2015). Its proposed Reddito di Inclusione Sociale (Income of Social Inclusion [REIS]) is based on a combination of adequate income support and access to social services, targeted at all individuals living in absolute poverty (Gori et al, 2016). To be fully operational, the measure would have required a €7.1 billion investment, proposed to be financed partly through additional resources and partly by merging resources from other forms of support that were already in place (Soddu, 2015).

In 2017, on the basis of the REIS proposal and cooperation with the alliance,[19] a new government-backed scheme to tackle poverty was eventually introduced. The Reddito di Inclusione (Inclusion Income [REI]) represented a major step forward in the fight against poverty in Italy. For the first time, a structural measure of minimum income was introduced and a permanent fund for the fight against poverty was established (Gori and Lusignoli, 2017). Many raised concerns about the limited impact that such a scheme might have on levels of absolute poverty (5.58 million individuals in 2017) when government estimates predicted that the measure could only reach 2.5 million individuals (Agostini, 2017; Gori and Lusignoli, 2017; Alleanza contro la povertà, 2018). Beginning operation in January 2018, the scheme was a means-tested, conditional measure – intended to become universal in the medium to long term – to cover all individuals in absolute poverty regardless of their household composition (Ministero del Lavoro e delle Politiche Sociali, no date[a]).[20]

The Italian general election of 2018 and the unprecedented government coalition that it ushered onto the political scene have triggered a shift that has led, in just a few months, to a reversal of social policy before any comprehensive evaluation of the REI could be carried out.[21] Despite the alliance's intervention warning against 'the temptation to reform the reform' and its recommendation to improve the measure already in place, the reddito di cittadinanza (citizen's income) has instead recently been introduced as a replacement for the REI (Alleanza contro la povertà, 2018). Although the Five Star Movement's flagship anti-poverty measure has been presented as a universal basic income scheme (linked to citizenship rights), it looks to be a de facto conditional MIS (Saraceno, 2018b).[22]

Shifting the focus from the specific realm of social policy, it is worth examining the recent development of a movement linked to urban food policies with its roots in the Milan Urban Food Policy Pact (MUFPP). In recent years, this urban dimension has been regarded as a cornerstone of efforts to rethink the food system with a view to environmental, economic and social sustainability. The work of the MUFPP was started by the Mayor of Milan, who launched a proposal for the pact that was finally signed during the Milan Universal Exposition in 2015 by more than 100 cities. The following day, it was presented to the UN Secretary General Ban Ki-moon during the celebration of World Food Day. The MUFPP is based on an awareness that food policies are closely intertwined with multiple other policy areas, ranging from health to social protection, and from spatial planning to energy and the environment. It therefore calls for the adoption of a multi-actor, interdisciplinary and inter-sectoral approach to policy design. In light of this, mayors and local government representatives in many cities are signing up to the MUFPP. This represents a commitment to adopt the voluntary actions of the Urban Food Policy Framework, which are intended to achieve more sustainable food systems from an urban starting point. Within this framework, cities can select and adapt recommendations to best suit their specific needs. They choose from a set of recommended actions grouped into six interconnected, overlapping categories: governance; sustainable diets and nutrition; social and economic equity; food production; food supply and distribution; and food waste (MUFPP, no date).

Although the MUFPP is still in its infancy, the prominence that it has gained, the multifarious initiatives launched under the framework and the variety of actors involved look promising in terms of activating synergies between different practice and policy spheres (Forster et al, 2015). In particular, under current arrangements for local welfare, the municipal level – which is responsible in Italy for a large share of the delivery of social services but faces considerable resource constraints – could benefit from the urban/municipal/inter-municipal dimension of many initiatives emerging through the MUFPP. This potentially leaves room for a debate on food and, more specifically, the right to food as a foundation on which actors can collectively design and enact new practical and policy solutions to address food poverty, encompassing health, food production and consumption, the environment, and social equity, all of which are crucial to the urban/geographical dimension.

Conclusions

In Italy, the crucial role played by food charity is the result of both a traditionally weak social assistance sector and the centrality of food assistance programmes based on surplus recovery and redistribution. Recent developments have confirmed such tendencies: a law on food waste and donations has been passed, complementing the new European FEAD, which assigns a primary role to charitable food provision. However, the Great Recession triggered such a drastic fall in living conditions that many (food) charities, while holding the line to provide immediate relief to the poor, have also begun to reflect on their position in this evolving context. As one component of a complex and multidimensional experience of poverty, food poverty acted as a warning sign, showing that increasing numbers of people were experiencing problems and that, if they existed, social safety nets were not doing their job. The awareness on the part of key actors in food charity of the necessity to bring the problem to public attention, and of their own limited capacity to address the increasing levels of need, has been decisive in fostering a debate on poverty and moving opinion forward. These elements have certainly played a role in recent social policy shifts that have contributed to filling the historical gap in Italy's welfare state, namely, the absence of a national strategy to tackle poverty. However, the latest data showing five million Italians living in poverty are not cause for hope that the worst is over and recovery to pre-crisis levels is being attained. In addition, the recent political shift and the policy reversal that followed have not allowed a comprehensive evaluation of the effects of implementing certain social policy measures.

In recent years, mayors and local government representatives from many cities have signed up to the MUFPP and its attempts to establish local food policies and implement urban-centred strategies on food. Although this movement is spreading at global, national and sub-national levels, with best practices already being shared among more than 180 cities worldwide, the specific form of these food policies strictly depends on the individual city, actors engaged, selected priorities and actions implemented.

It remains to be seen whether these new arrangements will give rise to local initiatives that are able to guarantee the right to food and ensure social equity. However, a combination of collectively designed approaches to food policy, complementing a broader, national strategy to tackle poverty, could tangibly increase the possibility of effectively tackling the structural causes of food poverty.

Notes

[1] The index encompasses six dimensions: poverty prevention; equitable education; labour market access; social cohesion and non-discrimination; health; and intergenerational justice.

[2] In Italian, the term 'food bank' is only used to refer to the FBAO ('Fondazione Banco Alimentare Onlus'), which is the national food bank foundation – a specific actor operating as an intermediary between donors and front-line agencies directly providing food aid.

[3] Absolute poverty is defined by the Italian National Institute of Statistics (I.Stat) as the economic capacity of a family – based on the age of its members and the location and type of municipal residence – to purchase a basket of goods and services considered essential for a dignified life (I.Stat, 2018a).

[4] Relative poverty is calculated on the basis of per capita spending and updated annually, referring to a nucleus of two persons. This nucleus of two is considered to be in relative poverty if it consumes less than the average single individual in any given year. Relative poverty therefore provides an assessment of inequality in the distribution of expenditure for consumption – poor households are identified as those that are disadvantaged compared to others (I.Stat, 2018a).

[5] These results were drawn from the cases of 197,332 individuals who talked to Caritas operatives across 1,982 counselling centres in 2017. This represented a slight decrease from the previous year in the number of people accessing help (down from 205,090). Each user can exhibit more than one type of problem.

Every year since 2006, the number of counselling centres collecting data in a systematic way has increased, so that every annual report has a different – but larger – empirical basis (Caritas Italiana, 2017a; De Lauso, 2018).

[6] The full name of the inquiry was 'Commissione parlamentare d'inchiesta sulla miseria in Italia e sui mezzi per combatterla, 1952–53' ('Parliamentary Inquiry on Extreme Poverty and on the Instruments to Combat It').

[7] Italy and Greece were the only member states of the EU where no national MIS existed for low-income individuals and families until 2017. In that year, a form of MIS was introduced in both countries. In Greece, the 'social solidarity income' – intended for families and individuals living in extreme poverty – is means tested and combines income support, access to services and support for labour market reintegration (European Social Policy Network, 2017). In Italy, the 'inclusion income' (Reddito di Inclusione [REI]) was introduced in 2017 but has now been replaced by the 'citizen income'. For a detailed explanation of the evolution of anti-poverty schemes in the Italian political context, see Madama et al (2014).

[8] Previous comprehensive national legislation dates back to the Crispi law of 1890.

[9] The AAI became a permanent authority, responsible for assistance activities that, according to the vision of its initiator, should have laid the groundwork for a broad, long-term food and nutrition strategy. Ideally, it was hoped that domestically produced food would gradually replace imported food in free school meal programmes, yielding benefits for agricultural production and the general Italian economy. However, when the moment came for the Italian government to take over responsibility for the broader management and sponsorship of the programme, the AAI was instead required to cut back on school meals spending, and the programme gradually declined. For a detailed overview of the role of the AAI, see Inaudi (2015).

[10] The MDP was also known as the Programme Européen d'aide alimentaire aux plus Démunies (PEAD).

[11] Accompanying measures range from needs assessment to counselling services and other forms of tailored assistance. Depending on the resources and capacities, some agencies are also able to provide basic health care, job search counselling and school support (Metis and Fondazione Giacomo Brodolini, 2018).

[12] Applicants can certify a state of deprivation by providing proof of a low income as measured by a composite indicator of economic conditions (ISEE), a specific document from their municipality/social services or a report of a home visit confirming deprived living conditions. However, means testing is only applied to those seeking regular provision. Emergency cases and cases involving homelessness do not require prior identification by a partner organisation (Ministero del Lavoro e delle Politiche Sociali, no date[b]; Metis and Fondazione Giacomo Brodolini, 2018).

[13] Ln 166/2016 takes its name from the MP who was spokesperson for the law – Maria Chiara Gadda. The text, in Italian, of the law is available at: www. gazzettaufficiale.it/eli/id/2016/08/30/16G00179/sg

[14] These services have been found operating within the territories of 157 and 186 Caritas dioceses, respectively, though they are not exclusively run by Caritas (Caritas Italiana, 2015a).

[15] Emporia of Solidarity include the initiatives within the Caritas network, though the name covers a whole range of similar initiatives run by different operators throughout Italy, which may also be referred to as social markets, social emporia

or just emporia (Maino et al, 2016). The first two were set up in 2008, but the most recent data reveal 180 emporia now taking part in the FEAD programme (Caritas Italiana and CSVNet, 2018). This section focuses on Caritas initiatives but several features can be generalised to other emporia.

[16] Emporia often provide both food and non-food items.

[17] SIA was a national measure for families in severe deprivation where at least one member was either a child, a daughter/son with a disability or a pregnant woman. The experimental implementation of SIA in a number of municipalities did not deliver the expected results. Several reasons lie behind Caritas's critical evaluation of the measure. Caritas took part in the evaluation process with other members of the Alliance against Poverty (REIS, no date).

[18] Scientific coordination is provided by Professor Cristiano Gori, Massimo Baldini, Alberto Martini, Maurizio Motta, Franco Pesaresi, Paolo Pezzana, Simone Pellegrino, Stefano Sacchi, Pierangelo Spano, Ugo Trivellato and Nadir Zanini (REIS, no date).

[19] A memorandum of understanding between the government and the Alliance against Poverty was signed in April 2017.

[20] To be eligible for the REI, potential recipients had to meet several requirements relating to income and financial and family status. The benefit was designed to bridge the gap between the actual household income and a net income threshold. Funding was increased from the original €1.7 billion to €2 billion in 2018 (around 0.1 per cent of GDP), with planned progressive increases to €2.7 billion in 2020. However, the REI incorporated the unemployment assistance scheme (ASDI) and previous SIA. The benefit amount depended on the number of family members, their level of income and other allowances received (Ministero del Lavoro e delle Politiche Sociali, no date[a]). The REI was conditional in that it was linked to participation by the family in a personalised activation project – a key aspect of the measure – involving a multidisciplinary team including municipal social services and employment services (Ministero del Lavoro e delle Politiche Sociali, no date[a]).

[21] See, for instance, the partial evaluation given by the Percorsi di secondo welfare research group (available at: www.secondowelfare.it/).

[22] The benefit of €780 a month is paid for a maximum of two years to individuals with no or low income from work and pension, and is conditional on the recipient accepting any offer of a job or professional training (see: www.redditodicittadinanza. gov.it/).

References

AGEA (Agency for Payments in Agriculture) (2013) 'Relazione piano di distribuzione degli alimenti agli indigenti 2013. Consuntivo delle attività realizzate al 30.04.2013' ['Food distribution plan report to the most deprived 2013. Final balance of the activities carried out as of 04/30/2013'], www.agea.gov.it/portal/pls/portal/docs/1/3806205. PDF

Agostini, C. (2017) 'Per combattere la povertà ora serve un piano triennale' ['A three-year plan now needed to combat poverty'], www.secondowelfare.it/povert-e-inclusione/per-combattere-la-poverta-serve-ora-un-piano-triennale.html

Alleanza contro la povertà (2018) 'Un impegno a combattere la povertà assoluta. La richiesta dell'Alleanza contro la povertà in Italia al nuovo Governo' ['A commitment to combat absolute poverty. The Alliance's request for the new government against poverty in Italy'], www.redditoinclusione.it/wp-content/uploads/2018/06/Piattaforma_Alleanza_2018.pdf

Arcuri, S. (2019) 'Food poverty, food waste and the consensus frame on charitable food redistribution in Italy', *Agriculture and Human Values*, 36(2): 263–75.

Azzurro, P. (2015) 'La donazione degli alimenti invenduti verso la semplificazione normativa', www.minambiente.it/sites/default/files/archivio_immagini/Galletti/Comunicati/alma_mater_bologna/Position%20paper%20sulla%20donazione%20degli%20alimenti%20invenduti.pdf

Baglioni, S., De Pieri, B. and Tallarico, T. (2017) 'Surplus food recovery and food aid: the pivotal role of non-profit organisations. Insights from Italy and Germany', *VOLUNTAS: International Journal of Voluntary and Nonprofit Organizations*, 28(5): 2032–52.

Bane, M.J., Coffin, B. and Thiemann, R.F. (eds) (2000) *Who will provide? The changing role of religion in American social welfare*, Boulder, CO: Westview Press.

Caraher, M. (2015) 'The European Union food distribution programme for the most deprived persons of the community, 1987–2013: from agricultural policy to social inclusion policy?', *Health Policy*, 119(7): 932–40.

Caritas Europe (2015) 'Caritas cares: Italy report. November 2015', www.caritas.eu/wordpress/wp-content/uploads/2018/08/150101-PU-End-poverty-in-europe-country-report-italy.pdf

Caritas Europe (2017) 'Caritas cares: Italy report. November 2017', www.caritas.it/caritasitaliana/allegati/7346/CaritasEuropa_Report_102017.pdf

Caritas Italiana (2012) 'Rapporto 2012 sulla povertà e l'esclusione sociale in Italia. I ripartenti. Povertà croniche e inedite. Percorsi di risalita nella stagione della crisi' ['2012 report on poverty and social exclusion in Italy. The restarts. Recovery paths in the crisis season'], www.caritasitaliana.it/materiali/Pubblicazioni/libri_2012/rapporto2012/Rapporto_Povert_2012_Caritas_Italiana.pdf

Caritas Italiana (2014) 'False partenze. Rapporto 2014 sulla povertà e l'esclusione sociale in Italia' ['False departures. 2014 report on poverty and social exclusion in Italy'], www.caritasitaliana.it/caritasitaliana/allegati/4776/Rapporto_2014_completo%20-%20def%20-%20light.pdf

Caritas Italiana (2015a) 'Povertà plurali. Rapporto 2015 sulla povertà e l'esclusione sociale' ['Poverties, plural. Report on poverty and social exclusion'], www.caritasitaliana.it/materiali/Pubblicazioni/libri_2015/Rapporto_Poverta/RapportoPoverta_2015_web.pdf

Caritas Italiana (ed) (2015b) 'Dopo la crisi costruire il welfare. Le politiche contro la povertà in Italia' ['Building the welfare state after the crisis. Policies against poverty in Italy'], http://s2ew.caritasitaliana.it/materiali/Pubblicazioni/libri_2015/Rapporto_politiche_poverta/Caritas_rapporto_politiche_poverta2015.pdf

Caritas Italiana (2016) 'Non fermiamo la riforma. Rapporto 2016 sulle politiche contro la povertà in Italia' ['Do not stop the reform. 2016 report on policies against poverty in Italy'], http://s2ew.caritasitaliana.it/materiali//Pubblicazioni/libri_2016/nonfermiamolariforma_ottobre2016.pdf

Caritas Italiana (2017a) 'Futuro anteriore. Rapporto 2017 sulla povertà e l'esclusione sociale' ['Future Perfect. 2017 report on poverty and social exclusion'], www.caritas.it/caritasitaliana/allegati/7346/Rapporto_Caritas2017_FuturoAnteriore_copertina.pdf

Caritas Italiana (ed) (2017b) 'Per uscire tutti dalla crisi. Rapporto 2017 sulle politiche contro la povertà in Italia. Reddito di inclusione: la sfida dell'attuazione' ['Getting everyone out of the crisis. 2017 report on policies against poverty in Italy. Inclusion income: the challenge of implementation'], www.caritasitaliana.it/materiali/Pubblicazioni/libri_2017/rapp_caritas_politichepoverta2017.pdf

Caritas Italiana and CSVNet (Coordinamento Nazionale dei Centri di Servizio per il Volontariato) (2018) '1° Rapporto Caritas Italiana-CSVNet sugli empori solidali in Italia' ['Caritas Italy-CSVNet 1st report on emporia of solidarity in Italy'], press release, http://s2ew.caritasitaliana.it/materiali/comunicati/novembre_2018/CS_congiunto_22-11-2018.pdf

Caritas Italiana and FBAO (Fondazione Banco Alimentare Onlus [Food Bank Foundation]) (2015) 'Manual of good practices for charitable organisations. In accordance with Article 8 of Regulation (EC) 852/2004', http://cdn.bancoalimentare.it/sites/bancoalimentare.it/files/manualecaritasbanco_eng_007.pdf

Caselli, D. (2015) 'La realtà della povertà in Italia' ['The reality of poverty in Italy'], in Caritas (ed) *Dopo la crisi costruire il welfare. Le politiche contro la povertà in Italia* [Building the welfare state after the crisis. Policies against poverty in Italy], pp 13–22, http://s2ew.caritasitaliana.it/materiali/Pubblicazioni/libri_2015/Rapporto_politiche_poverta/Caritas_rapporto_politiche_poverta2015.pdf

CIES (Commissione Indagine Sull'Esclusione Sociale) (no date) 'Commissione di Indagine Sull'Esclusione Sociale', http://sitiarcheologici.lavoro.gov.it/CIES/Pages/20120620.aspx

Coop (no date) 'Recupero prodotti – da spreco a risorsa' ['Food products' recovery – from waste to resource'], www.coopfirenze.it/sezione-soci/coop-buon-fine

Culpepper, P.D. (2014) 'The political economy of unmediated democracy: Italian austerity under Mario Monti', *West European Politics*, 37(6): 1264–81.

De Lauso, F. (2018) 'Il volto dei poveri incontrati nei Centri di Ascolto Caritas' ['The face of the poor met in the Caritas Listening Centers'], in Caritas (ed) *Rapporto sulle politiche contro la povertà in Italia. Povertà in attesa* [*Report on policies against poverty in Italy. Poverty waiting*], pp 31–89, www.caritasitaliana.it/caritasitaliana/allegati/7847/Cap_02_Rapporto_2018.pdf

Del Pino, E. and Pavolini, E. (2015) 'Decentralisation at a time of harsh austerity: multilevel governance and the welfare state in Spain and Italy facing the crisis', *European Journal of Social Security*, 17(2): 246–70.

De Schutter, O. (2013) 'Food banks can only plug the holes in social safety nets', www.theguardian.com/commentisfree/2013/feb/27/food-banks-social-safety-nets

Dowler, E. (2002) 'Food and poverty in Britain: rights and responsibilities', *Social Policy & Administration*, 36(6): 698–717.

Emporio della Solidarietà di Prato (2015) 'Bilancio sociale 2015' ['Final balance 2015'], www.emporio.prato.it/images/articles/bilancio%202015.pdf

Esping-Andersen, G. (1990) *The three worlds of welfare capitalism*, Cambridge: Polity Press.

European Social Policy Network (2017) 'ESPN flash report 2017/68. The national roll-out of the "Social Solidarity Income" scheme in Greece', https://ec.europa.eu/social/BlobServlet?docId=18246&langId=en

Eurostat Database (no date) 'Inability to afford a meal with meat, chicken, fish (or vegetarian equivalent) every second day – EU-SILC survey', http://appsso.eurostat.ec.europa.eu/nui/show.do?dataset=ilc_mdes03&lang=UK

FBAO (Fondazione Banco Alimentare Onlus [Food Bank Foundation]) (no date) 'Banco Alimentare', www.bancoalimentare.it/it

FBAO (2014) 'Emergenza alimentare: la nostra priorità' ['Food emergency: our priority'], www.bancoalimentare.it/it/Emergenza-Alimentare-la-nostra-priorita

FBAO (2015) 'Spreco alimentare. Dalle parole ai fatti' ['Food waste: from words to action'], www.bancoalimentare.it/en/node/3779

Ferrera, M. (1996) 'The "Southern model" of welfare in social Europe', *Journal of European Social Policy*, 6(1): 17–37.

Ferrera, M., Fargion, V. and Jessoula, M. (2012) *Alle radici del welfare all'italiana: origini e futuro di un modello sociale squilibrato* [*At the roots of Italian welfare: Origins and future of an unbalanced social model*], Venice: Marsilio.

Forster, T., Egal, F., Getz Escudero, A., Dubbeling, M. and Renting, H. (2015) 'Milan Urban Food Policy Pact: selected good practices from cities', www.ruaf.org/sites/default/files/MUFPP_SelectedGoodPracticesfromCities.pdf

Frigo, A. and Tola, M. (2017) 'La povertà alimentare: il FEAD' ['Food poverty: the FEAD'], in Caritas (ed) *Per uscire tutti dalla crisi. Rapporto 2017 sulle politiche contro la povertà in Italia. Reddito di inclusione: la sfida dell'attuazione* [*Getting everyone out of the crisis. 2017 report on policies against poverty in Italy. Inclusion income: the challenge of implementation*], pp 27–32, www.caritasitaliana.it/materiali/Pubblicazioni/libri_2017/rapp_caritas_politichepoverta2017.pdf

Galli, F., Cavicchi, A. and Brunori, G. (2019) 'Food waste reduction and food poverty alleviation: a system dynamics conceptual model', *Agriculture and Human Values*, 36(2): 289–300.

Garrone, P., Melacini, M. and Perego, A. (2015) 'Surplus food management against food waste. Il recupero delle eccedenze alimentari. Dalle parole ai fatti' ['Surplus food management against food waste. The recovery of food surpluses. From words to action'], www.bancoalimentare.it/sites/bancoalimentare.it/files/executive_summary_surplus_food_managemnt_against_food_waste.pdf

Gori, C. (2012) 'Politiche sociali, il piatto piange' ['Social policies: the kitty is short'], www.ilsole24ore.com/art/commenti-e-idee/2012-10-22/politiche-sociali-piatto-piange-074705.shtml?uuid=AbsAaWvG&refresh_ce=1

Gori, C., Baldini, M., Martini, A., Motta, M., Pellegrino, S., Pesaresi, F., Pezzana, P., Sacchi, S., Spano, P., Trivellato, U. and Zanini, N. (2016) Il reddito d'inclusione sociale (REIS): la proposta dell'Alleanza contro la povertà in Italia.

Gori, C. and Lusignoli, L. (2017) 'Alleanza contro la povertà e REI' ['Alliance against poverty and REI'], in Caritas (ed) *Per uscire tutti dalla crisi. Rapporto 2017 sulle politiche contro la povertà in Italia. Reddito di inclusione: la sfida dell'attuazione* [*Getting everyone out of the crisis. 2017 report on policies against poverty in Italy. Inclusion income: the challenge of implementation*], pp 45–54, www.caritasitaliana.it/materiali/Pubblicazioni/libri_2017/rapp_caritas_politichepoverta2017.pdf

Gori, C. and Marsico, F. (2015) 'Il rapporto Caritas sulle politiche contro la povertà. Oggi e domani' ['Caritas report on policies against poverty'], in Caritas (ed) *Dopo la crisi costruire il welfare. Le politiche contro la povertà in Italia* [*Building the welfare state after the crisis. Policies against poverty in Italy*], pp 9–12, http://s2ew.caritasitaliana.it/materiali/Pubblicazioni/libri_2015/Rapporto_politiche_poverta/Caritas_rapporto_politiche_poverta2015.pdf

Inaudi, S. (2015) 'Assistenza ed educazione alimentare: l'Amministrazione per gli Aiuti Internazionali 1947–1965' ['Nutrition assistance and education: the Administration for International Aid 1947–1965'], *Contemporanea*, 18(3): 373–400.

I.Stat (Italian National Institute of Statistics) (2014) 'Anno 2013. I consumi delle famiglie' ['Year 2013. Households' consumption'], www.istat.it/it/files//2014/07/Consumi-delle-famiglie1.pdf

I.Stat (2017) 'Anno 2015. La spesa dei comuni per i servizi sociali' ['Year 2015. Municipal expenditures for social services'], www.istat.it/it/files/2017/12/Report_spesa-sociale2015.pdf

I.Stat (2018a) 'La povertà in Italia. Anno 2017' ['Poverty in Italy. Year 2017'], www.istat.it/it/files/2018/06/La-povert%C3%A0-in-Italia-2017.pdf

I.Stat (2018b) 'Spese per consumi delle famiglie. Anno 2017' ['Spending for households' consumption. Year 2017'], www.istat.it/it/files/2018/06/Spese-delle-famiglie-Anno-2017.pdf

I.Stat (2019) 'Anno 2016. La spesa dei comuni per i servizi sociali' ['Year 2016. Municipal expenditures for social services'], www.istat.it/it/files/2019/01/Report-spesa-sociale-2016.pdf

I.Stat Database (no date) 'I.Stat', www.istat.it/it/

Jessoula, M., Kubisa, J., Madama, I. and Zielenska, M. (2014) 'Understanding convergence and divergence: old and new cleavages in the politics of minimum income schemes in Italy and Poland', *Journal of International and Comparative Social Policy*, 30(2): 128–46.

Kazepov, Y. (2008) 'The subsidiarization of social policies: actors, processes and impacts: some reflections on the Italian case from a European perspective', *European Societies*, 10(2): 247–73.

Lorenz, S. (2012) 'Socio-ecological consequences of charitable food assistance in the affluent society: the German Tafel', *International Journal of Sociology and Social Policy*, 32(7/8): 386–400.

Madama, I. and Jessoula, M. (2015) 'Alleanza contro la povertà e reddito minimo: perché può essere la volta buona' ['Alliance against poverty and minimum income; why it might be the right time'], in Caritas (ed) *Dopo la crisi costruire il welfare. Le politiche contro la povertà in Italia* [*Building the welfare state after the crisis. Policies against poverty in Italy*], pp 91–104, http://s2ew.caritasitaliana.it/materiali/ Pubblicazioni/libri_2015/Rapporto_politiche_poverta/Caritas_ rapporto_politiche_poverta2015.pdf

Madama, I., Natili, M. and Jessoula, M. (2013) 'COPE work package 5 – the national arena for combating poverty: national report: Italy, http://cope-research.eu/wp-content/uploads/2013/05/National_ Report-Italy.pdf

Madama, I., Jessoula, M. and Natili, M. (2014) 'Minimum income: the Italian trajectory: one, no one and one hundred thousand minimum income schemes', *Working Paper-LPF*, 2014(1): 1–28.

Maino, F., Lodi Rizzini, C. and Bandera, L. (2016) *La povertà alimentare in Italia. Le risposte del secondo welfare* [*Food poverty in Italy: Responses from the second welfare*], Bologna: Il Mulino.

Metis and Fondazione Giacomo Brodolini (2018) 'FEAD country fiche Italy', www.lavoro.gov.it/temi-e-priorita/europa-e-fondi-europei/ focus-on/fondo-di-aiuti-europei-agli-indigenti%E2%80%93Fead/ Documents/2018-FEAD-Country-Fiche-Italy.pdf

Ministero del Lavoro e delle Politiche Sociali (no date[a]) 'Reddito di Inclusione (REI)' ['Inclusion income'], www.lavoro.gov.it/temi- e-priorita/poverta-ed-esclusione-sociale/focus-on/Reddito-di- Inclusione-ReI/Pagine/default.aspx

Ministero del Lavoro e delle Politiche Sociali (no date[b]) 'Programma Operativo per la fornitura di prodotti alimentari e/o assistenza materiale di base (PO-I) 2014–2020' ['Operational programme for food provision and/or basic material assistance PO-1 2014–2020'], www.lavoro.gov.it/temi-e-priorita/europa-e-fondi-europei/ focus-on/fondo-di-aiuti-europei-agli-indigenti%E2%80%93Fead/ Documents/PROGRAMMA-OPERATIVO-FEAD.pdf

Ministero del Lavoro e delle Politiche Sociali (2015) 'Relazione di attuazione FEAD – OP1 2015' ['FEAD – OP1 implementation report'], www.lavoro.gov.it/temi-e-priorita/europa-e-fondi-europei/ focus-on/fondo-di-aiuti-europei-agli-indigenti%E2%80%93Fead/ Documents/FEAD-Rapporto-attuazione-giugno-2015.pdf

MIPAAF (Ministero delle Politiche Agricole, Alimentari e Forestali) (2013) 'Povertà alimentare, De Girolamo: trovate risorse per far partire fondo indigenti. Ora stimolare anche la filiera contro lo spreco di cibo' ['Food poverty, De Girolamo: found the resources to set up a fund for the poor. Now stimulate the supply chain against food waste'], www.agricolae.eu/poverta-alimentare-de-girolamo-trovate-risorse-per-far-partire-fondo-indigenti-ora-stimolare-anche-la-filiera-contro-lo-spreco-di-cibo/

MIPAAF (2015) 'Expo: presentate le azioni del Governo per ridurre sprechi e potenziare aiuti agli indigenti, Martina: 1 milione di tonnellate di alimenti salvati dallo spreco entro il 2016. puntiamo su un modello che incentivi il recupero' ['Expo: presented the government's actions to reduce waste and increase aid to the needy, Martina: 1 million tons of food saved from waste by 2016. We will focus on a model that encourages recovery'], www.politicheagricole.it/flex/cm/pages/ServeBLOB.php/L/IT/IDPagina/9378

Morlicchio, E. (2012) *Sociologia della povertà* [*Sociology of poverty*], Bologna: Il Mulino.

MUFPP (Milan Urban Food Policy Pact) (no date) 'Milan Urban Food Policy Pact', www.milanurbanfoodpolicypact.org/

Natili, M. (2016) 'Changing welfare in Southern Europe? Political competition and the evolution of regional minimum income schemes in Italy and Spain', *Social Policies*, 3(2): 331–48.

Natili, M. (2018) 'Explaining different trajectories of minimum income schemes: groups, parties and political exchange in Italy and Spain', *Journal of European Social Policy*, 28(2): 116–29.

Natili, M., Jessoula, M., Madama, I. and Matsaganis, M. (2018) 'The right(s) and minimum income in hard times: Southern and Eastern Europe compared', *European Societies*, 21(1): 33–51.

O'Connor, C., Gheoldus, M. and Jan, O. (2014) 'Comparative study on EU member states' legislation and practices on food donation: executive summary', www.eesc.europa.eu/resources/docs/executive-summary_comparative-study-on-eu-member-states-legislation-and-practices-on-food-donation.pdf

Pavolini, E. (2015) 'How many Italian welfare states are there?', in U. Ascoli and E. Pavolini (eds) *The Italian welfare state in a European perspective: A comparative analysis*, Bristol: Policy Press, pp 285–307.

Pavolini, E., León, M., Guillén, A.M. and Ascoli, U. (2015) 'From austerity to permanent strain? The EU and welfare state reform in Italy and Spain', *Comparative European Politics*, 13(1): 56–76.

Ranci, C. (1999) *Oltre il welfare state. Terzo settore, nuove solidarietà e trasformazioni del welfare* [*Beyond the welfare state. Third sector, new solidarities and welfare transformation*], Bologna: Il Mulino.

Ranci, C., Pellegrino, M. and Pavolini, E. (2005) The third sector and the policy process in Italy: between mutual accommodation and new forms of partnership, http://eprints.lse.ac.uk/29011/1/4TSEP.pdf

REIS (Reddito di Inclusione Sociale [Income of Social Inclusion]) (no date) 'Home page', www.redditoinclusione.it/

Riches, G. (1997) 'Hunger, food security and welfare policies: issues and debates in First World societies', *Proceedings of the Nutrition Society*, 56(1A): 63–74.

Santini, C. and Cavicchi, A. (2014) 'The adaptive change of the Italian Food Bank Foundation: a case study', *British Food Journal*, 116(9): 1446–59.

Saraceno, C. (1994) 'The ambivalent familism of the Italian welfare state', *Social Politics: International Studies in Gender, State & Society*, 1(1): 60–82.

Saraceno, C. (2018a) 'Il lavoro non basta a proteggere dalla povertà' ['Work is not enough to protect from poverty'], www.neodemos. info/articoli/il-lavoro-non-basta-a-proteggere-dalla-poverta/

Saraceno, C. (2018b) 'Così il reddito di cittadinanza può migliorare il Rei' ['How the citizenship income could improve the REI'], www.lavoce.info/archives/51860/cosi-reddito-cittadinanza-puo-migliorare-rei/

Schraad-Tischer, D., Schiller, C., Matthias Heller, S. and Siemer, N. (2017) 'Social justice in the EU – index report 2017: Social Inclusion Monitor Europe', www.bertelsmann-stiftung.de/fileadmin/files/ BSt/Publikationen/GrauePublikationen/NW_EU_Social_Justice_ Index_2017.pdf

Secondo Welfare (2013) 'Focus sulla povertà alimentare' ['Focus on food poverty'], https://secondowelfare.it/povert-alimentare/focus-poverta-alimentare.html

Segrè, A. and Azzurro, P. (2016) *Spreco alimentare: dal recupero alla prevenzione. Indirizzi applicativi della legge per la limitazione degli sprechi* [*Food waste: From recovery to preventing. Guidelines for application of the law*], Milan: Fondazione Giangiacomo Feltrinelli.

Soddu, F. (2015) 'Reddito minimo: Includiamo, senza cappelli', *Italia Caritas: Mensile di Caritas italiana. Organismo pastorale della CEI*, 4: 10–13, http://s2ew.caritasitaliana.it/materiali/Media/ Italia_Caritas/2015/IC04_maggio15.pdf

Streeck, W. and Thelen, K. (eds) (2005) *Beyond continuity. Institutional change in advanced political economies*, Oxford: Oxford University Press.

Tomei, G. and Caterino, L. (2013) *Un'indagine sulla Povertà Alimentare. Secondo Rapporto sull'esclusione Sociale in Toscana* [*A survey on food poverty. Second report on social exclusion in Tuscany*], Pisa: Pisa University Press.

Vampa, D. (2017) 'From national to sub-national? Exploring the territorial dimension of social assistance in Italy', *Journal of Social Policy*, 46(2): 269–89.

4

Food banks in the Netherlands stepping up to the plate: shifting moral and practical responsibilities

Hilje van der Horst, Leon Pijnenburg and Amy Markus

Introduction

This chapter examines how responsibilities for securing citizens' food needs have been understood and exercised over time in the Netherlands, and how such responsibilities have recently been affected by the emergence of food banks. In order to assess responsibilities for food needs in this relatively rich society, it is necessary to take into account some general circumstances. First, welfare provisions have been diminished due to financial limitations, neoliberal policies and a globalising economy. As a result, income protection has been reduced. Second, people now need more complex bureaucratic skills, as well as financial literacy, to access welfare provisions and to avoid accumulating problematic debt and experiencing the ensuing restrictions on their household budget. Nevertheless, Dutch policy still assumes a theoretical responsibility for guaranteeing a level of income that ensures access to basic necessities, including food. In addition, governmental aid is provided through income measures, discounts on expenses and even refunds on certain large expenses, not through in-kind assistance like that offered by food banks. The Netherlands regards food as a human right but emphasises that this right is secured through existing provisions and services, not through providing food itself.

Nevertheless, due to various complex factors, people are falling below minimum levels of subsistence. Out of solidarity and respect for human dignity, food banks and their volunteers are picking up the slack (Pijnenburg, 2018). The question is how this phenomenon of charitable food aid might reconfigure responsibilities relating to citizens' food needs.

Hunger brings with it an urgent moral imperative to act. Disputes about who is responsible for dealing with this issue are deemed to be of less immediate concern. The first priority is for some party to step up to the plate to alleviate hunger. Since 2002, food banks have taken on this task in the Netherlands. In effect, they have assumed a certain amount of responsibility for responding to the food needs of families. A private charity organisation assuming such responsibility not only reorders the practical ways in which households in poverty access food, but also transfigures moral understandings of responsibility itself.

With regard to the responsibilities of the state, the current literature points to an iterative process between welfare states and food charities. On the one hand, welfare states limit welfare provision in terms of both secured income levels and coverage. This de facto creates a space in which food banks and other charities can start to assume responsibility for securing access to food. On the other hand, food banks have drawn substantial criticism for actually *allowing* states to shrink their responsibility towards citizens even further (Poppendieck, 1998; Dowler and O'Connor, 2012; Riches and Silvasti, 2014; Lambie-Mumford, 2017). Some authors argue that where food banks address the harshest forms of food insecurity, states can allow gaps in the safety net of welfare provision to emerge and spread, and also neglect structural problems, furthering the neoliberal retreat of government (Riches, 2002). These authors maintain that this situation is unsatisfactory because this form of food provision falls short in the areas of human dignity (Van der Horst et al, 2014) and nutrition (Neter et al, 2016).

In the Netherlands, the initial political response to food banks' assumption of responsibility was criticism. In the context of a well-developed welfare state, food banks were considered to be a disgrace, throwing the country back to a past when poor households were dependent on charity and subject to discipline (Verschuren, 2015). Indeed, food banks were regarded as taking responsibility where the state should act to tackle structural problems and reach impoverished households. However, since that first response, criticism has diminished and governmental institutions have come to adapt their policies and practice to accommodate the existence of food banks and their services. A majority of local governments now facilitate food banks through funding and in-kind support,[1] suggesting the further institutionalisation of charitable support (see also Williams et al, 2016).

There is a strong perception internationally that food charity is a form of welfare replacement. However, there is little empirical knowledge of the ways in which state welfare and charitable food assistance relate to each other, and how responsibilities are understood and practised. This requires a multilevel understanding. Food banks are embedded in locally situated practices and complex histories of responsibilities for ensuring access to food and other basic needs. This chapter examines just how such responsibilities for securing citizens' ability to fulfil their basic needs, most notably, food, have developed over time in the Netherlands, and how they have recently been affected by the emergence of food banks. The analysis is based on existing research, policy documents, newspaper articles and websites, and is illustrated with quotes from a set of 15 interviews with food bank volunteers, aldermen and municipal policy officers conducted by one of the authors (Markus, 2018).

Welfare state: from pillars to participation society

In order to contextualise how responsibilities between the state and third sector organisations have developed in the Netherlands, this chapter identifies four periods: (1) the period of pillars; (2) the period of welfare expansion; (3) the period of welfare retreat; and (4) the period of societal responsibilisation. The first period – the period of pillars – started in 1848, when both freedom of religion and freedom of organisation were introduced and third sector organisations proliferated. Both Roman Catholics and orthodox Protestants exploited the new civil liberties to found organisations operating in all kinds of domains, including social life and welfare. These organisations then formed associations based on a shared religious denomination – Catholic or Protestant. Such associations, operating nationally, came to be known as 'pillars'. Next to the two religious pillars, a socialist pillar and a liberal pillar emerged, though they were never as all-encompassing as their ecclesiastical peers (Hoogenboom, 2011). During this period of pillars, third sector organisations and various elites, typically operating locally, assumed responsibility for poor relief. While the Dutch welfare state is currently among the most comprehensive in the world, it was late to develop, partly due to the central role played by the pillars (De Swaan, 1988), as faith-based organisations resisted the involvement of the state in providing aid (Hoogenboom, 2004). Thus, responsibility for ensuring food security lay explicitly with these pillars and access to food aid was based on a person's affiliation with such a pillar.

After the Second World War, the second period started, which can be characterised as the period of welfare expansion. During this period, the state assumed more responsibility and the influence of the pillars diminished. The welfare state expanded quickly, with state pensions, social security, disability allowances and a minimum wage all being introduced during this period. Recipients moved from being dependent on charity offered by organisations linked to their religion to a position of having certain rights aligned with citizenship, regardless of their religious or political affiliation.

After 25 years of welfare state expansion, the third phase – of neoliberal welfare retreat – commenced. Individual responsibility and, later, community and social network responsibilities became important elements of both discourse and practice (De Bruijn et al, 2016). The Dutch government of the 1980s, in line with policies initiated by the Thatcher government in the UK and under Reagan's presidency in the US, implemented various austerity measures under the umbrella of its so-called 'no nonsense policy'. Cost-saving measures included cutting the benefits and salaries of civil servants and teaching staff. The social safety net that had been established over the preceding decades became more restricted.

This period of welfare retreat led to concerns about rising poverty. This 'new poverty' was recognised in the budget debate of the Dutch Parliament in 1989. The United Nations (UN) World Summit for Social Development of 1995 reinforced the warnings and emergency signals concerning 'new poverty' that had already been entering the public debate from below for some time. The issue even ended up being mentioned in the 1995 'annual speech' given by Her Majesty Queen Beatrix of the Netherlands. Strikingly, the speech, which always reflects the position of the Dutch government, explicitly called on non-governmental actors to assume responsibility for addressing this issue:

> Incidentally, many native citizens also find themselves in a comparably weak socio-economic position. The government calls on citizens, businesses, other public authorities and civil society organisations to work together to tackle social exclusion and silent poverty in our society in a concerted and decisive manner. The cohesion we need is at stake if large numbers of people feel excluded. (Authors' translation)[2]

Thus, the period of welfare retreat, rather fluidly, gave way to the fourth period – that of societal responsibilisation.

The focus on the responsibilities of communities and social networks was further sharpened under the rubric of the 'participation society' in 2013, which was launched in an international climate of retreating governments and post-crisis economic conditions (Cohen and Fuhr, 2017). This was the latest attempt to increase the responsibility of citizens to care for themselves and their social environment. Critics emphasise that the ability of citizens to carry out this responsibility, especially for their social environment, was overestimated (Boutellier and Van der Klein, 2014). Six years later, one of the architects of the policy – former Minister for Education, Culture and Science Jet Bussemaker (Dutch Labour Party) – acknowledged this in a newspaper interview (Kammer and Van Lonkhuyzen, 2019). In fact, throughout this period, the government remained active as both a provider and facilitator. In Tonkens's (2015) analysis, the government in the Netherlands was not really retreating, but rather 'reshaping' its relationship with citizens, moving from the role of provider to the role of facilitator.

Local government officials reflected on this fourth period when interviewed (Markus, 2018). For example, an alderman of a small municipality characterised the role of local government as neither to provide nor to retreat, but rather to facilitate a local network, embodying the ideals of the participation society:

> So that welfare state, we can actually no longer afford it the way it was. So it is becoming a societal issue more and more and we have to mobilise our own network more and more as well…. I think we, as a municipality, must facilitate that network. We should not be that network. But we should facilitate. (Markus, 2018)

Nevertheless, there was still a strong feeling among interviewees that the state has a responsibility to ensure that citizens have sufficient income, whether through work or social security (Markus, 2018). Interviewees differed in their evaluation of the sufficiency of the current welfare system. One alderman was more critical and suggested that the central government is not taking enough responsibility for ensuring that people have sufficient means for their basic expenses: 'On the other hand, still, one of the biggest causes why people have to turn to the food bank is because they simply have too little income. And that, you cannot change in the municipality, that is really somewhat on the Hague's [central government's] plate though' (Markus, 2018). Thus, while the Netherlands has experienced a period of welfare retreat since the 1980s, the government is still seen as responsible for social welfare, though ideas about how to fulfil this responsibility differ.

Poverty and food security

Even if welfare provisions in the Netherlands are still extensive in comparison with other countries, certain populations are now less protected, and possibly more at risk of food insecurity, than they were prior to the period of welfare retreat. These groups include unemployed people and migrants. In general, welfare levels have not kept pace with income, and income protection – in terms of both social security measures and labour market security – has been on a significant downward trend, especially since the 1990s (Vrooman, 2016).

About one person in 17 is estimated to be affected by poverty in the Netherlands. Poverty is assessed by calculating the income that households require to fulfil their basic needs. The total number of individuals affected ranges between 800,000 when using a strict definition in which only the basic necessities are counted and 1.2 million when a definition is applied that includes a small sum for social participation (Hoff et al, 2016). This means that in order to make ends meet, these people need to forgo or limit spending on other necessary expenses. When choosing between heating their home, purchasing new shoes for children having a growth spurt or buying food, people may opt to economise on food beyond an acceptable threshold. Being in a situation where such a choice is necessary hardly suggests that one is food secure.

There are several drivers of poverty in the Netherlands, and changes to the labour market constitute the first of these. The Netherlands is increasingly seeing the emergence of 'working poor' (about one in 20 workers) as a result of low-paying jobs and limited capacity to work due to health issues or caring responsibilities (Snel, 2017). The percentage of people who have flexible employment contracts without much income protection has grown, as has the number of self-employed workers, including many in low-skilled jobs (NVVK, no date; CBS, 2019).

Against this background of reduced income security and income levels at the bottom of society, there has also been a significant increase in individual debt. The number of people seeking assistance because of indebtedness fluctuates but grew between 2012 and 2017 (NVVK, no date, 2017). The level of debt is also on the increase, reaching a per person average of €42.100 in 2017 (NVVK, 2017). Although substantial, the number of people asking for help with their debts is a small proportion of the total number experiencing debt problems, which is estimated to be 5 per cent of the population (Madern, 2014).

While low income is a risk factor for indebtedness, problematic debts are not confined to low-income households. Since 2011, the percentage of people asking for debt counselling and debt restructuring who receive income from work has surpassed the percentage of people whose income consists of welfare benefits. When people enter the process of debt restructuring, their household income after repayments is equivalent to about 90 per cent of what would be received in social security. This process lasts three years, after which any remaining debts are absolved. The programme relieves people of the burden of finding ad hoc solutions to repay creditors in order to prevent, for example, eviction or having their water and electricity supplies cut off. However, it does mean that people have only the most basic income on which to survive. People in debt – whether in restructuring or other programmes, or paying off creditors from their own budgets directly – constitute the main group at risk of food insecurity and suffer the associated shame and stress (Hoogland and Berg, 2016).

In an interview, a food bank volunteer described the kinds of situations that lead people into financial problems, and highlighted the complexity of bureaucracy in this area (cf Tonkens and Verplanke, 2016). There is a role to be played by the government in preventing these problems, but according to this volunteer, ad hoc solutions – such as those offered by the food bank – will also continue to be necessary:

> And we are now of course at a turning point with new resources, at the tax office, doing returns. With that, some people fall through the cracks. And I think you should work to avoid that, but you should also tackle the consequences when prevention fails. And there is now such an acceleration in information and everything related to that that it produces victims. (Markus, 2018)

Even with the developments outlined previously, the Netherlands is one of the countries that ranks lowest on measures of material deprivation and food insecurity in Europe. However, this does not tell the whole story of food insecurity in the Netherlands. Households struggling to balance their budgets save money through their food choices. Calorie-dense foods have become relatively cheaper. Ice cream, sugar and confectionery all decreased in cost between 2010 and 2017. Crisps and sauces increased in price but only by a few percentage points. In contrast, healthy foods became 22 per cent more expensive between 2010 and 2017 (CBS, 2018). This explains why foods that are less calorie dense and more nutrient rich might be less accessible to people in poverty who are trying to make ends meet (Bere et al, 2008; Miller et al, 2016).

The right to food in the Netherlands

Since the redrafting of the constitution in 1983, the Netherlands has recognised both classic freedom rights, also known as 'first-generation' rights, and 'second-generation' economic, social and cultural (ESC) rights. Therefore, it seemed that the Dutch constitution had fully acknowledged and implemented the basic rights set out in the International Covenant on Economic, Social and Cultural Rights (ICESCR), which was ratified by the Netherlands in 1978. Article 11 of the ICESCR relates to the human right to food.

However, the full picture is not so simple (Vlemminx, 2010). During the ratification debates in the 1970s, the Dutch government interpreted the rights of the ICESCR not as 'fixed' criteria, but as indications that had to be defined in more detail by means of politics and policy. When discussing the constitutional reform in 1983, the Dutch government had ensured that there was room for manoeuvre with regard to the inclusion of the ESC rights by arguing that the relevant regulatory and executive authorities had sufficient policy space to cover these rights. It was of the opinion that the ESC rights were already almost fully realised in the new constitution and that no further judicial control or enforcement was needed. While operating within a monistic system – where international treaties like the ICESCR are directly applicable – the Dutch government simultaneously continued to hamper, or even block, the possible effects of implementing the ICESR.

After an in-depth study of the right to food in the Netherlands and Belgium, Wernaart (2013) concluded that the Netherlands distinguishes quite strictly between civil and political rights, on the one hand, and ESC rights, on the other. While civil and political rights are directly applicable, ESC rights are not considered directly applicable (Wernaart, 2013: 272). Rather, conditions are created that formally give people access to those rights but the substantive use and realisation of these rights is difficult and depends on people's individual responsibility.

A similar approach can be identified in an exchange between the government and the UN Economic and Social Council about the existence of food banks in relation to food security. This committee asked the Dutch government in 2010 what concrete measures had been taken to address the emergence of food banks and the apparent food insecurity that this suggested. After stating that the existing Dutch system of social security guarantees a minimum income 'that enables people to meet their basic needs, including food, clothing and shelter', the Dutch government replied: 'As far as food banks are concerned, the Government has agreed with the VNG [Association of Dutch Municipalities] to improve cooperation between municipalities and local food banks to encourage those who use food banks to avail themselves of municipal provisions.'[3] Thus, primary responsibility for access to food is interpreted in terms of local government providing help with income and expenses.

This response reflects a rather strong belief in the sufficiency of existing provision. A similar conviction seems to exist at the local governmental level, despite interviewees increasingly being confronted with people for whom the available resources are not adequate to prevent them from needing food aid. By holding on to the idea of a 'functioning system of protection', the need for food assistance is seen in the context of individual circumstances and setbacks, rather than at the level of the social welfare system.

This high level of confidence in the welfare system also leads to the notion that the government cannot be involved in emergency food aid because this would amount to an admission that the system is inadequate. Such reasoning about the risk of undermining one's own system by creating an extra 'fix' can be observed in an interview with a policy adviser from a small municipality, who stated that there is a problem with a state correcting errors in a system for which it is responsible. Correcting errors would mean that there are problems with the welfare system itself, which this adviser maintained is not the case. Rather, such issues should only be understood as problems and 'situations' encountered at the level of the individual: 'No, because by that you actually suggest [that] our laws are not in order, that we have a basic subsistence level that is not in order. And that is not the case. No, it is more about the situations around it that people can get caught in' (Markus, 2018). Doubt about the capacity of the state to ensure food security is especially evident in interviews with food bank volunteers (Markus, 2018). One volunteer pointed to a paradox when a state is responsible for ad hoc solutions for gaps in the safety net:

> So I do not know well, should the state take care of that? I don't know whether the state has the capacity to do that, and what kind of apparatus you have to build for that. This is an apparatus supporting another apparatus, because we

have good social arrangements in the Netherlands, so, yes,
I find it hard. (Markus, 2018)

Thus, even in the face of people falling through such gaps, this interviewee supports the view that the existing social security measures are, in fact, good.

Food banks stepping up to the plate

Having outlined the background to food insecurity, the idiosyncratic development of the third sector in the Netherlands and the general attitude of the Dutch government towards the basic right to food, this chapter now examines the way in which food assistance has developed in the country. Food banks have existed in the Netherlands since 2002. The first food bank opened in Rotterdam, with more quickly following in other cities. In 2008, a national association of Dutch food banks was set up to facilitate the operation of local food banks and link them together in a shared mission.

Although substantial local variations can be observed, all member food banks are bound by centrally agreed principles and objectives. Food banks that are members of the association have two goals: to offer food to the poorest people; and to prevent the wastage of food that has gone beyond its shelf life or that does not meet producers' aesthetic standards but that is still safe for consumption. Thus, food aid is just one of the aspects of a dual mission. Using food surplus is not a means, but rather a goal in itself. Local variations exist with regard to the importance accorded to the goal of waste reduction. While some food banks depend solely on surplus food, others complement this through food drives at supermarkets.

Both of these goals are crucial in understanding the Dutch context. Making the goal of reducing food waste equal in importance to the goal of providing food aid has a major impact on the composition of the food aid. Recipients of the aid cannot expect a consistent supply made up of common food staples. Rather, the composition of food parcels depends on what can be 'harvested' by volunteers. In addition, although local food banks collaborate in regional distribution centres in order to distribute food more evenly, some local food banks are more successful than others at complementing this supply with locally sourced donations. This means that the parcels offered by different food banks also vary in size.

In addition, food banks that are members of the national association have no religious or political links or orientation. This secular nature is striking, especially given the history of aid being organised in the context of the religious pillars, as discussed earlier in this chapter. Nevertheless, there are definite links between local food banks and churches. As Noordegraaf (2010) showed, active volunteers in the church are also often involved in food banks, and churches give food banks cash donations and, less often, in-kind help (for example, allowing church facilities to be used for the distribution of food aid).

All food banks work with volunteers, and it is notable that their main motivation is not political or religious. Rather, observing that some people cannot reach a decent standard of living, even in the Netherlands, is an important starting point for many volunteers' decision to help out at a food bank (Pijnenburg, 2018). When asked about their support for the food bank, volunteers often explain that they are driven by a simple feeling that 'certain things are simply wrong'. Solidarity and respect for human dignity form the normative backbone of the food bank as a civil society organisation.

Currently, there are 168 local food banks, often operating at multiple locations where the food is handed out to recipients. Van Steen and Pellenbarg (2014) counted 435 'food pantries' of this kind in 2014; by 2017, there were 530.[4] In addition, there are eight regional distribution centres where food is stored and allocated to the various food banks. As mentioned previously, food banks also collect food locally to supplement the centrally distributed food. Since 2013, food banks have cooperated through Voedselbanken Nederland (the already mentioned national Association of Dutch Food Banks). All people active in food banks and in the national organisation are volunteers (totalling 11,000 in 2017). A large majority of food banks in the Netherlands are members of the association, though there are some initiatives that run independently, including initiatives for Muslim food banks, food banks for the elderly and food banks for children.

To apply to receive aid from a food bank, people have to contact the food bank directly themselves or be referred by a professional (such as a social worker). Eligibility criteria are set by the General Assembly of the Association of Dutch Food Banks (Voedselbanken Nederland, 2018). In order to qualify, the discretionary income of the applicant (*after* fixed charges like rent, tax and insurance, *but before* the daily expenses of food, clothing and so on) is calculated either by a food bank volunteer or an external professional. To determine this income, the food bank adds together a sum per household and a sum per individual. In 2018, a household could receive food assistance if its discretionary income fell below €130 plus €85 per person in the household per month. Thus, for a single-person household, this discretionary income would be €215 (€130 + €85). A household of a single parent and one child would qualify when the discretionary income falls below €300. The discretionary income is calculated by taking the household's net income, including any allowances, and subtracting fixed expenses. Thus, people can be eligible to use a food bank because of low income but also because of high fixed expenses.

Households receive one food parcel per week, often adjusted for the size of the household. Food assistance is restricted to a maximum period of three years, and eligibility is checked with a reassessment of the household budget every six months. On average, a parcel contains 20–25 food units (with units being ill-defined but largely reflecting package sizes that are common in retail, for example, a litre of milk or a kilogram of pasta) and represents a retail value of about €35, though this varies according to the amount of surplus food donated. The operational costs of one parcel (including transport and refrigeration costs) are estimated at €5.[5]

There is not a great deal of detailed evidence available on those who turn to food banks for assistance. Each food bank records only very basic information. In 2017, food banks assisted 132,500 people. As not all households receive help throughout the year, the number of people accessing assistance at any one time will be lower than that. At 31 December 2017, this number was 79,000 individuals, or 30,500 households. The biggest groups are single-person households (42 per cent) and single-parent households (30 per cent).[6]

The number of people served by food banks was on the rise until 2014, when it began to fall. Since 2016, the number of people receiving assistance through food banks has remained stable.[7] Explanations for this pattern are informed guesses at best. Initial growth in users could be explained by the fact that the number of food banks was also growing, with the fastest expansion happening until 2014. Thus, new food banks opening brought them within reach of a greater share of the population. With food banks now offering services in 96 per cent of municipalities, the potential for further growth from increasing accessibility is limited. The fall in user numbers since 2014 could be related to the improvement in economic conditions, reducing some of the risk factors for households becoming unable to meet their basic needs. On the other hand, not all people who would qualify for food aid make use of this assistance. This may be due to disabilities or mental health issues (Waltz et al, 2018), but the negative emotional effects of food banks, the associated stigma or the quality of the food offered there may also have an impact (Van der Horst et al, 2014).

In 2006, only four years after the first Dutch food bank opened, Desain et al (2006) conducted a survey of 430 food bank users and asked them about their reasons for seeking such help. The interviewees provided a multiplicity of explanations. A majority of responses can be subsumed under the categories of 'high living expenses' and 'insufficient income'. Other factors that had an impact on income and outgoings included additional expenses and limits on income-earning capacity due to causes such as unemployment, illness, divorce, addiction and care for a newborn or family members who were not part of the household. While some people mentioned problems with welfare benefits (either a decrease or a delay due to a long processing period), those ranked rather low on the list (see Table 4.1).

Several years later, Kromhout and Van Doorn (2013) looked at food bank users in the city of Utrecht. They found several notable characteristics, though these could not necessarily be generalised to the Netherlands as a whole. Recipients are predominantly (67 per cent) of Dutch descent; three quarters reported health problems, both physical (for example, heart and vascular diseases) and mental health problems (for example, depression); and almost all respondents reported problematic debts, ranging between €1,000 and €100,000.

Although these findings do not provide a complete picture and have some overlapping categories, they do seem to confirm what is known about poverty and the drivers of insecurity in the Netherlands. People experience financial problems and accumulate debts as their

Table 4.1: Reasons behind need for food assistance

Reason	N	%
High housing and living expenses	239	56
Structurally insufficient income to meet expenses	163	38
Unemployment	163	38
Ease with which one can access credit/loans (including mail order)	111	26
Introduction of the euro	105	25
Disability and illness	92	21
Divorce	85	20
Lower welfare allowance	71	17
Long processing time for benefits	59	14
Addiction	18	4
Caring for family at a distance	18	4
Birth of a child	17	4
Other causes	104	25

Note: More than one explanation could be indicated.

Source: Desain et al (2006)

income is insufficient to meet their expenses. The reasons for this situation are manifold but include incomes being under pressure due to the flexibilisation of employment contracts, social security not being fully indexed to inflation and higher demands on people's bureaucratic and financial skills in applying for benefits, as well as rising prices and housing costs. The ultimate consequence of this is that some people end up without sufficient means to cover their basic expenses.

Political response to food assistance and food charity

The Netherlands was one of the countries in the EU that did not support the Food Distribution Programme for the Most Deprived Persons of the Community (MDP). Given the existence of food banks in the country, this raised some eyebrows. The national Association of Dutch Food Banks (Voedselbanken Nederland) has been especially vocal in its criticism of the government's position. The MDP was launched in 1987 as part of the EU's Common Agricultural Policy (CAP) and was 'designed to release products that were available in Community intervention stocks to charitable organisations for free distribution to persons in need' (European Court of Auditors, 2009: 4). It had two main objectives: 'a social one (to make a significant contribution to the well-being of deprived persons) and a market one (stabilisation of the markets of agricultural products through the reduction of intervention stocks)' (European Court of Auditors, 2009: 4).[8]

As long as the MDP programme was implemented within the limits set by this dual objective, the Dutch authorities seemed to have had little objection to the programme. However, this changed in the mid-1990s when intervention stocks decreased and market purchases had to be made in order to compensate. This was made possible by the adoption of Commission Regulation EEC, No 3149/92 of 29 October 1992 and Council Regulation EC, No 2535/95 of October 1995. From then on, the official Dutch point of view has been to insist, above all, on the *principle of subsidiarity* within the EU. The Dutch government considers the fight against poverty and social exclusion to be an issue for the social policies of individual member states. The changes made step by step under the banner of the EU's CAP were regarded as gradually smuggling in a social policy in disguise, which was seen as undesirable when such policy was deemed to be a national matter. The MDP programme expired at the end of 2013 and was succeeded by the Fund for European Aid to the Most Deprived (FEAD) programme for the time period 2014–20. At the time of writing, preparations for the next programme – the European Social Fund Plus (ESF+) – are in full swing. The Dutch response to these programmes has remained basically the same. With regard to the proposed FEAD programme, Dutch Minister of Foreign Affairs Frans Timmermans wrote in 2012 to the second chamber of the Dutch Parliament: 'Since 1995, the Netherlands, under various cabinets, has not been in favour of the EU providing food to the most deprived persons and sees no reason in the current proposal to review its position'.[9] The main reasons given were subsidiarity ('Poverty policy, including care for the most disadvantaged, is a national matter'), the apparent ineffectiveness of such investment and the Netherlands' focus 'on work as a means to combat poverty'(authors' translation).[10] The ESF+ (for the time period 2021–27) combines various programmes that are already in existence: the FEAD, European Social Fund (ESF), Youth Employment Initiative (YEI) and Employment and Social Innovation Programme (EaSI). Although not without reservations, the Dutch government's attitude towards this proposal is moderately positive and emphasises the focus on 'the challenges identified … namely guiding people with a large distance to the labour market to work and keeping the labour force permanently employable'.[11] However, as stated in the official announcements of the Dutch House of Representatives (the Tweede Kamer or 'TK'), 'the provision of basic physical facilities should not be regulated at European level' (TK 21 501–31, no 498).[12]

To recap, the recent Dutch government's attitude was that people were sufficiently assured of the right to food. In addition, the primary means of this assurance were income policy and social security. Furthermore, the state assumed responsibility and rejected involvement from the EU. Poor relief was seen as a matter for the state. Such a way of thinking can also be recognised in the government's response to the proliferation of food banks.

This stance was clearly illustrated in 2008 in a debate that took place in the second chamber after a newspaper had reported that food banks had apparently become a permanent feature of Dutch society.[13] Then acting Secretary of State and Labour Party member Ahmed Aboutaleb stated that food banks should not take on the role played by official governmental services, and municipalities should point out to those who make use of food banks that they are entitled to government social security.[14] Also in 2008, he reinforced the same message at a conference with food banks and Dutch municipalities (to which the Dutch government referred in 2010 in its answers to the UN Economic and Social Council).

The core elements of Dutch government policy on poverty and food, which took shape in the period 1980–2017, can be deduced from these statements and summarised as follows:

- The answer to poverty (old or new) has to be found in work (and creating jobs).
- Dependence on social security services needs to be counteracted by policies that stimulate and activate people to (look for) work.
- People using food bank services need to be made aware that various social security services are available.
- From a long-term/structural perspective, food banks are a 'shame to society' and/or the wrong answer to the problem of poverty.
- From a short-term/practical perspective, food banks do satisfy an urgent need, though in a very limited and temporary way.

These core elements appear in all the debates about food banks and the responsibility for providing sufficient (good) food.

With regard to the arguments about work (the first two elements in the list), for example, there remains a concern about fairness vis-a-vis low-income earners who do not receive food from food banks (Markus, 2018). In an interview, while overestimating the average value of food parcels (which is €35), a policy officer in a large municipality worried that additional food aid, on top of other provisions, would be problematic as it could mean that the total means of someone on welfare with food aid would surpass that of someone on the minimum wage without food aid:

> The food bank gives, off the top of my head, food packages of €50 or €60 per week. That is more than €200 per month, which people get, on top of their benefits. We, of course, always have a solidarity story. Those who earn just over the minimum and barely manage, they are greatly annoyed. (Markus, 2018)

As the section on poverty and food security earlier in this chapter showed, it is an understatement to say that the central elements listed do not entirely correspond to the real situation in the Netherlands. In particular, the tension between the second and third elements, focusing on social security services, provides a bureaucratic breeding ground for problems that can push citizens into impossible situations and send them from pillar to post. On the 15th anniversary of the first Dutch food bank in 2017, almost all political parties vacillated between the extremes of declaring the existence of food banks a shame, on the one hand, and a blessing, on the other (Boverhuis, 2016; see also Van Doorn and Keinemans, 2016).

Since 2014, cooperation between the Association of Dutch Food Banks and the Alliance for Sustainable Food has been facilitated by the Ministry of Social Affairs and the Ministry of Agriculture, Nature and Food Quality. The objective is to facilitate easier and faster contact and exchange of goods between companies in the food sector and food banks. A noteworthy and surprising fact is that the coalition agreement between the political parties that formed the government at the time of writing stated that there should be more scope for supermarkets and the hotel and catering industry to donate surpluses to food banks (VVD et al, 2017). This is in line with a 2016 conclusion of the Council of the European Union (2016) to:

> foster discussions involving all Members to explore the ways and means to strengthen management of the food supply chain and foster cooperation between actors in order to minimise the amount of food that is unsold by food manufacturers, retailers and caterers, in cooperation with other actors in the food supply chain, including food banks and other charitable organisations.

The food bank has apparently become such an established part of the response to poverty that it is important enough to be part of talks to form the governing cabinet. Over the years, a more or less cooperative relation has been built up between food banks and local government. As previously mentioned, the 2008 conference that brought municipalities and food banks together was the first step in this direction.

Municipalities vary in their responses to poverty, their budgets and their generosity. Municipalities are in charge of administering social security, though they are bound by nationally defined standards and social security levels. This means that they control access and enforce compliance with rules. In the case of unforeseen expenses (for example, a broken washing machine or the need to furnish a new house), municipalities can pay *Bijzondere Bijstand* (additional welfare). On top of this, they can also exempt households from local taxes and give other discounts. Many municipalities provide additional support to families with children and give discounts on recreational activities such as sports. In addition, municipalities are in charge of debt counselling and debt alleviation. Lastly, municipalities can use their budgets to subsidise organisations that address poverty, including food banks.

Research in 2010 showed that 40 per cent of the 217 municipalities surveyed gave some kind of financial support to a local food bank (Britt et al, 2010). In 2017, the national Association of Dutch Food Banks (Voedselbanken Nederland) reported that 76 per cent of food banks received some form of support from their municipality, indicating that food banks had become a more established and interconnected part of the municipal approach to poverty (see also Van Doorn and Keinemans, 2016). Forms of support and collaboration differ but a majority of food banks and municipalities will direct people to each other's services (food banks to municipalities and vice versa). Food banks may display leaflets about available municipal assistance, while municipal officers may make regular visits to food banks in order to reach people in need of assistance.

Responsibility and social justice

The central issue addressed in this chapter is how responsibilities for securing citizens' food needs have been understood and practised over time in the Netherlands, and how such responsibilities have recently been affected by the emergence of food banks. In examining this issue, it has become clear that there is a separation between moral and practical responsibilities. Morally, some people in the Netherlands point to the responsibility of 'society' to help neighbours in need, others to the government's responsibility to prevent poverty. Still others see a moral responsibility to ensure fairness for people in low-income work who do not qualify for additional aid. While some point to the financial and legal limitations that government has to reckon with, others highlight the incongruity of a government relying on charitable help to remedy gaps in a system that is actually the government's own responsibility. Lastly, there are those who simply focus on the fact that people are running into 'situations' that lead to ad hoc problems of food insecurity that need a response. Food banks are seen as most capable of providing this, and are thus in a position to step up to the plate.

Are food banks undermining or replacing state responsibility? Recent policy statements suggest that the state is not (yet) absolving itself of its responsibility. When asked, the government consistently accepts responsibility and rejects both the notion that food banks are necessary and the idea that the EU could play a role in this area. In support of the conclusion that government responsibility is not being taken over by food banks, one could also present the fact that while the number of food bank users grew up to 2016, the number has stabilised since then, at least for now, at a point well below its peak.

The opposite thesis – that food banks have partly replaced the state in the area of food security – can be supported by the phenomenon of local municipalities appearing to cooperate with and support food charity because they understand that food banks fulfil a role that is missing from their own services. Food banks are seen as providing a complementary service, remedying the kinds of circumstances to which the government cannot respond. By regarding the system of social security as more or less sufficient – and blaming individual 'circumstances' rather than any characteristics of the system as the cause of food insecurity – the government is de facto allowing the need for charitable food assistance to continue. By servicing those who 'fall through the cracks' of the system, food banks may make it easier for the state to permit such gaps to persist. It is certainly not hard to imagine more structural circumstances that lie behind so-called 'individual misfortunes'.

Furthermore, the current phase of societal responsibilisation – optimistically called the 'participation society' – offers a moral justification for increased cooperation with food banks at the local government level. Civil society initiatives are applauded, and local municipalities see it as their role to support such initiatives when they emerge.

There is little reflection on the particular shape that food charity takes through food banks in any of the sources reviewed for this chapter, including the interviews with those locally responsible for poverty policy. There are fundamental challenges to human dignity when food assistance is linked to the objective of food waste reduction, as is the case in the Netherlands (Van der Horst et al, 2014). While the *existence* of food banks has been a cause for moral outcry, there has been no such response to the *form* that this food charity takes. For the sake of human dignity, it is necessary to start imagining other forms.

Notes
[1] See: https://voedselbankennederland.nl
[2] See: www.troonredes.nl/troonrede-19-september-1995/
[3] United Nations Economic and Social Council, E/C.12/NLD/Q/4-5/Add.1, available at: https://tbinternet.ohchr.org/_layouts/15/treatybodyexternal/Download.aspx?symbolno=E%2FC.12%2FNLD%2FQ%2F4-5%2FADD.1&Lang=en
[4] See: https://voedselbankennederland.nl/wp-content/uploads/2019/03/Feiten_en_-_Cijfers_per_31-12-2018-DEF.pdf

5   See: https://voedselbankennederland.nl
6   See: https://voedselbankennederland.nl
7   See: https://voedselbankennederland.nl
8   Intervention stocks are defined in the European Court of Auditors (2009: 6) report as 'agricultural products bought-in under public intervention measures aiming to stabilise markets and ensure a fair standard of living for the agricultural community'.
9   See: https://zoek.officielebekendmakingen.nl/kst-22112-1519.pdf
10   See: https://zoek.officielebekendmakingen.nl/kst-22112-1519.pdf
11   See: https://zoek.officielebekendmakingen.nl/kst-21501-31-498.html
12   See: https://zoek.officielebekendmakingen.nl/kst-21501-31-498.html
13   *Het Parool*, 23 September 2008, available at: www.parool.nl/nieuws/voedselbank-is-normale-instantie-geworden~b38e8627/?referer=https%3A%2F%2Fwww.google.com%2F
14   TK 2008–09, Aanhangsel van de Handelingen, no 268, available at: www.tweedekamer.nl/downloads/document?id=0a2598de-f640-4d14-b6d0-812bf51b330d&title=Het%20bericht%20dat%20de%20voedselbank%20%27normaal%27%20is%20geworden.pdf

References

Bere, E., Van Lenthe, F., Klepp, K.I. and Brug, J. (2008) 'Why do parents' education level and income affect the amount of fruits and vegetables adolescents eat?', *The European Journal of Public Health*, 18(6): 611–15.

Boutellier, J.C.J. and Van der Klein, M. (2014) *Praktijken van sociale verantwoordelijkheid. Over de inzet van burgers in de 'participatiesamenleving'* [*Practices of social responsibility. On the efforts of citizens in the 'participation society'*], Utrecht: Verwey Jonker Instituut.

Boverhuis, J. (2016) '"Pleisters plakken" en "vruchten plukken"' ['"Pasting bandaids" and "picking fruits"'], https://eenvandaag.avrotros.nl/geld-en-werk/item/pleisters-plakken-en-vruchten-plukken/

Britt, A., Van den Heuvel, A., Kornalijnslijper, N. and Vianen, C. (2010) *Quickscan Voedselbanken, 2e meting* [*Quickscan food banks, second count*], The Hague: SCW/KWI.

CBS (Statistics Netherlands) (2018) 'Nieuws' ['News'], www.cbs.nl/nl-nl/nieuws/2018/03/gezonder-eten-stijgt-meer-in-prijs-dan-ongezonder-eten

CBS (2019) 'Nieuws' ['News'], www.cbs.nl/nl-nl/nieuws/2019/07/aantal-flexwerkers-in-15-jaar-met-drie-kwart-gegroeid

Cohen, S. and Fuhr, C. (eds) (2017) *Austerity, community action, and the future of citizenship*, Bristol: Policy Press.

Council of the European Union (2016) 'Outcome of proceedings', http://data.consilium.europa.eu/doc/document/ST-10730-2016-INIT/en/pdf

De Bruijn, D., Nourozi, S., Van Xanten, H., Turnhout, S., De Jong, F. and Van der Veer, K. (2016) *Wat knelt? Knelpunten bij burgerinitiatieven in zorg en ondersteuning [What is difficult? Points of tension with citizen initiatives in care and support]*, Utrecht: Movisie en Vilans.

Desain, L., Van Gent, M.J., Kroon, P., Langendijk, F. and Van Waveren, B. (2006) *Eindrapport klantenanalyse voedselbanken [Final report customer analysis food banks]*, Amsterdam: Regioplan.

De Swaan, A. (1988) *In care of the state: Health care, education, and welfare in Europe and the USA in the modern era*, Oxford: Oxford University Press.

Dowler, E.A. and O'Connor, D. (2012) 'Rights-based approaches to addressing food poverty and food insecurity in Ireland and UK', *Social Science & Medicine*, 74(1): 44–51.

European Court of Auditors (2009) *Special report no 6, European Union food aid for deprived persons*, https://op.europa.eu/en/publication-detail/-/publication/17d29833-ac93-42e2-8a3e-bb70c3955b49/language-en.

Hoff, S., Wildeboer Schut, J.M., Goderis, B. and Vrooman, C. (2016) *Armoede in Kaart [Mapping poverty]*, The Hague: Sociaal en Cultureel Planbureau.

Hoogenboom, M. (2004) *Standenstrijd en zekerheid. Een geschiedenis van oude orde en sociale zorg in Nederland (ca 1880–1940) [Elites and security. A history of old order and social care in the Netherlands (ca 1880–1940)]*, Amsterdam: Boom.

Hoogenboom, M. (2011) 'Particulier initiatief en overheid in historisch perspectief' ['Private initiative and government in historical perspective'], *Beleid en Maatschappij*, 38(4): 388–401.

Hoogland, H. and Berg, J. (2016) 'Financiële problemen gaan samen met stress en schaamte' ['Financial problems go along with stress and shame'], *Sociaal Bestek*, 78(3): 30–1.

Kammer, C. and Van Lonkhuyzen, L. (2019) 'Oud-minister Bussemaker vindt dat participatiemaatschappij is mislukt', www.nrc.nl/nieuws/2019/02/15/oud-minister-bussemaker-vindt-dat-participatiemaatschappij-is-mislukt-a3654219

Kromhout, M. and Van Doorn, L. (2013) *Voedselbanken in Utrecht. Deelnemers in beeld [Food banks in Utrecht. Participants in the picture]*, Utrecht: Hogeschool Utrecht.

Lambie-Mumford, H. (2017) *Hungry Britain: The rise of food charity*, Bristol: Policy Press.

Madern, T.E. (2014) *Overkoepelende blik op de omvang en preventie van schulden in Nederland [Overarching view of the extent and prevention of debt in the Netherlands]*, Utrecht: Nibud.

Markus, A. (2018) 'Beter een brood in de zak dan een pluim op de hoed. Hoe verantwoordelijkheid voor de voedselvoorziening verdeeld is tussen gemeente en voedselbank' ['Better a bread in the bag than a feather on the hat. How responsibility for food supply is divided between municipality and food bank'], master's thesis, Wageningen University.

Miller, V., Yusuf, S., Chow, C.K., Dehghan, M., Corsi, D.J., Lock, K., Popkin, B., Rangarajan, S., Khatib, R., Lear, S.A., Mony, P., Kaur, M., Mohan, V., Vijayakumar, K., Gupta, R., Kruger, A., Tsolekile, L., Mohammadifard, N., Rahman, O., Rosengren, A., Avezum, A., Orlandini, A., Ismail, N., Lopez-Jaramillo, P., Yusufali, A., Karsidag, K., Iqbal, R., Chifamba, J., Martinez Oakley, S., Ariffi, F., Zatonska, K., Poirier, P., Wei, L., Jian, B., Hui, C., Xu, L., Xiulin, B., Teo, K. and Mente, A. (2016) 'Availability, affordability, and consumption of fruits and vegetables in 18 countries across income levels: findings from the Prospective Urban Rural Epidemiology (PURE) study', *The Lancet Global Health*, 4(10): e695–703.

Neter, J.E., Dijkstra, S.C., Visser, M. and Brouwer, I.A. (2016) 'Dutch food bank parcels do not meet nutritional guidelines for a healthy diet', *British Journal of Nutrition*, 116(3): 526–33.

Noordegraaf, H. (2010) 'Aid under protest? Churches in the Netherlands and material aid to the poor', *Diaconia*, 1(1): 47–61.

NVVK (Dutch Association for Debt Assistance and Social Banking) (no date) 'Jaarverslagen' ['Annual reports'], www.nvvk.eu/page/392

NVVK (2017) 'Jaarverslag' ['Annual report'], http://jaarverslag.nvvk.eu/2017/uitgelicht/index.html

Pijnenburg, L. (2018) 'The single story about the foodbank', in S. Springer and H. Grimm (eds) *Professionals in food chains*, Wageningen: Wageningen Academic Publishers, pp 229–33.

Poppendieck, J. (1998) *Sweet charity? Emergency food and the end of entitlements*, New York, NY: Viking.

Riches, G. (2002) 'Food banks and food security: welfare reform, human rights and social policy. Lessons from Canada?', *Social Policy & Administration*, 36(6): 648–63.

Riches, G. and Silvasti, T. (eds) (2014) *First world hunger revisited: Food charity or the right to food?*, New York, NY: Palgrave Macmillan.

Snel, E. (2017) 'Werkende armen in Nederland' ['Working poor in the Netherlands'], *Mens en Maatschappij*, 92(2): 175–201.

Tonkens, E. (2015) 'Vijf misverstanden over de participatiesamenleving' ['Five misunderstandings about the participation society'], *Tijdschrift voor Gezondheidswetenschappen*, 93(1): 1–3.

Tonkens, E. and Verplanke, L. (2016) 'Sociale zekerheid. Een gelaagd begrip: Materiele, emotionele en relationele zekerheid in de eenentwintigste eeuw' ['Social security. A layered concept: material, emotional and relational security in the twenty-first century'], in P. van Lieshout (ed) *Sociale (on)zekerheid: De voorziene toekomst*, Amsterdam: Amsterdam University Press, pp 185–201.

Van der Horst, H., Pascucci, S. and Bol, W. (2014) 'The "dark side" of food banks? Exploring emotional responses of food bank receivers in the Netherlands', *British Food Journal*, 116(9): 1506–20.

Van Doorn, L. and Keinemans, S. (2016) 'Het ongemak van de voedselbanken' ['The inconvenience of the food banks'], in L. Linders, D. Feringa, M. Potting and M. Jager-Vreugdenhil (eds) *Tussen regels en vertrouwen. Veranderende rollen in de verzorgingsstaat*, Amsterdam: Van Gennep, pp 93–106.

Van Steen, P.J. and Pellenbarg, P.H. (2014) 'Food banks in the Netherlands', *Tijdschrift voor Economische en Sociale Geografie*, 105(3): 370–2.

Verschuren, P. (2015) *Genadebrood. De onstuitbare opmars van de voedselbank* [*Bread of grace. The unstoppable advance of the food bank*], Groningen: Uitgeverij Passage.

Vlemminx, F. (2010) 'The Netherlands and the right to food: a short history of poor legal cuisine', in O. Hospes and I. Hadiprayitno (eds) *Governing food security. Law, politics and the right to food*, Wageningen: Wageningen Academic Publishers, pp 123–35.

Voedselbanken Nederland (2018) 'Voedselbank Reglement' ['Food bank regulations'], https://voedselbankennederland.nl/wp-content/uploads/2018/09/20180908-VBN-Voedselbank-Reglement.pdf

Vrooman, J.C. (2016) *Taking part in uncertainty: The significance of labor market and income protection reforms for social segmentation and citizens' discontent*, The Hague and Utrecht: The Netherlands Institute for Social Research (SCP) and Utrecht University.

VVD, CDA, D66 and Christen Unie (2017) 'Vertrouwen in de toekomst. Regeerakkoord 2017–2021' ['Trust in the future. Coalition agreement 2017–2021'], www.kabinetsformatie2017.nl/documenten/publicaties/2017/10/10/regeerakkoord-vertrouwen-in-de-toekomst

Waltz, M., Schippers, A., Gittins, E. and Mol, T. (2018) 'Disability, access to food and the UN CRPD: navigating discourses of human rights in the Netherlands', *Social Inclusion*, 6(1): 51–60.

Wernaart, B. (2013) *The enforceability of the human right to food: A comparative study*, Wageningen: Wageningen Academic Publishers.

Williams, A., Cloke, P., May, J. and Goodwin, M. (2016) 'Contested space: the contradictory political dynamics of food banking in the UK', *Environment and Planning A: Economy and Space*, 48(11): 2291–316.

5

Redistributing waste food to reduce poverty in Slovenia

Vesna Leskošek and Romana Zidar

Introduction

Food poverty is an area that has been overlooked in Slovenia, attracting very little public attention. There was barely any media discussion of food poverty in 2014/15, despite a temporary shortage of food supplies from intervention stocks of the European Union's (EU's) Food Distribution Programme for the Most Deprived Persons of the Community. At the same time, the redistribution of food waste has been increasing in importance and scope. Instead of household food poverty, the focus of public discussion is on national food security and food safety issues, such as sustainable development, food self-sufficiency, the use of pesticides and the scale of organic food production. Moreover, the discussion of food consumption and food waste is thematised within the framework of ecological discourse by emphasising the unacceptability of wasting food because of the negative consequences of food waste for the environment (Bašič Hrvatin, 2014). For these reasons, measures that were taken in France several years ago to force supermarkets to redistribute their food surpluses to those at risk of food poverty have gained considerable public attention, with active discussions also taking place on social media and in daily newspapers (Šoštaršič, 2013). There is broad public support for the idea that surplus food and waste food should be given to the poor (Lončar, 2015), with such activity enhancing the positive image of the actors involved in the food redistribution system (Stenmarck et al, 2016).

This chapter presents the results of the first study of charitable food assistance in Slovenia. Taking into account the fact that nothing was previously known about the link between waste or surplus food and food poverty in Slovenia, the aim of the study was to identify the main actors – and their positions – in the redistribution chain in order to understand the modes of operation and the extent of the system. The authors are interested in the role of the state in facilitating the redistribution chain as part of its anti-poverty policy, and a key question is whether policy changes indicate that the welfare system in Slovenia is undergoing a transformation. This chapter briefly introduces the main actors identified in the study to enable a better understanding of the findings. Three types of organisation were identified in the redistribution chain: donors (the sources of food donations); distributing organisations (delivering donated food to recipients); and food banks (members of international food bank organisations). Additionally, an important role for the Slovene Lions Club[1] was identified, acting as a mediator between donors and distributing organisations. Donors are supermarkets, hypermarkets, grocery stores and, to a smaller extent, restaurants, bakeries and primary producers. The biggest distributing organisations are Red Cross Slovenia and Caritas Slovenia, which are authorised by the state to distribute food parcels supplied from EU intervention stocks. Other distributing organisations are non-governmental organisations (NGOs) whose primary mission is to provide services to people living in vulnerable situations, including homeless people, victims of violence, people with mental health problems, drug users and elderly people. This chapter identifies only two food banks, which have a very limited area of operation.

The mode of operation in the redistribution chain is outlined later in the chapter. The earlier sections present data on poverty and food policies, and summarise the frameworks of the emerging food redistribution industry in Slovenia in order to illustrate the national context. The chapter then outlines findings from the research conducted with a sample of donors and distributing organisations of surplus and waste food. The final section draws conclusions concerning the operation of the food redistribution system and its potential effects on anti-poverty measures and policies in the country.

Poverty in Slovenia[2]

The first reports on hunger in Slovenia referred to the period of the First World War, when food rationing was introduced and closely monitored by military-run centres mainly distributing food, but also clothes, shoes and other consumer goods. The devastating consequences of the famine at that time are shown by data that the average weight of soldiers was below 50 kilograms (Štepec, 2018). Hunger continued in the interwar period and after the Second World War. In April 1945, the United Nations Relief and Rehabilitation Administration (UNRRA) provided aid in the form of necessities such as food, clothes and raw materials to Yugoslavia worth more than US$5 billion in total. Extensive aid was required to meet people's urgent needs, and operations continued until 1947 when the UNRRA mission was closed (Ajlec, 2013).

Little is known about hunger and poverty in Slovenia during the socialist period. Statistical data on poverty are scarce and only available for certain years. Between 1947 and 1955, some 10,000 to 15,000 people per year received financial social assistance (Statistical Office of the Republic of Slovenia, 1953, 1955), and between 1970 and 1986 (Statistical Office of the Republic of Slovenia, 1980–87), the figure was 10,000 people per year. The first Slovene survey on the quality of life was conducted in 1984 and the second in 1991, with both including questions on subjective perceptions of poverty. In 1984, 22.1 per cent of respondents claimed not to have enough money to cover their basic living expenses, compared with 59.9 per cent in 1991 (Novak, 1993). The high level in 1991 may be attributed to the turbulence of the late 1980s when the country was in economic and political crisis. Under pressure from international monetary organisations, import restrictions were introduced. There were shortages of petrol, coffee, medicines, cooking oil and other goods. The number of people receiving social assistance started to rise from 1987 to 1990, when it reached 15,704 (Statistical Office of the Republic of Slovenia, 1991). No data can be found on aid provided by NGOs because their overall number and activities were limited during socialism. The national Red Cross provided some aid in the form of clothes and other necessities for basic survival, but no further details are available.

Several cultural and political events triggered the change of the socio–political system from socialism to capitalism.[3] A key difference between the previous political system and the current one is the understanding of social inequality. While inequality was ignored during socialism, under capitalism, it has been embraced as the main demarcation from socialism (Dragoš, 2010). A fundamental change in Slovenia's welfare policy came in 2005, a year after the country had become a full member of the EU, when the 'Slovene reform programme for achieving the Lisbon Strategy goals' (hereafter referred to as 'the Reform programme') was drafted (Republika Slovenija, 2005). The programme's main goal was to introduce structural reforms, with the most important being changes in the welfare system. It was declared that the role of the welfare state had to be reformed if Slovenia was to accelerate the social changes needed to boost the economy (Republika Slovenija, 2005: 7). This implied an alteration in the relationship between the state and its citizens, greater entrepreneurism, and a transfer of responsibility for social security from the state to civil society organisations, individuals and private sector companies. To achieve this, it was necessary to 'marketise social services and apply entrepreneurial logic, which would secure the shift from the welfare state to welfare society in which individuals accept responsibility for their social security' (Republika Slovenija, 2005: 23).

The biggest change that the government sought to achieve was to encourage the unemployed and recipients of financial social assistance[4] to actively seek work, improve their skills and accept casual and temporary jobs. The previous collective system of social protection would have to be transformed into a system of individual needs and responsibilities. To this end, several goals were set, including: the introduction of an activation paradigm; the expectation that people receiving financial social assistance would search for a job and accept any job offered (up to three levels below their educational qualifications); the prevention of fraud; and enhanced cooperation between employment services and social services. These principles were first codified in the Act Amending the Social Assistance Act (OG RS, 105/2006) adopted by Parliament in 2006.[5] The key changes brought by the new legislation were the increased conditionality and the obligation to accept any kind of job on offer. These changes triggered a considerable drop in the number of recipients of assistance. In 2003, around 90,000 people[6] received financial social assistance. In 2006, this number had dropped to an average monthly total of 52,910. In 2007, the number of recipients fell further to 43,179, and by July 2008, it was 36,355 (Ministry of Labour, Family, Social Affairs and Equal Opportunities, no date).

Additional changes were introduced in the Social Assistance Benefits Act 2010 (OG RS, 61/2010) after a campaign promoting additional limitations for accessing financial social benefits carried out in 2009 when the country was led by a social-democratic government. The changes were motivated by various factors that reflect both the political and economic trends in the EU and the situation in Slovenia. The changes were introduced at the outset of the economic crisis, and the cuts in welfare expenditure were labelled a preventative measure. The other reason was ideological and relates to changes in welfare policies across the EU where the discourse on welfare fraud was used to justify welfare cuts (for example, Connor, 2007; Fuchs, 2009; Lundström, 2011; Matsaganis, 2011; Jesilow, 2012). This discourse on welfare fraud reflects the understanding of social justice in workfare regimes, chiefly meaning minimising the state's responsibility and maximising that of citizens (Wacquant, 2003). The paradigmatic change from welfare to workfare and the introduction of an activation policy imposed measures to personalise or individualise responsibility for one's own survival (Torfing, 1999; Attas and De-Shalit, 2004; Bauman, 2005).

The campaign in Slovenia was also built on arguments about welfare fraud, with the recipients of social benefits portrayed as passive, idle and work-shy (Parliament of the Republic of Slovenia, 2010; Leskošek, 2014). In reality, the campaign was carefully conceptualised to achieve consensus on curbing rights and restricting access to benefits. Indeed, the public did begin to believe that those in receipt of benefits were exploiting both the state and taxpayers, with the success of the campaign reflected in public opinion (see Table 5.1). The result was a broad public consensus on the need to limit access to social benefits in order to stop people cheating the welfare system.

The new Social Assistance Benefits Act (OG RS, 61/2010) introduced several measures to enhance control over recipients, increasing the power in the hands of social services staff. They were given direct online access to more than 30 databases containing recipients' information (including their bank account details). Approximately 40 fault-based grounds were introduced for denying social benefits or terminating them. Most relate to the manner in which a person lost their previous job. Social services staff are authorised to refuse or terminate the right to financial social assistance if they assess that the user is behaving contrary to legal expectations, which include regular visits to the employment office, actively seeking work and not rejecting any job offered.

Conditionality has impacted on the number of recipients. The amended legislation came into force at the height of the economic crisis in 2012 when the unemployment rate had almost doubled. One impact of the crisis in Slovenia was a rise in the number of people at risk of poverty (see Table 5.2). Between 2012 and 2015, a second

Table 5.1: Attitudes towards recipients of financial social benefits

	Statement	Agree	Disagree
Social rights	Social security benefits in Slovenia make people lazy	51.6	25.4
	Expenditure on social security in Slovenia makes people less willing to help each other	45.6	30.1
	Most of the unemployed are not really looking for a job	44.0	30.4
	Many people manage to obtain cash benefits they are not entitled to	64.5	14.6

Source: The 2016 European Social Survey, in Toš (2017: 148–9)

Table 5.2: Percentage of persons living below the at-risk-of-poverty rate, by gender

	2008	2009	2010	2011	2012	2013	2014	2015	2016	2017
Total	12.3	11.3	12.7	13.6	13.5	14.5	14.5	14.3	13.9	13.3
Men	11	9.8	11.3	12.2	12.5	13.5	13.7	13	12.5	12.0
Women	13.6	12.8	14.1	15	14.6	15.4	15.2	15.6	15.2	14.5

Source: SORS (Statistical Office of the Republic of Slovenia), 2019

round of legislative amendments had the effect of increasing the share of people living below the poverty line.

Due to austerity measures, relatively tight eligibility criteria and the fact that the minimum income[7] was not indexed to living costs, the number of recipients of financial social assistance decreased. At the same time, growth can be observed in the number of food parcels being distributed. In 2013, the number of food aid recipients was 156,442 (see Table 5.4 later), up from approximately 105,000 in 2008 (IFRC, 2016). The media reported on the problem of the growing need for food assistance as an indication of rising poverty, juxtaposing this with revelations about food being wasted in the public sector. Access to school meals was problematised, and donations were collected for children whose parents could not afford to pay for lunch. In 2015 and 2016, one of the most visible organisations for collecting donations for school lunches – Petka za nasmeh (Gimme 5 For A Smile!) – organised a countrywide lobbying campaign to change the relatively high eligibility criteria for free school lunches in order to give more children access. At the same time, a media and public discussion was taking place that criticised the amount of food waste in public institutions like schools, residential homes for the elderly and hospitals, portraying it as a waste of public money (Gradišar, 2017). Such media efforts influence public opinion, creating moral panic about the right of poor people to refuse, dislike or even throw away food they receive for free.

Origin of charitable food: food waste and surplus food donation policy

Little is known about food aid delivery programmes in the era before Slovenia joined the EU in 2004. There is limited information on food aid distributed by the Red Cross and Caritas as the only organisations then providing in-kind aid, such as clothes, shoes and hygiene products. Both organisations collaborated with different supermarkets and raised funds from individual donors to buy food. In 2005, the Red

Cross provided 35,000 food parcels (Red Cross, 2006). There is no evidence of the distribution of waste food before 2005. As discussed previously, food waste only became a politicised public issue later, when the economic crisis increased the numbers of people living below the poverty line and the government decided to introduce austerity measures limiting access to financial social assistance. In 2005, the Slovene Ministry of Agriculture amended national legislation in order to implement the EU's Food Distribution Programme for the Most Deprived Persons of the Community. At the level of distribution, the Ministry of Labour, Family, Social Affairs and Equal Opportunities is authorised to select the charitable organisations responsible for the distribution of food aid, which include the national Red Cross and Caritas.

As mentioned earlier, the first effects of the 2009 financial crisis on the Slovene economy were higher rates of unemployment, poverty and people unable to make ends meet. Having not previously been considered a political or public issue, food poverty suddenly became much more visible. The consequences of cuts to social assistance schemes included rising numbers of people having to seek food aid from humanitarian organisations, and more and more families being unable to afford school lunches for their children. The crisis brought a sudden collision of two seemingly separate issues: measures to alleviate poverty at the systemic and practical levels; and managing food waste generated by different elements of the food supply chain. In these circumstances, the topic of food waste, rather than food poverty as a social problem, became immensely politicised. Changes were not only visible in public and political discourse, but also part of policy solutions across the EU. Policy diffusion – the process by which policy choices are transferred from one country to another through open coordination (Dolowitz and Marsh, 2000; Meseguer and Gilardi, 2009; Obinger et al, 2013) – has been well researched and is an important factor contributing to the replication of neoliberal ideas, concepts and practices.

EU prevention policies and interventions that have been adopted in Slovenia as part of the 'zero-waste initiative' aim to reduce the food waste of two main target groups: the food industry and individual households (Stenmarck et al, 2016). To manage food waste that cannot be avoided or addressed through prevention measures, the redistribution of edible waste food from the food industry to the poor is regarded as a sustainable solution. Such redistribution is considered to be not only a poverty alleviation measure, but also the most cost-effective and sustainable solution to benefit the environment and society at large. In order to create an environment to enable the donation of food, incentives contained in the 'EU food donation guidelines' (hereafter 'the Guidelines') (European Commission, 2017) were adopted in 2017. The Guidelines reflect EU policy on utilising edible waste food from the food industry as part of overall poverty relief measures, stating that 'the best destination for food surplus, which ensures the highest value use of edible food resources, is to redistribute this food for human consumption where safe to do so ... to those in need' (European Commission, 2017: 2).

The Guidelines introduced the term 'food surplus', which refers to the 'surplus food that might otherwise be wasted' and define the term 'food redistribution' as the process by which surplus food is 'recovered, collected and provided to people, in particular to those in need' (European Commission, 2017: 4). It is quite clear that the Guidelines seek to reframe edible waste food by renaming it 'surplus' to avoid any negative connotations or questioning of the proposed policy solution. While food waste may be considered to be spoiled, the term 'food surplus' should not raise any questions about the quality or appearance of donated waste food, or, indeed, donors' underlying good intentions. Interestingly, the 'European Parliament resolution of 16 May 2017 on the initiative on resource efficiency: reducing food waste, improving food safety' (hereafter 'the EP Resolution') (European Parliament, 2017) argues for the need to reduce food waste on moral grounds. It presents World Food Programme statistics on the malnourishment of children in the developing world, and World Bank data on poverty, calling on member states to remove administrative barriers for food businesses and create incentives to enable them to donate edible waste food to the poor. The EP Resolution considers food donations by businesses to be an act of social solidarity (European Parliament, 2017: 8). However, the food industry stands to obtain clear financial benefits from making such donations through tax reliefs and a reduction in indirect costs, such as the costs of biological waste management and disposal. The EP Resolution also considers food donations by businesses to be an act of environmental and social responsibility, giving companies that donate a reputational advantage in the highly competitive food industry.

Importantly, such policies and guidelines are currently being adopted at the national level in several countries, including Slovenia, where an amended Agriculture Act that encompasses all the main solutions from the Guidelines was passed in June 2017 (Official Gazette of the Republic of Slovenia, 2017). The Act introduces three categories of actors that can now participate in food donation:

donors, distributing organisations and recipients. Donors can be any organisation or business in the food supply chain (primary production, food processing and manufacturing, retail and other distribution, and the catering and hospitality sectors). Distributing organisations can include humanitarian organisations, disability organisations and state social services that deliver food to recipients. Recipients are: the unemployed, underemployed or working poor who are entitled to in-cash social assistance; those over 65 years of age and entitled to income support; disabled people; or those assessed by professionals as living in vulnerable situations. The Act foresees the state funding of technical equipment for distributing organisations to facilitate the process but fails to recognise the importance of healthy and balanced diets as a consideration in the process of redistributing donated food, despite this particular aspect being briefly mentioned in the Guidelines.

In summary, several intertwined processes have boosted food charities' use of waste and surplus food in responding to food poverty in Slovenia. Welfare cuts and changes in social assistance legislation have restricted people's access to social benefits. These cuts were justified not only by reference to the economic crisis and the resulting shortage of finances for welfare, but also with moral arguments about preventing fraud and the need to motivate and activate recipients who have become dependent on state money. This situation has led to increased demand for food donations. At the same time, national legislation has enabled NGOs to step into the process of redistributing waste and surplus food, with this being seen as a good response to the problem of food waste, on the one hand, and food poverty, on the other. In order to understand how these changes have transformed the practices of tackling poverty and especially hunger, it is necessary to gather insights into the emerging business of food surplus redistribution. This will be discussed in the next section, where the results of the research into the food redistribution system in Slovenia are presented.

Methodology

A scoping study was conducted to identify relevant actors and their position in the food redistribution chain in order to understand the modes of operation and the extent of the business. Two types of organisations were identified: donors and the distributing organisations of donated food to end recipients. An online questionnaire was developed to obtain data on both types of organisations. A shortlist of distributing organisations was created from the database of all organisations providing programmes and services to people in vulnerable situations (homelessness, illicit drug use, survivors of domestic abuse and people facing mental health issues). This database is available from the Ministry of Labour, Family, Social Affairs and Equal Opportunities. Also included were the two largest humanitarian organisations in the country authorised by the state to distribute food parcels to the poor: the Red Cross and Caritas.

The approach taken to finding information on donors was different because there is no central register of food donations, and no systemic or systematic monitoring of the surplus food and waste food redistribution chain. Information on donations of surplus food was sought from the web pages of supermarkets, hypermarkets and food manufacturers (for example, bakeries and restaurants). Online news was also searched for mentions of food donations in the years 2015–18. The majority of organisations did not respond to invitations to provide information (see Table 5.3). Some donors sent emails explaining that their corporate policies do not allow responses to surveys, or that the survey demanded the disclosure of their business strategy, which could potentially endanger their business results. A representative of Lidl –

Table 5.3: Sample and questionnaire

Type of organisation	Number of invited organisations	Number of respondents	Completed questionnaires	Main themes addressed
Distributing organisations	50	26	20	Types of food donations received; from whom; frequency and amount of donations; logistics; donors' special requirements; situational questions, for example, protocols in the case of spoiled food; reasons for participation in the food donation chain; and how donations contribute to the well-being of recipients
Donors	27	19	7	Types of food donated; to whom; how contacts and decisions are made; the frequency and amount of donations; logistics; special requirements for distributing organisations; situational questions, for example, protocols, hazard analyses and critical control points (HACCP); benefits of being a donor; and opinions about recipients

one of the biggest discount supermarkets in the country – agreed to participate in a phone interview.

The research plan included an interview with the Slovene Lions Club – a major intermediary and redistribution organisation, as discussed earlier in the chapter. Unfortunately, it did not respond to inquiries. Information was obtained from the club's web page and from survey responses where the Lions Club was frequently mentioned as an important actor in the overall organisation of the business.

A search for information on food banks yielded two that promote themselves as such. Again, information was collected from their web pages and newspaper articles in which they were mentioned. An interview was conducted with a representative from the Ministry of Agriculture to further strengthen the relevance of the collected data. Pertinent secondary data collected from websites, media and scientific and policy papers were also reviewed.

The scope and modes of operation of food charity in Slovenia

As noted earlier in this chapter, the distribution chain for food charity in Slovenia is relatively opaque, making any attempt to specify the scope and modes of operation quite challenging. Food banks were added to the previously identified donors and distributing organisations to give a total of three main groups of actors in the redistribution chain.

Donors of surplus food and food waste

Supermarkets and grocery shops are the most frequent donors, followed by restaurants and other business entities such as food producers. However, supermarkets donate only some of the food that is labelled as surplus or waste. Most food that is close to its expiry date is offered to customers at reduced prices. When the food becomes inedible (for example, rotten fruit and vegetables), it is disposed of in landfills. Hypermarkets and supermarkets favour donating food to the Lions Club, which runs a food redistribution project and organises the delivery of collected food to social welfare organisations. The Lions Club co-founded the social enterprise restaurant Pod strehco (Under One Roof[8]), which offers cheap meals made of donated food. Most food that enters the distribution chain is close to its use-by date and does not require refrigeration. Examples include pre-prepared food like sandwiches and salads, as well as, to a lesser extent, canned food and fresh products like fruit, vegetables or baked goods.

Supermarkets are well aware that the transport of surplus and waste food from suppliers to consumers represents an additional cost for distributing organisations but they are unwilling to cover these expenses because it could negatively impact on their balance sheets. They expect distributing organisations to have all the equipment necessary for transport and to be able to comply with hazard analyses and critical control points (HACCP) protocols. The reason donors prefer to cooperate with organisations like the Lions Club is that they have the capacity to ensure smooth logistics and distribution without disturbing supermarkets' regular business activities. Supermarkets are not fond of small-scale, individual arrangements for redistributing surplus food since these may interfere with their core business activities.

By cooperating with organisations that currently redistribute surplus and waste food, supermarkets are preparing for the possible future adoption of measures to ban food waste in Slovenia. Some supermarkets are adapting their stock management practices by introducing the just-in-time ordering of perishable goods such as fresh fruit, vegetables or baked goods to prevent excessive food waste. Supermarkets are also cooperating with each other and government institutions to simplify and optimise the logistics of distributing surplus food to recipients. It is in business owners' interests to deal with food waste effectively and efficiently, without interfering with their core business operations. At the same time, managing food waste and food surpluses through relatively inexpensive charity solutions is considered to be part of their corporate social responsibility (CSR) activities and an opportunity to build a positive brand image, which they then try to promote in all possible ways through various CSR campaigns. For example, since 2015, Lidl has been leading the Food Is Not To Be Wasted[9] campaign in cooperation with the national eco-schools programme, in which 32 kindergartens, 49 primary schools and 15 high schools are participating.[10] The campaign's main objectives are to raise awareness among children of the problem of food waste and to reduce the amount of food wasted in the participating institutions. However, it is important to note that Lidl – the initiator and main sponsor of the campaign – sells mostly pre-packed food itself, such as pre-packaged fruit and vegetables, which contributes to the country's enormous quantities of unrecyclable trash, including plastic wrap and styrofoam.

Restaurants constitute another category of donors, and some of them distribute their surplus food with the assistance of the Lions Club. One of the most visible restaurants donating surplus food is a vegetarian restaurant in the capital of Slovenia, which forms part of the global organisation Food for Life (Hare Krishna) that distributes its own food. Food for Life provides cooked meals to a shelter for the homeless and the NGO Stigma, which offers services to active drug users. Most other restaurants send their waste and surplus food to biogas and composting plants.

Distributing organisations

Distributing organisations are not primarily food delivery operations. They started distributing surplus food because they were offered donations of food to give to their service users. Their primary role is providing welfare services to different groups of people (homeless people, illicit drug users, survivors of domestic abuse and people facing mental health problems), and they provide lunches or snacks as an additional service. The majority have started to distribute surplus food over the last five to seven years. Only the Red Cross and Caritas regularly provide food parcels consisting of dry (flour, rice, sugar and pasta) and canned food, and people have to collect them from the organisation. Other distributing organisations provide various forms of food, the most common being breads and savoury pastries, frozen foods, followed by hot or cold meals from canteens, cafeterias or supermarket hot food counters, then fresh vegetables, fruit and dairy products to a smaller extent, and lastly canned foods. A few distributing organisations also receive fresh pastries from bakeries and pastry shops. How the food is served depends on the type of organisation. Some provide hot lunches in day centres or shelters, others give out sandwiches or baked goods, and some occasionally hand out dried basic foods such as rice, pasta, flour and cooking oil.

The amounts of food delivered to recipients vary between organisations, from 10 kilograms to three tons per month. As mentioned earlier in the chapter, Red Cross Slovenia and Caritas Slovenia are authorised by the state to distribute food parcels supplied from EU intervention stocks. The data presented in Table 5.4 were collected from Red Cross annual reports and are not completely accurate since the methodology for presenting data in the yearly reports has changed over time. In some cases, the total includes the overall number of recipients of donated food, regardless of the source; in others, only the recipients of food donations from EU intervention stocks are counted. In 2015, the Red Cross started to distribute surplus foods. The organisation receives hot meals and other types of surplus food produced daily by kindergartens, schools, restaurants and supermarkets. This activity was initiated by the Lions Club. The data

Table 5.4: Food redistribution by Red Cross Slovenia

	2011	2012	2013	2014	2015	2016
Number of recipients	–	144,863	156,442	154,981	132,000	129,035
Supply of food (tons) from EU intervention stocks (until 2013) and from the Fund for European Aid to the Most Deprived (FEAD) (from 2014 on)	3,755	2,203	2,125	1,055		2,550 (including December 2015)
Food parcels from FIHO* and It Is Nice To Share**	51,904	52,830	33,517	44,108	53,066 – 531 tons	43,815 – 438 tons (excluding It Is Nice To Share)
Food parcels given as support for those in bankruptcy	393	2,039				
Food parcels from local donations (tons)	275	242	251	507	430	425
Apples, pears and tomatoes (tons)				533	571	700
Surplus food (tons)					–	174

Notes: * FIHO is the Foundation for Financing Disability and Humanitarian Organisations in the Republic of Slovenia and receives funds from the national lottery.
**A food donation project.

Source: Annual business reports of Red Cross Slovenia (2012, 2013, 2014, 2015, 2016, 2017)

presented in Table 5.4 show how the need for food charity expanded in the years of economic crisis in Slovenia.

In 2017, the Red Cross delivered a total of 4,221 tons of food. In addition, in the same year, Caritas Slovenia distributed a total of 3,457 tons of food to 94,884 recipients, of which 2,350 tons came from Fund for European Aid to the Most Deprived (FEAD) stocks. Since recipients might receive food packages from both humanitarian organisations,[11] the Caritas data cannot simply be added to those for the Red Cross to calculate a total.

Only 35 per cent of all distributing organisations that participated in the survey needed special equipment to distribute food (for example, boxes for transportation, serving pans, food warmers and refrigerators), which they bought with assistance from donations or using their own funds. No respondent had purchased technical equipment with support from the Ministry of Agriculture at the time of the survey. The primary reason is that the first call[12] for tenders from NGOs and humanitarian organisations was only published in May 2018. In June of that year, 13 organisations – mainly branches of the Red Cross, Caritas, the Lions Club, Food for Life and a few NGOs working with the homeless – were given funding for such equipment.

Distributing organisations report that the sources of donations vary, with hypermarkets and supermarkets (for example, Mercator, Spar, Hofer, Lidl and Jager) leading the way, followed by primary producers (farmers, dairies, bakeries and the meat-processing industry), smaller grocery shops, public institutions (homes for the elderly, schools and kindergartens), small restaurants and large cafeterias (for example, Sodexo). The donors approach distributing organisations differently – making contact either directly or through intermediaries, with the Slovene Lions Club being most frequently mentioned. The results show that 95 per cent of all donors impose no special requirements on the distributing organisations, with only 5 per cent of them requiring distributing organisations to comply with HACCP standards and use all the technical equipment needed for the safe handling of the food involved.

The survey indicated that the donor–distributor relationship is relatively complicated, with a few sets of issues outlined in the research. On the distribution side, most distributing organisations face a number of challenges. The most pressing is how to manage the collection and distribution of surplus food, with issues relating to a lack of funds to cover transport and staff costs. Another important issue is distributing organisations' inability to refuse a food donation, where they face a similar situation to recipients. As already noted, the research reveals that recipients – who are most likely poor, socially excluded and marginalised individuals – are, in a way, expected to demonstrate gratitude for 'the gift' without commenting on its appropriateness, and are certainly not expected to reject it. Any deviations from this expected behaviour may be labelled morally inappropriate and could bring wider social consequences, not only for the individual, but also for the social group to which they belong. In addition, this creates social pressure on distributing organisations, which are in no position to refuse food donations because this could pose a substantial risk to their reputation, public image and potential partnerships. Slightly more than 50 per cent of distributing organisations surveyed had never refused a food donation, even when they considered the donation to be unsuitable for human consumption. One fifth had occasionally refused a donation, but only when the smell, appearance or taste indicated that the food was spoiled. Another 20 per cent of respondents reported that donors had allowed them to select food for distribution to recipients, and only 5 per cent had rejected a food donation on the grounds that it was unhealthy for recipients. Some organisations replied that they accept every type of food donation because recipients 'take and consume anything'. A few distributing organisations reported accepting any donation but later throwing away food they considered spoiled or unfit for human consumption. Only a few had decided to inform donors that the food was spoiled, and none of them had informed the food safety inspection service. However, the majority of distributing organisations rarely face such situations because most of the donated food has a long shelf life.

The survey results also show that distributing organisations believe that the responsibility for problems caused by spoiled food should be shared equally among all actors in the food donation supply chain but that recipients should take full responsibility for any cases of consuming spoiled food. This means that if people consume food even though it looks, smells and tastes odd, then it is their responsibility if they experience any health issues.

Food delivery is becoming an important and regular activity for distributing organisations, and this demands greater attention from management, suitable logistics and additional funding to ensure such operations run smoothly. In the past, the majority of social welfare organisations were not involved in the redistribution of surplus and waste food, and they either did not offer food (for example, in day centres for homeless people or people with mental health problems) or they bought it in (as in shelters for women suffering domestic violence or homeless people, where cooked meals are provided). When asked why they now engage in the redistribution of surplus and waste food, there were three typical answers. Most stated that surplus food should be redirected to people experiencing poverty since they cannot purchase food in sufficient quantities to meet their needs. As a second reason, the immorality of wasting food was highlighted, and the third was that food redistribution was seen as an opportunity they took when donors approached them. The paradox of the current situation is that distributing organisations are sometimes throwing unsuitable food away, which goes to landfills, because they do not want to spoil their relationship with their donors and jeopardise future cooperation.

On the other hand, the distributing organisations were much more decisive when it comes to recipients, maintaining that they should meet certain criteria to be eligible for food charity assistance. The most common criterion was that they should provide proof that they are receiving financial social assistance or be referred to the distributing organisation by social services. The distributing organisations that work with specific groups of people – for example, maternity homes or day centres for homeless people or people with mental health problems – only give food to their service users. It appears that distributing organisations in Slovenia are adopting a culture of means testing to prove entitlement to social assistance. The main reason for this is to prevent fraud by requiring recipients to provide proof of being genuinely poor. A total of 40 per cent of organisations believe that the food they provide to final recipients can significantly improve their situation and well-being, with 25 per cent of respondents being undecided on this issue of improvement, while 35 per cent believe that such food donations do not help to improve the situation or well-being of recipients, but are necessary for their survival. Approximately half of the respondents also believe that recipients do not manage their income well and have poor eating habits, mainly because they have low awareness of healthy diets.[13] Nevertheless, most respondents believe that the eating habits of their service users/recipients would improve if they had the resources to purchase food, and if more fresh fruit, vegetables and dairy products were included in food donations.

The survey included an open question asking respondents about their concerns and suggestions with regard to the redistribution of surplus and waste food. Some of them answered that distributing food donations to service users improved the quality of the organisation's services and enabled it to address users' needs in an effective and efficient way. For those respondents, food redistribution is an opportunity to reach people who would not usually access the organisation's services and learn more about their needs. In organisations offering accommodation (for example, maternity homes), food donations are of less practical use because the energy-dense, nutrient-poor food usually donated is not suitable for everyday consumption by users. Some respondents suggested that municipalities should provide plots of land for cultivation by people experiencing food poverty so that they can make efforts to grow their own food.

Food banks

Two food banks were identified in the research: Sibahe and Food for Life. The first is local, while the second is part of Food for Life Global, which promotes itself as an international food bank network. Sibahe operates at the local level in collaboration with the European Federation of Food Banks (FEBA). Despite having been quite active and visible in the media between 2012 and 2014, it has not expanded its operations. On the other hand, while Food for Life is part of a global network of vegan humanitarian restaurants, it has only one location in Slovenia – in Ljubljana – meaning that it is geographically limited to one municipality. Food for Life, together with the Ministry of Health, implemented the programme Healthy and Accessible Food, aimed at helping poor and low-income households, safe houses and programmes accommodating female survivors of domestic violence, youth crisis centres, and programmes for asylum seekers and homeless people. The main activity of the programme was to provide cooking classes and recipes to prepare 'tasty, healthy and accessible meals that follow healthy nutrition guidelines'.[14] All recipes were vegetarian.

The Lions Club: between businesses and charity

The research shows that the Lions Club has a distinctive role in the redistribution process. According to its website, it collects food surpluses from 70 grocery shops in 27 cities all over the country. Food is delivered to different distributing organisations, such as safe houses, shelters for homeless people, Red Cross local branches and Caritas dioceses. In 2017 alone, the club delivered food for 2 million meals (Lions District Slovenia, 2017). In many ways, food redistribution is a demanding process. Donors are willing to donate as long as they incur no additional expenses or disturbance to their business processes. To comply with the needs and demands of the business sector, distributing organisations should run waste food takeover operations smoothly and discreetly to the extent that ensures minimum disturbance to the regular business operations of the donors. In order to do this, they must engage a number of volunteers, appropriate vehicles, special food containers and financial resources to cover their expenses. Only a handful of organisations in the humanitarian and social services sphere in Slovenia have the capacities to do so. The research shows that the Lions Club is currently the chief organiser of the redistribution process. Membership of the Lions Club is mainly held by people from the business community who understand the needs of supermarkets, have mastered business processes and also understand that the circular economy needs consumers. As one of the most active organisations, the club collaborates with many distributing organisations, as well as supermarkets and restaurants. The Lions Club supported the establishment of the first restaurant preparing meals made exclusively from waste and surplus food, and it is recruiting more distributing organisations as well as businesses, acting as a middleman to organise a smooth and effective donation process.

Discussion

This section discusses the study's main research question about the role of the state in enabling food distribution to people living in poverty in relation to the traditional redistribution role of the welfare state. Analysis of the Slovene redistribution chain for waste and surplus food points to certain parallels that can be drawn between food as an in-kind benefit provided by NGOs or private companies, and the financial social benefits paid by the state to reduce poverty. Earlier sections of the chapter have emphasised this strong connection between food distribution and financial assistance. Even before the effects of the economic crisis hit Slovenia between 2009 and 2015, there were plans to 'modernise' and 'rationalise' the welfare state. It was regarded as being too generous, making people dependent on financial support from the state and pushing them away from the labour market. Low levels of income inequality were seen as an undesirable remnant of socialism and the result of an overly generous welfare state that addressed issues of inequality with correctives such as financial social assistance. The low rate of people at risk of poverty was also seen as a sign of the welfare state's excessive generosity (Republika Slovenija, 2005). This resulted in changes to legislation on social assistance, introducing increased conditionality and punishments for non-compliance with conditions or the failure to prove that one was actively seeking work. Although major cuts to social assistance programmes were made at a time of economic crisis, it can still be argued that they were not necessary because the government decides it own priorities. Different European states responded to the crisis in different ways. Some actually increased spending on social security to prevent any escalation of poverty (OECD, 2017); however, Slovenia was not among this group. In fact, it did the opposite: the government reduced social security spending, arguing that we all had to 'tighten our belts' in the name of future prosperity and economic growth. The irony is that some Slovenes grew richer during the crisis (Credit Suisse, 2014), which may say a great deal about the ideology that 'we are all in the same boat' and perceptions of the true state of inequality.

The data on poverty and food distribution presented in this chapter actually point to something complex and fundamental. The reductions in financial social benefits were an intentional choice, made in the knowledge that such cuts lead to increased poverty. The government was well aware of the negative effects that cuts to the social security system would have on people's capacity not only to make ends meet, but also to afford the most basic necessities, including food. Its actions contributed to more people sinking into deeper poverty. The move was presented by the government as a necessary step to push people labelled as 'work-shy' to engage in any form of paid work, no matter how precarious it might be. Since 2005, the majority of national governments have been pushing the false belief that greater inequalities contribute to prosperity as people have to struggle to find jobs regardless of their quality. People need only to try hard to ensure that they will succeed. Failure to find a job is nothing more than a sign of individuals' incompetence and lack of moral responsibility towards society. It is interesting to note the way in which the government framed its policy changes as an act of justice, carefully crafting a narrative of the state protecting hard-working citizens from being the victims of welfare fraudsters. The government was also priming people to adopt a belief that, as citizens, they can no longer rely on the state to protect them against market risk. Replacing cash benefits with in-kind benefits is a necessary step in this transformation of the welfare state into a workfare state – and to what Gray (2004) describes as 'unsocial Europe'. Using food aid as a substitute for financial benefits is part of this strategy, and is heavily supported by business and public opinion. Even some NGOs make food aid conditional on recipients providing documentation to confirm their entitlement to such help. All this shows how the narrative of frauds and cheating, and the legitimisation of conditionality – which is itself a dehumanising ideology – is slowly internalised by professionals, becoming integral to the operations of civil society organisations. Konings (2015) writes that the main strength of capitalism is its ability to convince us to organise our own oppression. Adopting conditionality principles, attributing moral codes to food surpluses and the belief that some people's choices of what they consume, how and when should be limited are textbook examples of such voluntary self-oppression.

Comparative data show that the conclusions of this study are in line with the analyses of other researchers around Europe. The authors have identified four conceptual frameworks that are particularly relevant to the analysis in this chapter:

1. *Commodification of food poverty*. The recovery of surplus and waste food is becoming a highly commodified area worldwide, with many actors participating in discussions of the subject, and a number of entities and individuals finding sustainable solutions to 'save the planet' and feed the poor at the same time. This is important in supporting government agendas and policies related to food waste and food poverty. As Silvasti and Riches (2014: 192) state: 'however strong human compassion or the moral imperative to feed hungry people, charitable food aid as a practical and effective response to hunger and poverty presents disturbing dilemmas'. It is unfortunate that strategies to achieve zero waste are being tested on populations that have no political, economic or cultural capital. Waste and surplus food from corporate businesses often acts as a pull factor that is offered as a solution to the problem of food poverty. In this sense, supply and demand are intertwined, mutually dependent and must be understood in the context of the marketisation of the welfare state and the depoliticisation of food poverty (Riches, 1999). Although the research presented in this chapter reveals that the everyday interactions and relationships in the donor–distributor–recipient triangle are quite complex, one conclusion dominates the analysis: food charity creates the illusion of a just system in which everyone gains and the CSR practices of business are exemplary.

2. *Moral discourses and the tendency to individualise responsibility for experiencing food poverty*. Lambie-Mumford (2017: 27) claims that this is a 'discursive shift: alongside the increasing emphasis on individual notions of responsibility and risk (for poverty), there has been a renewed and increasing emphasis on the notion of "deserving" and "undeserving" poor people'. This prevailing discourse was omnipresent in this survey, with a number of respondents sharing their opinions concerning various personal traits of recipients that contribute to their poor dietary habits, obesity and poverty, disregarding or trivialising the fact that food

donations mainly consist of energy-dense pre-prepared foods that are poor in nutrients. Poor people's inability to maintain a healthy, balanced diet and their failure to access healthy foods are addressed through educational activities teaching people how to lead healthy lives. Such an approach assumes that 'people are the problem', while suggesting that food poverty could be eradicated by changing people's lifestyles. This indicates how individualisation (blaming and shaming) is leading to responsibilisation (teaching the poor how to cook healthy meals because poverty is a consequence of personal traits) and shifting the focus away from the fact that the root causes of poverty should be addressed and that people need accessible, robust public services, programmes and funds that provide a decent standard of living, rather than surplus food and cookery classes.

3. *Increased conditionality and obstacles to claiming cash benefits.* The driver of waste food redistribution activities in Slovenia is the welfare reform that has increased the conditionality of financial social benefits, tightened eligibility criteria and lowered the amounts available. This is not an exclusively Slovene issue and has been recognised in much research and many publications (for example, see Chapter 8). Although the lack of data makes it impossible to precisely assess the true extent of food poverty in Slovenia, the growing demand for food aid reported by the Red Cross and Caritas is an indicator of the problem. Such demand is a direct consequence of reduced access to financial social benefits. The legislation on social assistance (discussed earlier in this chapter in the section on poverty in Slovenia) was drastically amended at the time of the economic crisis. This meant that people suffered rising unemployment at the same time as social assistance schemes were being cut, leading to increased demand for food charity. At that time, charity food delivery programmes were presented as the right way forward as they resolved more than one problem: food hunger on the side of recipients and food waste on the side of business. As soon as the food redistribution chain was created, it was also normalised in the sense of becoming part of policies to tackle poverty in the country. The donation of waste and surplus food was viewed as an act of solidarity without consideration of the rights of recipients, affecting understandings of social justice (for example, Riches and Silvasti, 2014; Caraher and Furey, 2017; Lambie-Mumford, 2017).

4. *The position of poor people in the circular economy.* The European Parliament and the European Commission are committed to

reducing food waste. This was established as one of the priorities of promoting a circular economy to help reduce pressures on the environment (European Commission, 2015; European Parliament, 2016). Food donations are an element of the circular economy as part of the promotion of zero-waste principles (reuse, repair, recycle, reduce). Currently, poor, low-income and food-insecure people are an indispensable part of this circle because they are the main consumers of waste and surplus food. There is a serious danger that welfare system reforms will entrench this position of poor people in the circular economy because, at least in Slovenia, social policy is substantially (if not totally) subordinated to economic policy.

Conclusions

The research shows that the major change in Slovenia relates to the role and meaning of financial social assistance. Increased conditionality and control over recipients – in combination with low amounts of basic minimum income – have caused an enormous drop in the number of recipients of welfare benefits. The introduction of eligibility restrictions in Slovenia was intended to have this effect, and the aim of the government was to lower social security costs in order to lower direct taxes on income, which will supposedly boost the economy. Financial social benefits are seen as contributing to negative personal traits – if they are too high, people become dependent on them, so benefits must be low enough to nudge people towards the labour market. To compensate for the lower levels of financial social assistance that no longer cover basic living costs, food aid or aid in kind is presented as a suitable solution. In some ways, this type of aid may be seen as more than just financial benefits, even though 'people dependent on food aid necessarily lose part of their freedom of choice and inherent human dignity, because they have to accept charity food in spite of their actual needs and preferences' (Riches and Silvasti, 2014: 9). These changes are also supported by the broad promotion of discourses about the immorality of generating food waste and consequent moves to combat this. Such moves are – in a similar way to attitudes to redistributing food to the poor – publicly constructed as acts of high moral and ethical value.

With ever more organisations engaging in the redistribution of surplus and waste food, the demand to push food forward to the 'needy' is growing, creating pressures on the receiving side. As Caraher and Furey (2017) warn, this creates a situation in which some citizens are able to choose food in socially acceptable ways while others have that choice made on their behalf, fulfilled by surplus food that is not considered saleable by the retail sector. As the results of the research presented in this chapter show, food donations bring relief to recipients but cannot be viewed as a long-term or sustainable solution. The right to choose food belongs to the individual and should not be questioned when it comes to poor consumers (Riches and Silvasti, 2014). The fact that Slovene consumers from the lowest quintile spend approximately one fifth of their household income on food and beverages, as opposed to one tenth for those in the highest quintile (SORS, 2015), demonstrates that food costs represent a substantial burden on the poorest. Nevertheless, this burden should not be reduced through the formalisation of food donations. The situation requires the development of robust social protection systems that cover basic human needs – such as appropriate nutrition and shelter – as well as public policies that address the underlying causes of poverty, economic, social and gender inequalities, pollution, climate change, and migration.

The EU and its member states are committed to meeting the target for food waste reduction adopted by the United Nations General Assembly as part of the 2030 Sustainable Development Goals (Target 12.3), aiming to reduce food waste in the retail and consumer sectors by 50 per cent, and reduce food losses occurring in food production and supply chains by the year 2030 (European Commission, 2016). Reducing food waste is undeniably an important global issue in helping to tackle the depletion of the world's limited natural resources. It should be comprehensively addressed at global, regional, national and local levels by developing, implementing and monitoring comprehensive policies that deal with the multifaceted, multi-actor nature of the issue of global food waste.

The public discourse on food waste reduction and prevention influences how the topic is presented, discussed or contested. Nevertheless, it is important to address the often hidden or overlooked agendas that the issue creates, especially in relation to food donations made by major supermarkets and restaurants to charities that cater to the needs of 'the less fortunate', and also with particular regard to NGOs that are authorised to provide services to and simultaneously advocate on behalf of vulnerable groups. Such organisations face a rather contradictory situation in which they distribute surplus food as a charitable response to food poverty, while calling for the elimination of the root causes of food poverty in the affluent Global North. In this sense, they are alleviating poverty in the short term with colourful

'Band-Aids' while being fully aware that such an approach is ineffective over any longer term due to the fact that it ignores the structural (economic, political, social and cultural) factors that lead to food poverty.

Notes

[1] The Lions Club is part of the worldwide organisation Lions Club International, which, among other activities, runs projects on food waste and food banks around the world. The Slovene club is registered as the association of District 129. Membership is by invitation. Its current activities include the promotion of healthy lifestyles, food donations, peace and international cooperation.

[2] Slovenia has historically been part of many different empires and countries (for example, the Roman Empire, Byzantine Empire, Habsburg Monarchy and Illyrian provinces). In 1918, Slovenia was liberated from the Austro-Hungarian Empire and became a founding member of the State of Slovenes, Croats and Serbs, which then became the Kingdom of Yugoslavia in 1929. In 1945, as a co-founder, Slovenia joined the Federal People's Republic of Yugoslavia or Socialist Federal Republic of Yugoslavia.

[3] The Slovene declaration of independence from Yugoslavia initiated the so-called Ten-Day War, followed by the signing of the Brioni Agreement on 7 July 1991. This aimed to enable negotiations on Yugoslavia's future but led to the bloody Balkan wars (Ambroso, 2006: 1–2).

[4] The amount of financial social assistance was calculated to provide for recipients' minimum needs. In 2003, the full amount of financial social assistance was €181.61 per month (50 per cent of the monthly threshold to be at risk of poverty for a single-person household), and in 2008, the full amount was €220 per month (40 per cent of the monthly threshold to be at risk of poverty for a single-person household).

[5] The amended Act also brought significant changes in relation to the accessibility of other forms of monetary social assistance, including child benefits, one-off financial social assistance and state scholarships.

[6] There is a significant difference between the number of recipients under socialism and capitalism, which is a complex phenomenon. After the political transition, Slovenia experienced a massive collapse of its heavy industry and an enormous increase in unemployment.

[7] Financial social assistance provides users with means for meeting minimum needs in the amount guaranteeing their subsistence. Subsistence is considered to be provided if the entitled person receives income, after the deduction of taxes and compulsory social security contributions, amounting to the minimum income. The persons who are entitled to cash social assistance do not have any income or receive income below the above stated amount. In the case of no income, the entitled persons receive the full stated amount; otherwise, they are entitled to receive the difference between their own income and the stated amount.

[8] The restaurant opened in 2013 and mainly relies on donations of food and money to operate. Customers can purchase two meals – one for themselves, plus one for a future customer who cannot afford to pay for a meal. The restaurant was established on the initiative of the Lions Club and in cooperation with the Red Cross, Caritas, the Association of Friends of Youth Moste and the Rotary Club.

The poor can have a free meal if they are referred by social services and receive a positive evaluation by a special commission operating on behalf of the Under One Roof restaurant.

9   See: www.boljsi-svet.si/projekt/hrana-ni-za-tjavendan/

10 In the framework of the Recycling Cooking campaign, a cookery contest is organised where the best recipe using waste food receives a special prize, and selected recipes are published in a cookbook.

11 Due to the Data Protection Act, organisations are not able to monitor whether recipients are receiving food parcels from both organisations. However, based on personal interviews with representatives from both organisations, this practice of 'double claiming' does occur. The extent of the practice is unclear.

12 See: www.mkgp.gov.si/si/javne_objave/javni_razpisi/?tx_t3javnirazpis_pi1%5Bshow_single%5D=1404

13 Beliefs about poor people's lack of competency to manage their finances and control their impulses and consumption habits are also part of the system of degradation and individualisation of the problem of poverty. The state is responding with a series of awareness-raising programmes that include training in managing one's personal budget, all sorts of programmes related to healthy lifestyles and diets, information booklets, and recipes using ingredients typically found in food parcels.

14 The project ran from 2013 to 2015. Recipes are still available on their website (see: https://ffl.si/zdravo-in-dostopno/).

References

Ajlec, K. (2013) 'UNRRA v Sloveniji' ['UNRRA in Slovenia'], *Contributions to Contemporary History*, 53(2): 79-99.

Ambroso, G. (2006) 'New issues in refugee research, research paper no 133: the Balkans at a crossroads: progress and challenges in finding durable solutions for refugees and displaced persons from the wars in the former Yugoslavia', www.unhcr.org/4552f2182.pdf

Attas, D. and De-Shalit, A. (2004) 'Workfare: the subjection of labour', *Journal of Applied Philosophy*, 21(3): 309–20.

Bašič Hrvatin, S. (2014) 'Kako mediji spodbujajo razmetavanje hrane?' ['How media encourage food wastage?'], in P. Raspor (ed) *Hrana in prehrana za zdravje: Koliko hrane zavržemo? [Food and diet: How much food is wasted?]*, Koper: Založba Univerze na Primorskem, pp 45-54.

Bauman, Z. (2005) *Work, consumption and the new poor*, Maidenhead: Open University Press.

Caraher, M. and Furey, S. (2017) 'Is it appropriate to use surplus food to feed people in hunger? Short-term Band-Aid to more deep rooted problems of poverty', http://foodresearch.org.uk/publications/is-it-appropriate-to-use-surplus-food-to-feed-people-in-hunger/

Connor, S. (2007) 'We're onto you: a critical examination of the Department for Work and Pensions' "Targeting Benefit Fraud" campaign', *Critical Social Policy*, 27(2): 231-52.

Credit Suisse (2014) 'Global wealth report', www.credit-suisse.com/about-us/en/reports-research/global-wealth-report.html

Dolowitz, D. and Marsh, D. (2000) 'Learning from abroad: the role of policy transfer in contemporary policy making', *Governance* 13(1): 5–24.

Dragoš, S. (2010) 'Tangencialnost in subsidiarnosti' ['Tangentiality and subsidiarity'], *Teorija in praksa* [*Theory and Practice*], 47(2/3): 392-404.

European Commission (2015) 'Communication on "Closing the loop – an EU action plan for the circular economy" adopted by the European Commission on 2 December 2015', https://eur-lex.europa.eu/legal-content/EN/TXT/?uri=CELEX:52015DC0614

European Commission (2016) 'EU platform on food losses and food waste', https://ec.europa.eu/food/sites/food/files/safety/docs/fw_eu-actions_flw-platform_tor.pdf

European Commission (2017) 'EU food donation guidelines', *Official Journal of the European Union*, 60(C361): 1–52.

European Parliament (2016) 'Circular economy package: four legislative proposals on waste', www.europarl.europa.eu/EPRS/EPRS-Briefing-573936-Circular-economy-package-FINAL.pdf

European Parliament (2017) 'European Parliament resolution of 16 May 2017 on the initiative on resource efficiency: reducing food waste, improving food safety', https://ec.europa.eu/food/sites/food/files/safety/docs/fw_lib_ep_resource-efficiency_reduce-fw-improv-fs_2017.pdf

Fuchs, M. (2009) 'Social assistance – no, thanks? The non take up phenomenon and its patterns in Austria and Finland after 2000', https://core.ac.uk/download/pdf/11867530.pdf

Gradišar, A. (2017) 'Bolnišnica zavrže letno 111 ton hrane, dom za starejše 22 ton' ['Hospital threw away 111 tons of food per year, homes for elderly 22 tons'], https://radioprvi.rtvslo.si/2017/10/bolnisnica-letno-zavrze-111-ton-hrane-dom-za-starejse-22-ton/

Gray, A. (2004) *Unsocial Europe*, London: Pluto Press.

IFRC (International Federation of Red Cross) (2016) *Think differently: Humanitarian impacts of the economic crisis in Europe*, Geneva: International Federation of Red Cross, https://media.ifrc.org/ifrc/wp-content/uploads/sites/5/2017/02/Report-02_Think-Differently-Report-2013_EN.pdf

Jesilow, P. (2012) 'Is Sweden doomed to repeat U.S. errors? Fraud in Sweden's health care system', *International Criminal Justice Review*, 22(1): 24-42.

Konings, M. (2015) *The emotional logic of capitalism: What progressives have missed*, Stanford, CA: Stanford University Press.

Lambie-Mumford, H. (2017) *Hungry Britain: The rise of food charity*, Bristol: Policy Press.

Leskošek, V. (2014) 'From welfare fraud to welfare as fraud', in T. Harrikari, P.L. Rauhala and E. Virokannas (eds) *Social change and social work: The changing societal conditions of social work in time and place*, Farnham and Burlington, VT: Ashgate, pp 49–65.

Lions District Slovenia (2017) 'Projekt donirana hrana' ['Project donated food'], www.lions.si/projekti/

Lončar, A. (2015) 'Hrana lačnim, namesto v koš' ['Food to the hungry instead of to the trash can'], https://manager.finance.si/8839780?cctest&

Lundström, R. (2011) 'Between the exceptional and ordinary: a model for the comparative analysis of moral panics and moral regulation', *Crime, Media, Culture*, 7(3): 313–32.

Matsaganis, M. (2011) 'The welfare state and the crisis: the case of Greece', *Journal of European Social Policy*, 21(5): 501–12.

Meseguer, C. and Gilardi, F. (2009) 'What is new in the study of policy diffusion?', *Review of International Political Economy*, 16(3): 527–43.

Ministry of Labour, Family, Social Affairs and Equal Opportunities (no date) 'Statistical data', www.gov.si/teme/denarna-socialna-pomoc/

Novak, M. (1993) *Dober dan revščina* [*Good afternoon, poverty*], Ljubljana: Socialna zbornica Slovenije.

Obinger, H., Schmitt, C. and Starke, P. (2013) 'Policy diffusion and policy transfer in comparative welfare state research', *Social Policy & Administration*, 47(1): 111–29.

OECD (Organisation for Economic Co-operation and Development) (2017) 'Government at a glance', https://data.oecd.org/gga/central-government-spending.htm#indicator-chart

Official Gazette of the Republic of Slovenia (2017) 'Zakon o spremembah in dopolnitvah zakona o kmetijstvu (ZKme-1D)' ['Act amending the Agricultural Act'], www.uradni-list.si/glasilo-uradni-list-rs/vsebina/2017-01-1446?sop=2017-01-1446

Parliament of the Republic of Slovenia (2010) 'Transcript of the 24th session of the Parliament of the Republic of Slovenia', www.dz-rs.si/wps/portal/Home/deloDZ/seje/evidenca?mandat=V&type=sz&uid=9E0B388CD068A4A7C1257743003563E9

Red Cross (2006) 'Business report 2003–2006', www.rks.si/sl/Porocilo_2003-2006_2/Porocilo_2003-2006_1/?rks-frontend=iapfsr8e6ldq9b442bb13f4u66

Red Cross (2012) *Annual business report, 2011*, Ljubljana: Red Cross Slovenia.

Red Cross (2013) *Annual business report, 2012*, Ljubljana: Red Cross Slovenia.

Red Cross (2014) *Annual business report, 2013*, Ljubljana: Red Cross Slovenia.

Red Cross (2015) *Annual business report, 2014*, Ljubljana: Red Cross Slovenia.

Red Cross (2016) *Annual business report, 2015*, Ljubljana: Red Cross Slovenia.

Red Cross (2017) *Annual business report, 2016*, Ljubljana: Red Cross Slovenia.

Republika Slovenija (2005) 'Slovene reform programme for achieving the Lisbon Strategy goals', www.mg.gov.si/fileadmin/mg.gov.si/pageuploads/DPK/SI_NRP_2005_SLO_kon__na_verzija__28.10.2005.pdf

Riches, G. (1999) 'Reaffirming the right to food in Canada: the role of community-based food security', in M. Koc, R. MacRae, L.J.A. Mougerot and J. Welsh (eds) *For hunger-proof cities: Sustainable urban food systems*, Ottawa: Sustainable Development Research Centre, pp 203-7.

Riches, G. and Silvasti, T. (eds) (2014) *First world hunger revisited: Food charity or the right to food?*, Basingstoke: Palgrave Macmillan.

Silvasti, T. and Riches G. (2014) 'Hunger and food charities in rich societies: what hope for the right to food?', in G. Riches and T. Silvasti (eds) *First world hunger revisited: Food charity or the right to food?*, Basingstoke: Palgrave Macmillan, pp 191–208.

SORS (Statistical Office of the Republic of Slovenia) (1953) *Statistical yearbook*, Ljubljana: Statistical Office of the Republic of Slovenia.

SORS (Statistical Office of the Republic of Slovenia) (1955) *Statistical yearbook*, Ljubljana: Statistical Office of the Republic of Slovenia.

SORS (Statistical Office of the Republic of Slovenia) (1980–87) *Statistical yearbook*, Ljubljana: Statistical Office of the Republic of Slovenia.

SORS (Statistical Office of the Republic of Slovenia) (1991) *Statistical yearbook*, Ljubljana: Statistical Office of the Republic of Slovenia.

SORS (Statistical Office of the Republic of Slovenia) (2015) 'Average annual allocated assets of households by quintiles', http://pxweb.stat.si/pxweb/Dialog/varval.asp?ma=0878702E&ti=&path=../Database/Demographics/08_level_living/03_household_budget/05_08787_alloc_assets_food/&lang=1

SORS (Statistical Office of the Republic of Slovenia) (2019) 'At-risk-of-poverty rate, % of persons, Slovenia, annually', https://pxweb.stat.si/SiStatDb/pxweb/en/10_Dem_soc/10_Dem_soc__08_zivljenjska_raven__08_silc_kazalniki_revsc__10_08672_stopnja_tveg_revcine/0867206S.px/table/tableViewLayout2/

Šoštaršič, M. (2013) 'Presežki hrane iz trgovin in gostilen bi bili dragocena pomoč' ['Food surpluses from groceries and restaurants would be a valuable assistance'], www.delo.si/zgodbe/nedeljskobranje/presezki-hrane-iz-trgovin-in-gostiln-bi-bili-dragocena-pomoc.html

Stenmarck, Å., Jensen, C., Quested, C. and Moates, G. (2016) 'FUSIONS: estimates of European food waste levels', www.eu-fusions.org/phocadownload/Publications/Estimates%20of%20European%20food%20waste%20levels.pdf

Štepec, M. (2018) 'Prehrana v času prve svetovne vojne' ['Nutrition during the First World War'], www.100letprve.si/i_svetovna_vojna/prehrana/

Torfing, J. (1999) 'Workfare with welfare: recent reforms of the Danish welfare state', *Journal of European Social Policy*, 9(1): 5–28.

Toš, N. (2017) *Vrednote v prehodu XI. Slovenija v evropskih in medčasovnih primerjavah ESS* [*Values in transition XI. Slovenia in European and intermodal comparisons, European Social Survey*], Ljubljana: Fakulteta za družbene vede.

Wacquant, L. (2003) 'Penalizacija revščine in vzpon neoliberalizma' ['The penalisation of poverty and the rise of neo-liberalism'], *Družboslovne razprave* [*Debates in Social Sciences*], 19(43): 65–75.

6

Food aid in post-crisis Spain: a test for this welfare state model

Amaia Inza-Bartolomé and Leire Escajedo San-Epifanio

Introduction

In order to frame the current phenomenon of food aid in Spain, it is important to identify the resources to which people resort when they can find no way to satisfy their basic needs through the labour market. Over the last decade, the Spanish income guarantee system has stagnated and cannot now meet the needs of many people living in poverty (FOESSA, 2014). The first strategy or resource for households – and a very valuable one for those facing specific difficulties, such as a mortgage payment, a particular bill or food expenses – is the family network, though not everyone has access to this. Particularly at the start of the economic crisis, this was a genuine form of micro-solidarity which showed that it is possible to cope with emergencies (Pérez de Armiño, 2014). However, after this initial stage, family networks showed signs of exhaustion (Martínez Virto, 2014a, 2014b), and the third sector took on a greater role in addressing the right to food of people who are at risk of exclusion.

It is also vital to note that third sector entities have played different roles in supporting such access to food. It is particularly important to distinguish between, on the one hand, cases where these organisations acted in collaboration with the existing food distribution network – which is organised in Spain by the Spanish Red Cross and the Spanish Federation of Food Banks (FESBAL) – and, on the other hand, certain organisations that obtain their own food donations to distribute, or negotiate discount card systems with commercial networks (to provide food at lower prices to deprived people). In the first case, where non-governmental organisations act as collaborators with the network, their role is largely predetermined by Spanish government legislation that regulates the distribution of aid from the Fund for European Aid to the Most Deprived (FEAD). Under the framework of the 2017 FEAD operational programme, the number of collaborating organisations receiving food from the 56 FESBAL food banks and the Red Cross was 5,977 (1,390 organisations that offer cooked meals and 4,587 organisations that distribute food) (MAPAMA, 2017). In the second case – where they act independently – their activities are not covered by state legislation.

As a result of certain factors that will be explained later in this chapter, the requirements governing the distribution of aid from the FEAD were extended to most other types of distribution of food to people in need in Spain, whether the source was the FEAD or not. One of the most remarkable requirements is the obligation on organisations to provide recipients of food aid with additional help relating to social inclusion measures. As will be explained in detail, one of the practical effects of this requirement is the removal – at least partially – of the responsibility for social protection from the state. This is transferred not just to the third sector, but even to the level of organisations created solely to address food inequalities.

Levels of food insecurity due to people's economic situation – which resulted in food assistance being introduced, in principle, as a short-term measure – have shown signs of becoming chronic since the economic crisis of 2008. In terms of the amount of food distributed, in 2005, the total was 31,000 tons. During 2008–10, this rose steadily to 83,000 tons and continued increasing to 103,517 tons in 2011, and then 152,932 tons in 2015. It reached a peak of 153,908 tons in 2016 before reducing slightly to 151,527 tons in 2017. In terms of the number of recipients, FESBAL assistance reached 980,296 people in 2010. This number also progressively increased, until it stabilised at a rate of 1.5 million recipients per year between 2015 and 2017 (FESBAL, 2017).

The main reason for this situation is that, as already noted, the responsibility to fulfil the right to food of people in danger of social exclusion was handed over to the third sector because the available state resources were not sufficient to meet the needs of all people living in poverty. Therefore, the need for food is now fulfilled by third sector organisations, which enjoy high levels of legitimacy. The stigmatisation involved in receiving food from charities is not an issue that has been given much attention in the public debate in Spain. Furthermore, in this period of economic difficulty, religious and/or voluntary organisations – as well as private initiatives making in-kind donations of food – have received very positive attention in the media. Overall, the official network of food banks (FESBAL, 2017), which has been mobilised to distribute an increasing amount of food over the past ten years, is very positively regarded by society, as well as by political and institutional organisations. The food banks associated with this network are non-profit entities that, among other commitments, declare themselves to be apolitical and volunteer-based organisations. Moreover, it should be highlighted that this network participates once or twice a year in what is known as the 'Great Food Drive'. For two or three days, food bank volunteers collect food donations made by individuals as they leave supermarkets. This type of initiative accounts for around 25 per cent of the food received by some provincial food banks throughout the year. In addition to this large-scale collection, there are food collection activities throughout the year, as well as constant donations of food and money thanks to initiatives promoted by a variety of companies. Even so, according to FESBAL (2017), the most significant proportion of food is obtained through agreements with both public and private organisations, companies and institutions of various kinds. The difficult situation of many citizens scraping a living is exacerbated by the positive and uncritical public perception of initiatives where enterprises reduce their food waste by donating surplus food.

This chapter first deals with responses to poverty by the national welfare state income guarantee system in Spain. This is a partially decentralised guarantee system, which has been affected everywhere by the austerity that has constrained public spending. The chapter then describes the main strategies of Spanish households for surviving food insecurity and how most in-kind food aid is distributed. Finally, with a new system being established in practice, this chapter addresses its implications for fundamental rights and social justice. Conclusions are presented on the basis of the impact that the collision between these twin phenomena has had: on the one hand, the ineffectiveness of the welfare system, which is exacerbated by the increase in demand and the impact of austerity; and, on the other, the way in which a new food distribution network has been set up in Spain. Although the third sector participates, the established food aid distribution system has two main drivers. The first is the implementation of the FEAD in Spain, offering strategic political support for the agri-food sector. The second is corporate philanthropy (of agri-food and non-food companies) and public support from individual citizens through the Great Food Drives.

The inefficiency of the welfare system has boosted the food distribution network, which operates through third sector organisations and even informal charities. Third sector organisations collect food from food banks in order to distribute it, and they must provide information about the people they assist. These organisations operate simply as a point of distribution. Hence, even while recognising the importance of this distribution of food to alleviate current need in Spain, some voices question the implications of the system for human rights and social justice (SiiS-Fundación Eguía-Careaga, 2009; Mata and Pallarés, 2014; Pérez de Armiño, 2014; Sales and Marco, 2014).

The income guarantee system, austerity and poverty in Spain

Regional decentralisation of social protection in Spain after Franco's dictatorship

Between 1939 (the year in which the Spanish Civil War ended) and 1975, Spain was subjected to a dictatorial regime known as Francoism. The country's transition to being a democratic state was preceded in the 1960s by a process of economic transformation, thanks principally to industrialisation and tourism. Overall, there were important changes in the social structure, with a remarkable demographic increase and, due to the economic situation, a parallel increase in wages. Although insufficient, a Law for the Basis of Social Security was introduced during this period (in 1967), providing guarantees of medical assistance, retirement benefits and some other benefits. However, it was not until the introduction of the democratic constitution of 1978 that progress was made towards the current social security system.

The democratic constitution is also an important landmark because it initiated a process of regional decentralisation. In 1978, from a highly centralised and unitary dictatorship, the Spanish state changed to an almost federal organisational model, with 17 autonomous communities (ACs) operating at a sub-national level. This is significant in terms of social protection as competences relating to this matter are assigned to both the central government and ACs. In particular, the constitution assigns 'the basic legislation and the economic system of social security' to the state – leaving the implementation of its services to the ACs – whereas 'social assistance' is left in hands of the ACs.[1] The social protection provided by the state includes contributory benefits, in addition to non-contributory and family benefits. The ACs manage social assistance, which can be described as 'residual' in the sense that it provides supplementary support in areas that the general social security system does not cover. Hence, the provision and administration of policies and programmes related to the 'safety net' are said to be characterised by the system's decentralisation (Moreno, 2007). A second characteristic of this distribution of powers is that the protection provided by the ACs is discretionary. Therefore, the mechanisms of protection and access requirements for benefits vary between different ACs. Finally, it is important to point out that each AC's expenditure per inhabitant on social protection is less related to the *needs identified per inhabitant* than to the *resources* that each AC has available *per inhabitant*.

Effects of post-crisis austerity

When examining the changes that the Spanish welfare state has undergone, it is necessary to bear in mind some general issues. Although the need to adapt to economic globalisation or demographic change was the same for all welfare regimes from the 1980s onwards, there were additional difficulties in the Mediterranean countries. These included the ideological legitimisation of the welfare state, fiscal pressures related to the convergence objectives of the Economic and Monetary Union, and increasing pressure on the social costs of unemployment within the framework of globalisation (Guillén et al, 2016). In addition, after the global economic crisis of 2008, Spain has had to implement a set of difficult reforms to conform to European Union (EU) measures. Among these, the monitoring of social policies has been a key aspect of ensuring fiscal consolidation, under the constant threat of even more drastic external austerity measures (González Begega and Del Pino, 2017). This process has forced far-reaching decisions to be taken in this area, without the required debate and consensus, inaugurating a period that has been defined as 'the hibernation of the social contract' until the austerity measures of the eurozone had been met. During this period, the government found sources of alternative legitimacy in the community institutions of economic government (EU economic governance institutions), outside the national political framework (González Begega and Luque, 2015).

The imposed need to reduce the public deficit has had a substantial impact on the structure and development of the Spanish welfare state, subjecting traditional areas of protection such as pensions, health care and unemployment benefits to intense pressure due to insufficient financial means. It has also impeded the momentum for expansion into new areas of protection relating to issues such as equality, conciliation and dependency (Guillén et al, 2016). Welfare reductions pushed social spending into the spotlight, and the implementation of charitable measures to provide social protection and privately run welfare services – at the expense of public services – was deemed to be acceptable. In this context, society in general, and labour union agents in particular, had limited capacity to mount a response (Laparra and Pérez Eransus, 2012). Overall, austerity policies have meant an increase in inequality, greater relative and absolute poverty, lower wages, and higher unemployment (Muñoz de Bustillo and Antón, 2015). In fact, it is no surprise that many jobs were destroyed during the crisis given the Spanish economic model, based on lower-skilled sectors, lower productivity and high levels of temporary employment. Austerity measures have also had a negative effect on the welfare system's internal equity, decreasing access, generosity, benefits and the balance between private and public components across the different ACs (Guillén et al, 2016).

The Spanish welfare state reacted to the crisis by trying to provide more protection for citizens. However, due to the logic of the system's internal operation, the role of social policies in the benefits provided to help people escape poverty became even more polarising. In particular, the crisis widened the gap between retired people – who were relatively better protected before the crisis – and younger people, who had greater difficulties and received less help from the welfare state in spite of being active within the labour market. Furthermore, the risk of becoming trapped in poverty for couples with children is high, and those who have escaped poverty thanks to social transfers often live in unstable conditions (Laparra and Pérez Eransus, 2012). Moreover, the crisis has disproportionately affected vulnerable groups, resulting in an extraordinary increase in inequality. This is reflected in the collapse of incomes at the lower end of the scale, with the poorest losing 25 per cent of their incomes between 2007 and 2015 (Marí-Klose and Martínez Pérez, 2015). The Gini coefficient for inequality in Spain has increased 2.3 per cent since 2008, which is comparatively very high – giving a total figure almost 4 per cent above the average for the eurozone (EAPN, 2017).

The levels of deprivation and debt experienced by many households make it difficult for them to meet their financial obligations. This has had a domino effect, which has been especially remarkable in the domestic sphere. For example, in Spain, severe defaults tripled between 2007 and 2010 (increasing from 0.3 per cent to 1 per cent), and housing expenses became an excessively large percentage of the household budget for 49.8 per cent of families (Laparra and Pérez Eransus, 2012). Although the initial effects of the economic crisis were alleviated by unemployment benefits and intra-family support, an increase in chronic financial difficulties has been recorded, with rises in long-term unemployment, particularly for people over 50. Likewise, there has been an increasing spiral of scarcity and vulnerability in the social sphere, creating the conditions for a second wave of impoverishment and social exclusion with even worse effects (Caritas, 2013).

In 2016, a total of 12,989,405 people – 27.9 per cent of the Spanish population – were at risk of poverty and/or social exclusion (AROPE). The AROPE indicator has increased 4.1 per cent since 2008, which means that in order to return to pre-crisis levels, it is necessary to reduce the number of people at risk by two million. In Spain, the income of 70 per cent of the population has not recovered to the level in 2008. Severe material deprivation (SMD) affects 5.8 per cent of the Spanish population, which equates to slightly more than 2.6 million people. Among the indicators of SMD, in 2016, 2.9 per cent of the population could not afford a meal with animal or equivalent plant protein every two days, which is 32 per cent higher than in 2008 (EAPN, 2017). This evolution of exclusion implies a risk of the dualisation of Spanish society – a marked division between those inside and outside the labour market – given that a more fragmented society means a context of greater difficulties for social intervention as the routes to incorporation become rarer, more complicated and more expensive (Laparra, 2014).

The income guarantee system against poverty

In Spain, the income guarantee system is structured around contributory protection (based on previous contributions) and non-contributory or assistance protection. The latter is activated to protect workers who have been left out of contributory protection, have depleted it or cannot continue to work due to age, illness or disability. If people who are still of working age and able to work use up their allocation of non-contributory or assistance protection, they may apply for a minimum monthly income from the AC where they live. Each AC has different access requirements, amounts of benefits, duration and coverage (CES, 2017). Another resource to help people in poverty – also under the jurisdiction of the ACs – is social emergency aid, granted in special cases and usually provided as a single payment aimed at addressing a specific basic need such as housing, food or an emergency such as eviction.

Since the crisis, the increase in the number of people receiving benefits, and the longer durations for which people are without income or a job, have revealed the complexities and inconsistencies of the system, demonstrating its limited contribution to reducing the high levels of poverty (Ayala et al, 2016). In addition, the lack of processes to aid transition between the different protection schemes suggests that many workers are left for long periods with no or very limited income, and without resources to support them in returning to the labour market (Rodríguez-Cabrero, 2015).

All ACs have responded to the effects of the crisis by introducing a wide variety of measures to address different needs, depending on the resources that they have available, the specific impacts of unemployment and the lack of income. However, this has been affected by the diversity of political responses to the problem of poverty, regardless of the different costs of living in each region (Ayala et al, 2016). Furthermore, delays in the application process and actual payment of the minimum income have now stretched to over six months. Hence, together with the tightening of access requirements and budget reductions, these aspects combine to worsen the social situation of people in need (Caritas, 2012).

Food insecurity and survival strategies of Spanish households

If the institutional configuration of a welfare regime is linked to a given culture, doctrine or value system, in the case of Spain, this is framed within the Mediterranean family-based regime, where the family, public institutions and civil society interact with remarkable complementarity. In particular, it is worth noting the existence of family practices of generous micro-solidarity within households, as well as in family social networks. These have contributed to maintaining a cohesion that involves a difficult balancing act (Moreno, 2012; Pérez de Armiño, 2014). As basic needs such as food, housing expenses, clothing and footwear are sometimes not covered by the welfare system, people who cannot afford them on their own are forced to resort to family or private social entities for help. In fact, in Spain, the main strategy to secure basic needs has been family help, followed by working in the submerged economy and turning to social organisations. Public social services come in fourth place, and support from community networks is fifth (Caritas, 2011). Related to this, it is remarkable that 67 per cent of the people who resort to Caritas have already accessed public social services – the trend of informally redirecting them is being established across most of Spain (Caritas, 2013).

The forms of support most frequently provided by families are food and financial help with housing expenses (Caritas, 2013). In general, family solidarity has helped to lessen the impacts of exclusion processes by supplementing low levels of social benefits and providing benefits in areas not covered by social protection programmes (Martínez Virto, 2014a). However, due to the extended duration of the crisis, the capacity of family solidarity to meet basic needs is becoming exhausted. Initial symptoms of such exhaustion have manifested as conflicts, mental disorders and addiction (Martínez Virto, 2014b). It is also important to note that the family 'safety net', assistance provided by local administrations and charitable aid all have many disadvantages when it comes to promoting social cohesion and equal opportunities (Marí-Klose and Martínez Pérez, 2015) because large segments of the population with irregular trajectories are constantly exposed to situations of vulnerability and remain outside the system.

As Riches (1997) points out, spending on food is the most flexible part of vulnerable people's budgets. Work by the Sociological Research Centre (CIS, 2011), using a battery of questions to measure the impact of the crisis on household habits, shows that 41.2 per cent of respondents had changed their eating habits to save money. As a matter of principle, after the crisis, individuals sought to optimise their resources, continuing to meet their basic needs by adjusting their food budget, buying sale or own-brand items, or developing self-sufficiency activities such as cultivating vegetables (Martínez Virto, 2014a). In addition, in terms of cuts in food budgets, there are remarkable differences in the vulnerability of households. Since 2007, the number of households receiving no benefits (contributory or non-contributory) has increased by 37.6 per cent, whereas the increase of households receiving benefits was 25 per cent (Laparra, 2014). As of 2008, 68 per cent of Spanish Caritas offices noted that food aid was their most in-demand service (delivered as food parcels or money to buy food), followed by financial help with housing and, in third place, unemployment benefits (Caritas, 2013).

In most cases, this food need could be classified as *transitory food insecurity*, which is short term, temporary and could be applicable to cases arising from the economic crisis and its effects (FAO, 2011). In such situations, people's ability to access enough food to ensure good nutrition suddenly becomes restricted as a result of the instability of household incomes. Unfortunately, in the case of action to meet the need for food in Spain, different initiatives have not collaborated to plan an integrated response to the problem from a local and community perspective (Llobet, 2014).

In Spain, changes in food consumption in the wake of the economic crisis imply an increase in food insecurity. In the period 2015–17, severe food insecurity affected 1.4 per cent of the total population (around

650,000 individuals) (FAO, 2018). Difficulties in obtaining sufficient food to provide adequate nutrition are increasing, as are unhealthy dietary habits, leading to an increase in problems such as obesity (Antentas and Vivas, 2014). Specifically, in a study about the violation of the human right to food in the AC of Catalonia (Observatori DESC, 2014), the austerity policies implemented are reported to have caused people in vulnerable situations difficulties in fulfilling this right due to insufficient and partial assistance-based measures established by institutions in response to growing food needs. Hence, neither sufficient amounts nor nutritional standards are guaranteed for those who cannot meet their own dietary needs. Another study from an AC in Northern Spain – Asturias – revealed the dominance of food programmes run by third sector organisations because of their ability to provide larger quantities of food. Nevertheless, people prefer not to resort to them until informal help from family or friends becomes insufficient to alleviate their food insecurity. This situation often occurs when the households of the extended family are suffering similar hardship and can no longer respond to the needs of their relatives. However, those in need still suffer from food insecurity in the sense that they face great difficulties accessing fresh foods in any kind of stable and continuous manner. Hence, they basically eat insufficient amounts of food with little variety, leading to a precarious and deficient diet (Otero, 2015). Unfortunately, there are not enough statistical measurements or reliable and high-quality analyses from a right-to-food approach to give reliable information about the conditions of food access and availability in Spain (Observatorio del Derecho a la Alimentación de España, 2018).

Overview of food aid in Spain: development and implementation

It is almost impossible to map all the public and private initiatives of in-kind food distribution in Spain due to the country's structure of 50 provinces and two autonomous cities, with very unequal population densities and income levels. However, organisations that have been participating in food distribution programmes partially supported by the EU since 2008 are easily traceable by the volume of their activities. Between 2000 and 2013, a series of Food Aid Plans for the Most Deprived Persons was implemented and financed in Spain within the EU Common Agricultural Policy framework. These plans were based on providing food that had been gathered within the framework of the European regulations (such as cereals, oil and milk powder) through the Spanish Agrarian Guarantee Fund (FEGA). In 2014, the EU passed Regulation (EU) 223/2014, which resulted in the creation of the FEAD for the years 2014–20. Among its measures, it allows food to be purchased for delivery to the most deprived people 'through organisations associated' with the programme, as set out in the operative programme published by the Spanish Ministry of Health, Consumer Issues and Social Welfare (MSCBS, 2014).

In its resolution of 16 May 2014, FEGA established that the 'organisations in charge of distributing food' for the 2014 plan would be the 56 food banks affiliated to FESBAL and the Spanish Red Cross. Both of these, in turn, run distribution operations through a network of thousands of collaborating entities. This would remain the same for subsequent years. The plan calls these collaborating entities 'beneficiaries', although they are technically third sector organisations and charities assisting people in need. Collaborating entities must provide evidence of their needs and the number of people they assist, and these data are used to calculate the amount of food that they will receive to distribute. The resolution classifies these intermediary organisations into two different types: 'consumption entities' – such as soup kitchens – where people are directly provided with meals to eat immediately; and 'delivery organisations', where people collect food to prepare and consume in their homes later.

There is a substantial difference between the functioning of FESBAL and the Spanish Red Cross in terms of the FEAD food donation programme. The Spanish Red Cross distributes donated food both to smaller entities and directly to people in need. As laid down in their statutes, the formal objectives of the FESBAL network's members are to fight against food waste and distribute free food by acting as suppliers to other entities; FESBAL food banks do not act as direct distributors to end recipients. According to their annual reports, some of the food they distribute comes from 'fighting food waste', some from the EU fund – now the FEAD programme – and some from private donations. In total, food from the FEAD programme accounts for just over 20 per cent of the annual amount, with the rest coming through the other channels.

Many agri-food companies make in-kind food donations to the FESBAL network at various points along their production and distribution chains. The reasons for this are quite complex. One major reason is likely to be to create an association with the positive image that the public has of the FESBAL network and the activities of its food banks in tackling food poverty. As mentioned in the introduction to this chapter, the public regards donating food to be distributed through food banks as a non-political and transparent expression of sheer altruism. Hence, it is logical that companies wish for an association with the FESBAL network to be part of their corporate image. While these actions can be framed as philanthropy, it is perhaps more appropriate to regard them as acts of corporate social responsibility (CSR) because corporations actively and voluntarily make contributions with the goal of improving society, as well as their own competitive position and added value. Remarkably, food coming from the FEAD, CSR activities, individual donations and Great Food Drives is physically stored in the same place – FESBAL's provincial headquarters. From there, more than 6,000 collaborating entities receive food for onward delivery.

Over the years, collaborating entities wishing to participate in European-funded food aid programmes have had to meet an increasing number of conditions. Any beneficiary entity wishing to participate in the programme must now be constituted as an associated distribution organisation and comply with the requirements set out in the participation guide published by the Spanish Ministry of Agriculture, Fisheries, Food and Environment in 2014 (MAPAMA, 2014). The requirements are not all easy to meet, requiring high levels of administrative, operational and financial capacity. In addition, organisations are also required to develop accompanying measures such as guidance on social resources, to provide detailed information on certain performance indicators and to report the number of people referred to them by public social services (or social workers at organisations also participating in the programme). A desire to continue providing food obtained from the network to people they help on a daily basis explains why many third sector collaborating entities have adapted to satisfy these requirements. In contrast, certain organisations that had been delivering food aid for some time have been excluded from the programme due to their inability to fulfil all the conditions. In 2016, 6,200 delivery organisations were certified as beneficiaries (both consumption and delivery entities), which was down from over 9,000 in 2008. Even if organisations could legally still operate after losing their certification, they would experience a drastic reduction in the amount of food they received due to losing access to supplies coming through the FESBAL network.

Third sector collaborating delivery entities assume a very particular role in this vast network. This does not mean that they neglect the other important tasks (mostly social support) that they carry out as social organisations to help people at risk of social exclusion. Moreover, as mentioned in the introduction to this chapter, both third sector delivery entities and other charities deliver food from the FEAD and also in-kind donations. This is relevant because it is obtained through the FESBAL network, independent of the FEAD programme. FESBAL food is quantified in the reports of food banks affiliated to the network.

At the user-facing level, delivery organisations carry out social inclusion tasks unrelated to food. Each entity is entirely autonomous in its decision-making about how best to assist its users. Conversely, at a macro level, a significant proportion of third sector entities collaborate with the FEAD programme while simultaneously receiving food that arrives in the FESBAL network through channels other than the FEAD (surplus food donations, fundraising campaigns and so on). The FESBAL network handles food from all these different sources. The amount of food in the FESBAL network is growing so large that the distribution network is starting to resemble that of a corporation, despite the fact that most of the tasks at food banks are carried out by volunteers. The distribution of all this food is organised at a macro level. Thus, the only decision that participating social entities can make is whether they participate in this system or not.

It is important to point out that the entities called 'food banks' in Spain must be clearly differentiated from delivery organisations. The term 'food bank' ('*Banco de Alimentos*') is a registered trademark in Spain, and it can only be used by associations or foundations that meet the requirements of the FESBAL network, including adherence to a code of ethics.[2] Other entities could perfectly fit the broad definition of food banks commonly used internationally to describe organisations whose main activity consists of receiving donated food and then distributing it. In general, such organisations in Spain describe themselves using alternative terms to avoid confusion with affiliates of the FESBAL network. Similarly, there are facilities such as social supermarkets and solidarity food pantries that do not distribute food to recipients free of charge, but sell it at a substantial discount. However, their reach is by no means as extensive as that of the FESBAL network.[3]

Due to food from all sources being physically stored together, the requirements of the Spanish FEAD programme for its collaborating entities and delivery organisations are actually applied to all delivery entities within the enormous FESBAL network. This means that the regulations cover all entities willing to distribute food gathered by the network, regardless of whether or not it comes from the EU programme. Beneficiary entities are required: to have the capacity to store and deliver food; to provide human and material resources; to provide assistance for social and labour integration; and to record and report the number of recipients that they assist (and confirm evidence of their need for assistance). In addition, the FEAD programme requires that entities gather various pieces of personal data from their end users, which, in accordance with current legislation, are sent to the coordination department of the FEAD programme. Whether these data are also gathered when the food comes from another source depends entirely on what is agreed between the provincial food bank and each delivery organisation. As there is no obligation to publish these types of data or make them publicly accessible, the authors have not been able to obtain conclusive information about this aspect.

However, there is another aspect that is worth highlighting. Of all the requirements mentioned, it is surprising that the FEAD programme requires (and the FESBAL network requests confirmation) that delivery organisations have human and material resources for delivery (which is logical), as well as resources to provide assistance with activities that promote social inclusion. This is striking because neither the FEAD programme nor, by its nature, the FESBAL network effectively provide support with the costs of delivering such social assistance. In Spain, Royal Decree 603/2016 regulates the granting of direct subsidies to organisations responsible for the distribution of food and the development of social support measures, within the framework of the operational programme of the FEAD. This decree establishes that social assistance measures should consist of: individualised information and personalised guidance on social resources, employment, health, education and so on; actions that lead to labour insertion; guidance and advice on employment; training and any other action that improves conditions of access to the labour market for the most disadvantaged people receiving food aid; the organisation of group information sessions on access to existing resources, as well as economic aid; general information on nutrition, balanced diets and healthy eating; advice on household economics; training and guidance in the effective management of the family budget; and, finally, actions that encourage social participation.

As mentioned earlier in this chapter, collaborating entities are required to distribute food to end users in a specific way, according to national guidelines. As collaborating entities, they are not allowed to make their own decisions on how they distribute food; however, they do have autonomy in designing their social assistance projects. Although Spain's decision to use the full amount of aid provided by the FEAD to purchase food means that it does not materially support social assistance, this can also be said for the whole FEAD programme across the EU. The European Commission approved a total of €3,800 million within the FEAD for 2014–20, and the assistance to be provided only comprises food, clothing and personal hygiene products for the most deprived people. No amount is given for social assistance whatsoever. It imposes that cost on recipient countries, stating that 'each country must co-finance its own FEAD programme with at least 15% of the cost and, in addition, the measures each country applies must include social inclusion measures' (MAPAMA, 2014). Rather than funding being provided for this social inclusion assistance, or state institutions taking on the task, organisations that wish to participate in the delivery of EU food aid are required to provide social assistance to end users as an additional service. Unlike food distribution, which is regulated at the national level, the specifications of this social assistance and the support that public authorities must provide have, for the moment, been left de facto – though with no explanation – in the hands of each AC (Escajedo San-Epifanio and Inza-Bartolomé, 2018).

Research carried out with 2,707 delivery organisations shows that 743 offered social support measures to end users receiving help through the FEAD, equivalent to 27.44 per cent of the total organisations. In the case of organisations working with the Red Cross, 41.5 per cent provided some measure of additional social assistance, but this proportion drops to 24.6 per cent among organisations affiliated with FESBAL. Almost 86 per cent of the entities that develop some form of additional help provide information and individualised guidance on, among others, social, employment, health and educational resources according to users' needs, as well as referring them to services that provide these resources. The next most developed services, provided by 61.2 per cent of organisations, consist of advisory activities and workshops in the field of assistance in job search and labour market insertion. Finally, around 44 per cent provide information and advice on nutrition and healthy eating, and 41.1 per cent offer advice on managing household budgets and other issues related to family economy (MAPAMA, 2017).

Implications of food aid for social justice

Not being able to access food in a socially acceptable way makes resorting to food aid stigmatising, and it is a determinant step for people slipping into vulnerability. According to Paugam's (2007) stages of the process of stigmatisation suffered by people in need, 'fragility' is the initial stage. At this stage, people cannot generate their own income through the labour market, although they try to avoid contact with social services or welfare organisations. Then they become aware of the distance between their situation and what their reference society considers desirable. This is a fundamental moment when considering the situation of the person in need. Although, at this first stage, the initial strategy to satisfy need is to ask family for help, this resource is quite limited in many cases, and in others, people do not even have this minimal safety net. This stage is the prelude to the stage of 'dependency', when people begin receiving help from public social services or social assistance organisations. Hence, people in need recognise their situation of poverty and loss of personal autonomy, as well as their exclusion from consumer society. According to Bauman (2015), this situation means that one is deprived of what would be considered a 'normal life'. As this stage, people in poverty become flawed consumers who are excluded from the market.

In particular, people who are dependent on food aid are aware that their dignity is negatively affected and that they lose part of their freedom of choice because they are forced to accept any charity food aid that they are offered regardless of their individual needs and preferences (Riches and Silvasti, 2014). The psychosocial consequences of this institutionalised dependence on charity include increased social stigma and feelings of helplessness related to poverty. With their personal freedom of choice eliminated from the process of acquiring food, end users feel humiliated, being relegated to a position where they must prove their right to receive what are basically society's leftovers (Tarasuk and MacLean, 1990). Several studies highlight the feelings of shame associated with becoming a recipient of aid from food banks: 'while shame can be a very private emotion … it is also an utterly social emotion' (Van der Horst et al, 2014: 1506). For example, in the case of Barcelona's soup kitchens, which are highly stigmatised services, in the transition from the fragility to the dependency stage, being sent to one of these soup kitchens has a great symbolic impact, accelerating the process of social disqualification for the person involved (Sales and Marco, 2014).

A study of food banks in the Basque Country (SiiS-Fundación Eguía-Careaga, 2009) highlights the existence of charitable patterns that do not prioritise inclusion and promote healthy habits. Furthermore, these patterns foster a stigma that people in need tend to avoid. Therefore, it cannot be said that these initiatives are based on principles of normalisation and universality. Moreover, in these cases, the intermediary entities apply their own criteria to screen recipients, and their aid overlaps with the benefits provided to recipients by public institutions. According to the conclusions of another Spanish study

(Mata and Pallarés, 2014), the fact that third sector entities are in charge of food aid means that they can judge applicants, deciding who receives certain benefits and who does not, as well as for how long and, if applicable, what recipients have to do in exchange. Additionally, third sector entities hold and manage confidential data, with consequent potential for fragmentation and micromanagement given the possibility of overlap between different entities, different eligibility criteria in different regions and so on.

Although food distribution through charity may be an important aspect of addressing food insecurity, it is by no means a solution on its own (Ronson and Caraher, 2016). Food banks are insufficient in fighting malnourishment. They also reproduce charitable mechanisms that may be harmful to recipients by fostering disempowerment, the loss of personal autonomy, stigmatisation and the persistence of poverty and social exclusion (Gascón and Montagut, 2015). In the same way, the proliferation of charity contributes to a society's failure to deal with poverty in a meaningful way, normalises deprivation, legitimises personal generosity as an answer to huge social and economic dislocation, and acts as a 'valve of moral security', reducing the discomfort caused by conspicuous misery (Poppendieck, 1999).

It has been pointed out that due to a new social policy oriented towards charity practices, social welfare in Spain is threatened with a certain degree of diminution. This makes the welfare state lose its redistributive nature and its subsequent purpose of generating citizenship. If the state contributes to the privatisation of social services that used to be universal, it leaves these services in the hands of the third sector and to the mercy of society's capacity for charity, transforming them from public benefits (rights) to private ones (ex gratia) (Mata and Pallarés, 2014). Overall, food aid as a resource is a result of the imbalance and inefficiency of institutionalised social redistribution mechanisms, which fall far short of providing adequate coverage in Spain. Additionally, public institutions have proved unable to react appropriately to the economic crisis with adequate measures that would have averted increases in poverty, rather than implementing austerity policies. People admitting their situation and asking for help is an important indicator of their stage of dependency, but public institutions have responded by retreating from their responsibility, leaving the problem of tackling food insecurity to the third sector alone. Often, this help is offered in a stigmatising manner and cannot be claimed as a right.

When the need for help is caused by insufficient economic transfers (when the income guarantee system is inadequate to prevent people falling into poverty), food aid measures that originally emerged to respond to emergencies and transitory situations become a distortion factor. Food aid's charitable nature makes it dependent on goodwill. No social inclusion mechanisms are implemented in tandem with food aid to provide a more integrated approach to the problems that cause people to demand food. Therefore, any institutionalised public mechanisms that are supposed to implement social justice are ineffective because they do not fulfil their responsibility to tackle poverty, which, in this case, manifests as a need for food. Thus, poverty-relief measures come to rely on third sector entities and a voluntary workforce, while public opinion praises these dynamics. In addition, food aid has some hidden aspects related to benefits for the food industry. Corporations increase their CSR activity through donations to food banks, which, in turn, brings benefits for their image and reputation (Caraher and Cavicchi, 2014). In Spain, for example, these companies are enjoying increased support and appreciation from a growing number of organisations and various public institutions at the national, regional and local levels (Pérez de Armiño, 2014).

Conclusions: the future role of food assistance in the Spanish welfare state

The third sector has become a food delivery agent in a huge network where neither the state nor corporate organisations are acting. While this task is linked to assisting people, it lacks an organisational engine at its core to address the underlying causes of need. In other words, the work of the food distribution network does nothing to address existing need beyond the short term, and does not reflect on the best way to address the fundamental problems. The core of this distribution network comprises: the implementation model of the FEAD (bidding to purchase products); (subsidised) programmes of access to fruits and vegetables based on agri-food policies (mainly agricultural); and food products donated by companies (CSR activity) and citizens. It is vital to take into account that end users' autonomy has no place in this system at all, and it is obvious that a paradigm shift is needed.

When philanthropy, CSR activity and even individual citizens' altruism perform a function for which the state is constitutionally responsible, it is necessary to ask where the political responsibility lies. As previously discussed in this chapter, the main distribution system for in-kind food aid is organised around two entities: the Spanish Red Cross and, in particular, the 56 food banks associated with FESBAL. Food banks are non-profit private entities that distribute food from the

FEAD programme, and also receive in-kind and monetary donations from corporations and citizens. In Spain, the configuration of the FEAD programme as 'food aid' only is an entirely political decision adopted by the central government for the 2014–20 period. The state's decision to distribute the FEAD aid in this way – accounting for slightly less than one quarter of the total food aid distributed by the network – should be subject to scrutiny and potential revision by the entire citizenry of Spain. In a social state, the necessary critical analysis of this network of private donations must focus on the inactivity of a state that witnesses the creation of pockets of poverty through this network and yet does nothing to solve the problem. Public opinion's uncritical praise for these food donations, and companies discharging their CSR through activities to support the work of food banks, merely reflect the ubiquity of this current model of food aid distribution. Would it be possible to provide assistance to people at risk of food deprivation in a better way? Undoubtedly, yes. Are public authorities planning to take any steps in this direction? Honestly, at the time of writing, no.

As has been confirmed throughout this chapter, Spain's income guarantee system has become ineffective in addressing food poverty, and the family – which has been most people's principal source of support – is showing clear signs of exhaustion. In this scenario, charities in Spain have found room to expand, and in-kind charity food aid has been organised on the basis of an operational model that clearly contrasts with the aforementioned ineffectiveness of the state. However, as previously discussed, the engine driving this network is doing nothing to identify and address people's real underlying needs. Several factors favour the continuation of donation and distribution at current levels. Perhaps surprisingly, many third sector entities collaborate with the food distribution network while also continuing to carry out their usual tasks. Aiming to introduce food aid delivery to their provinces, public sector institutions have made financial donations or provided logistical support to create local food banks. In cases where a food bank was already in existence, such public sector funding has been directed to increasing its organisational and functional capacity. Therefore, in Spain, with a certain amount of common ground between third sector entities and public institutions regarding in-kind food distribution, the relationship has essentially become one based on collaboration.

In the aftermath of government austerity, what underlies the situation of poverty and exclusion examined in this chapter is an income guarantee system providing an institutional response that is clearly insufficient to fulfil citizens' basic social rights, such as the right to food. Moreover, the state system has been relying on the third sector as a way to avoid its own responsibility to fulfil these rights, with the approval of the general public. The problem is that systematically referring people to food aid can only perpetuate their situation. With social services incapable of providing an integrated solution, and help from close relatives showing signs of exhaustion, charity is legitimised through the rise of micro-solidarity provided via the third sector. This chain of events fits perfectly into the framework of the Mediterranean family-based welfare state. Society and the third sector avoid appealing to public authorities to fulfil the state's responsibilities to fairly redistribute resources and to implement an effective solution to the persistence of poverty after this period of economic crisis and austerity. This avoidance might imply an acceptance of the delegitimisation of the entire welfare system, its ineffectiveness and the state's shirking of its responsibilities.

People receiving food aid have actually suffered a triple rejection at different levels: first, from a normal labour market where work pays wages that are sufficient to provide a decent standard of living; second, from the normal consumer society; and, third, from the condition of being a full citizen because the associated rights are not currently fulfilled through institutionalised state mechanisms. The general invisibility of these effects of food poverty reinforces the processes of exclusion that affect people in need. A second indicator reveals that the food aid system has been built without regard for the problems that it is supposed to solve. As explained in detail earlier in this chapter, the system has expanded its network without taking into account the requirements of individual ACs, which may not even have enough resources to cover the social expenditure required to meet existing need.

The expansion of the food distribution network has been driven autonomously, supported not only by the government decision regarding the 2014–20 FEAD programme, but also by CSR and public/individual altruism. It cannot be denied that solidarity and CSR play an important role in all societies. However, in Spain, both the government and the ACs should ask themselves if it is appropriate to leave an obligation that is theirs to be fulfilled by acts of solidarity. Solidarity and CSR activity are voluntary actions by individuals and companies so it is logical that they should act individually with full autonomy. What happens with these actions in the medium and long term will depend entirely on who carries them out, as is presently the case. As the Canadian philosopher John Ralston Saul argues, a key factor that can indicate the weakening of a nation's democracy and citizenship is an increase in the function of charity and praise for voluntary work (Ralston Saul, 1998, cited by Rieff, 2015). Some traces of this might be found in Spain in the widespread positive views of in-kind food distribution and even in some statements by ruling authorities (Escajedo San-Epifanio, 2018). Emergency aid is vital wherever there are no other alternatives to deal with exceptional situations. However, in the medium and long term, the welfare state must assume – or resume –its obligations and work to redistribute welfare and wealth in line with people's rights, freedoms and dignity.

Funding

This research received funding from the University of the Basque Country (UPV/EHU), 'US17/22 project – Jaki-Zubiak. Building food bridges' (2017–19), Principal Researchers: L. Escajedo San-Epifanio, E.M. Rebato Ochoa, and the project ELIKADURA-EGOKIRANTZ (Sortarazi – Asociación Claretiana para el Desarrollo Humano NGO, and URBAN ELIKA Group), funded by the Basque government 'Call for knowledge management activities regarding social intervention' (2018).

Notes

[1]   Spanish Constitution, article 148.1.20.
[2]   Food banks in Spain are non-profit organisations with the legal form of non-political and non-religious foundations or associations. As the FESBAL website explains, these food banks are organised like companies and strive to manage the resources entrusted to them with maximum efficiency.
[3]   See: www.fesbal.org

References

Antentas, J.M. and Vivas, E. (2014) 'Impacto de la crisis en el derecho a una alimentación sana y saludable. Informe SESPAS' ['Impact of the crisis on the right to safe and healthy food'], *Gaceta Sanitaria*, 28(S1): 58–61.

Ayala, L., Arranz, J.M., García Serrano, C. and Martínez Virto, L. (2016) *El sistema de garantía de ingresos en España: Tendencias, resultados y necesidades de reforma* [*The income guarantee system in Spain: Trends, results and reform needs*], Madrid: Ministerio de Sanidad, Servicios Sociales e Igualdad.

Bauman, Z. (2015) *Trabajo, consumismo y nuevos pobres* [*Work, consumerism and the new poor*], Madrid: Gedisa.

Caraher, M. and Cavicchi, A. (2014) 'Old crises on new plates or old plates for a new crises? Food banks and food insecurity', *British Food Journal*, 116(9), https://doi.org/10.1108/BFJ-08-2014-0285

Caritas (2011) *VI Informe sobre las demandas atendidas a través de la red confederal de Acogida y Atención primaria* [*VI report on the demands addressed through the confederal network of Shelter and Primary Care*], Madrid: Caritas.

Caritas (2012) *VII Informe del Observatorio de la Realidad Social de Caritas. De la coyuntura a la estructura. Los efectos permanentes de la crisis* [*VII report of the Caritas Social Reality Observatory. From the conjuncture to the structure. The permanent effects of the crisis*], Madrid: Caritas.

Caritas (2013) *VIII Informe del Observatorio de la Realidad Social de Caritas. Empobrecimiento y desigualdad social* [*VII report of the Caritas Social Reality Observatory. From the conjuncture to the structure. Impoverishment and social inequality*], Madrid: Caritas.

CES (Consejo Económico y Social) (2017) *Informe. Políticas públicas para combatir la pobreza en España* [*Report. Public policies to fight poverty in Spain*], Madrid: CESl.

CIS (Centro de Investigaciones Sociológicas) (2011) *Barómetro de diciembre* [*December barometer*], Estudio n° 2923, Madrid: CIS.

EAPN (European Anti-Poverty Network) (2017) *El estado de la pobreza. Seguimiento del indicador de riesgo de pobreza y exclusión social en España 2008–2016. 7° Informe*, [*The state of poverty. Monitoring of the poverty risk and social exclusion indicator in Spain 2008–2016. 7th report*], Madrid: EAPN-España.

Escajedo San-Epifanio, L. (2018) 'El despilfarro de alimentos y el derecho humano a una alimentación adecuada en la Unión Europea: Una lectura en clave jurídico-constitucional' ['The waste of food and the human right to adequate food in the European Union: a reading in legal-constitutional key'], in L. Escajedo San-Epifanio, E. Rebato and A. López Basaguren (eds) *Despilfarro alimentario y derecho a la alimentación* [*Food waste and the right to food*], Valencia: Tirant lo Blanch, pp 29–59.

Escajedo San-Epifanio, L. and Inza-Bartolomé, A. (2018) 'EU welfare states, food poverty and current food waste policy: reproducing old, inefficient models?', in S. Springer and H. Grimm (eds) *Professionals in food chains*, Wageningen: Wageningen Academic Publishers, pp 205–10.

FAO (Food and Agriculture Organization of the United Nations) (2011) *Una introducción a los conceptos básicos de la seguridad alimentaria* [*An introduction to the basics of food safety*], Rome: FAO.

FAO (2018) *El estado de la seguridad alimentaria y la nutrición en el mundo* [*The state of food security and nutrition in the world*], Rome: FAO.

FESBAL (Federación Española de Bancos de Alimentos) (2017) *Memoria 2017* [*2017 memorandum*], Madrid: FESBAL.

FOESSA (Fomento de Estudios Sociales y de Sociología Aplicada) (2014) *VII Informe sobre exclusión y desarrollo social en España 2014* [*VII report on social exclusion and development in Spain*], Madrid: Caritas Española.

Gascón, J. and Montagut, X. (2015) *Bancos de alimentos ¿Combatir el hambre con las sobras?* [*Food banks. To fight hunger with leftovers*], Barcelona: Icaria-Asaco.

González Begega, S. and Del Pino, E. (2017) 'From letting Europe in to policy conditionality: welfare reform in Spain under austerity', http://ipp.csic.es/sites/default/files/content/workpaper/2017/2017_01_ippwp_gonzalezbegegadelpino.pdf

González Begega, S. and Luque, D. (2015) 'Crisis económica y deterioro de los pactos sociales en el sur de Europa: Los casos de España y Portugal' ['Economic crisis and deterioration of social pacts in Southern Europe'], *Revista Internacional de Sociología*, 72(1), https://doi.org/10.3989/ris.2014.03.17

Guillén, A.M., González-Begega, S. and Luque, D. (2016) 'Austeridad y ajustes sociales en el sur de Europa. La fragmentación del modelo de bienestar mediterráneo' ['Austerity and social adjustments in Southern Europe. The fragmentation of the Mediterranean welfare model'], *Revista Española de Sociología*, 25(2): 261–72.

Laparra, M. (ed) (2014) *La fractura social se ensancha: Intensificación de los procesos de exclusión en España durante 7 años. VII Informe sobre exclusión y desarrollo social en España 2014* [*The social fracture widens: Intensification of the processes of exclusion in Spain for 7 years. VII report on exclusion and social development*], Madrid: Fundación FOESSA.

Laparra, M. and Pérez Eransus, B. (eds) (2012) *Crisis y fractura social en Europa. Causas y efectos en España* [*Crisis and social fracture in Europe. Causes and effects in Spain*], Barcelona: Obra Social La Caixa.

Llobet, M. (2014) 'La innovación social en la seguridad alimentaria en Quebec. Algunas lecciones para el contexto español' ['Social innovation in food security in Quebec. Some lessons for the Spanish context'], *Documentación Social*, 174: 71–94.

MAPAMA (Ministerio de Agricultura, Pesca, Alimentación y Medio Ambiente) (2014) 'Guía para las Organizaciones Asociadas de Reparto participantes en el Programa de Ayuda Alimentaria 2018 del Fondo de Ayuda Europea para las personas desfavorecidas' ['Guide for associated distribution organizations participating in the food aid programme 2018 of the European Aid Fund for Disadvantaged People'], PO FEAD 2014–2020 en España, www.bancodealimentosdevalladolid.es/sites/default/files/documentos/guia_oar_2018.pdf

MAPAMA (2017) 'Programa de distribución de alimentos en beneficio de las personas más desfavorecidas. Programa Operativo FEAD (2014–2020)' ['Food distribution programme for the benefit of the most disadvantaged people. FEAD operational programme'], www.fega.es/sites/default/files/Informe_Fega_Desfavorecidos_2017.pdf

Marí-Klose, P. and Martínez Pérez, A. (2015) 'Empobrecimiento en tiempos de crisis: Vulnerabilidad y (des)protección social en un contexto de adversidad' ['Impoverishment in times of crisis: vulnerability and lack of social protection in an adversity context'], *Panorama Social*, 22: 11–26.

Martínez Virto, L. (2014a) *Sobreviviendo a la crisis. Estrategias de los hogares en dificultad* [*Surviving the crisis. Strategies of households in difficulty*], Barcelona: Edicions Bellaterra.

Martínez Virto, L. (2014b) 'Una crisis interminable: Estrategias para resistir y primeros síntomas de sobrecarga en las familias' ['An endless crisis: strategies to resist and first symptoms of overload in families'], *Zerbitzuan*, 57: 121–36.

Mata, A. and Pallarés, J. (2014) 'Del bienestar a la caridad. ¿Un viaje sin retorno?' ['From welfare to charity. A one-way trip'], *Aposta. Revista De Ciencias Sociales*, 62: 1–23.

Moreno, L. (2007) 'Europa social, bienestar en España y la "malla de seguridad"' ['Social Europe, welfare in Spain and the "safety net"'], in Á. Espina (ed) *Estado de Bienestar y competitividad. La experiencia europea* [*Welfare state and competitiveness. The European experience*], Madrid: Fundación Carolina/Siglo XXI, pp 445–511.

Moreno, L. (2012) *La Europa asocial. ¿Caminamos hacia un individualismo posesivo?* [*The asocial Europe. Do we walk towards possessive individualism?*], Barcelona: Península.

MSCBS (Ministerio de Sanidad, Consumo y Bienestar Social) (2014) 'Programa Operativo del Fondo de Ayuda Europea para las Personas más Desfavorecidas' ['Operational programme of the European Aid Fund for the Most Disadvantaged People'], FEAD, www.mscbs.gob.es/va/ssi/familiasInfancia/inclusionSocial/fead/programaOperativoFead2014.pdf

Muñoz de Bustillo, R. and Antón, J.I. (2015) 'Turning back before arriving? The weakening of the Spanish welfare state', in D. Vaughan-Whitehead (ed) *The European social model in crisis: Is Europe losing its soul?*, London: Edward Elgar, pp 451–506.

Observatori DESC (Derechos Económicos, Sociales y Culturales) (2014) *Informe sobre el derecho a la alimentación adecuada en Cataluña*, [*Report on the right to adequate food in Catalonia*], Barcelona: Observatori DESC.

Observatorio del Derecho a la Alimentación de España (2018) 'El derecho a la alimentación en España. Desafíos y propuestas' ['The right to food in Spain. Challenges and proposals'], www. derechoalimentacion.org/sites/default/files/pdf-materiales/ Derecho_alimentacion_desafios_propuestas_COMPLETO.pdf

Otero, S. (2015) 'Alimentación y pobreza. Estrategias de aprovisionamiento y gestión de la inseguridad alimentaria' ['Food and poverty. Strategies of provision and management of food insecurity'], http://digibuo.uniovi.es/dspace/bitstream/10651/33017/6/TFM_ OteroEstevez%2CSonia.pdf

Paugam, S. (2007) *Las formas elementales de la pobreza* [*The elementary forms of poverty*], Madrid: Alianza.

Pérez de Armiño, K. (2014) 'Erosion of rights, uncritical solidarity and food banks in Spain', in G. Riches and T. Silvasti (eds) *First world hunger revisited: Food charity or the right to food?*, Basingstoke: Palgrave Macmillan, pp 131–45.

Poppendieck, J. (1999) *Sweet charity: Emergency food and the end of entitlement*, New York, NY: Penguin Books.

Ralston Saul, J. (1998) *Reflections of a Siamese twin: Canada at the end of the twentieth century*, Toronto: Penguin Books.

Riches, G. (1997) 'Hunger and welfare state: comparative perspective', in G. Riches (ed) *First world hunger: Food security and welfare politics*, London: Macmillan Press, pp 1–13.

Riches, G. and Silvasti, T. (2014) 'Hunger in the rich world: food aid and right to food perspectives', in G. Riches and T. Silvasti (eds) *First world hunger revisited: Food charity or the right to food?*, Basingstoke: Palgrave Macmillan, pp 1–14.

Rieff, D. (2015) *El oprobio del hambre: alimentos, justicia y dinero en el siglo XXI* [*The reproach of hunger: Food, justice and money in the twenty-first century*], Madrid: Taurus.

Rodríguez-Cabrero, G. (ed) (2015) *ESPN thematic report on minimum income schemes*, Brussels: European Social Policy Network.

Ronson, D. and Caraher, M. (2016) 'Food banks: Big Society or shunting yards? Successful failures', in M. Caraher and J. Coveney (eds) *Food poverty and insecurity: International food inequalities*, London: Springer, pp 79–88.

Sales, A. and Marco, I. (2014) 'Ayuda alimentaria y descalificación social. Impacto de las diferentes formas de distribución de alimentos cocinados sobre la vivencia subjetiva de la pobreza en Barcelona' ['Food aid and social disqualification. Impact of the different forms of distribution of cooked food on the subjective experience of poverty in Barcelona'], *Documentación Social*, 174: 171–89.

SiiS-Fundación Eguía-Careaga (2009) *Programas de reparto de alimentos en Gipuzkoa. Situación actual, diagnóstico de necesidades y propuesta de líneas de intervención* [*Food distribution programmes in Gipuzkoa. Current situation, diagnosis of needs and proposal of lines of intervention*], Donostia: SiiS.

Tarasuk, V.S. and MacLean, H. (1990) 'The institutionalization of food banks in Canada: a public health concern', *Canadian Journal of Public Health*, 81(4): 331–2.

Van der Horst, H., Pascucci, S. and Bol, W. (2014) 'The "dark side" of food banks? Exploring emotional responses of food bank receivers in the Netherlands', *British Food Journal*, 116(9): 1506–20.

7

Food banks and the UK welfare state

Hannah Lambie-Mumford and Rachel Loopstra

Introduction

In 2016/17, The Trussell Trust Foodbank Network – the UK's largest food bank organisation – gave food to adults and children a total of 1,182,954 times, up from 128,697 in 2011/12 (The Trussell Trust, 2017). This growth in food bank use has been interpreted as a symbol of the failure of the unprecedented welfare state reform and public finance austerity implemented in the UK over the same period.

In response to the rise in food bank use, there has been an increase in public and professional interest in hunger and voluntary emergency food provision generally since 2010. The national newspaper *The Guardian* declared 2012 to be 'the year of the food bank' (Moore, 2012), and many of the country's leading news and media outlets have presented stories about hunger and the proliferation of food banks (Morris, 2013; Boyle, 2014; Galluzzo, 2014; Mould, 2014; Wells and Caraher, 2014). In national politics, food banks have been debated in Parliament, sparked the establishment of two All-Party Parliamentary Groups and been the subject of a parliamentary inquiry in 2014 (Hansard, 2013; All-Party Parliamentary Inquiry into Hunger and Food Poverty, 2014; Register of All-Party Parliamentary Groups, 2017). This inquiry was followed by a Commission on Food and Poverty led by the Fabian Society – a prominent UK think tank (Tait, 2015). Non-governmental organisations (NGOs) and emergency food charities themselves – including The Trussell Trust, FareShare and the Independent Food Aid Network (IFAN) – have widely publicised their statistics, commissioned research (for example, Perry et al, 2014; Loopstra and Lalor, 2017) and formed campaigning groups (such as End Hunger UK[1]).

Research into the issue has burgeoned. When the UK government first commissioned a review of the evidence on food aid, there was very little peer-reviewed literature on the topic in the UK (Lambie-Mumford et al, 2014). Now, leading social policy journals have published important studies on the drivers of contemporary food aid provision, and recent reforms to welfare entitlements, which have increased conditionality and reduced state provision, have been identified as key drivers of food aid use. Social and cultural geographers have explored the complexities of interactions and embedded contestations in food aid projects (Williams et al, 2016), and health geographers have described the lived experiences of food bank users with health conditions who are unable to access an adequate diet (Garthwaite et al, 2015). Sociologists and practical theology scholars have also begun to explore the Christian ethos underpinning the activities of many food aid providers (Cameron, 2014; Allen, 2016; Power et al, 2017). Research has covered different parts of the UK, not always referring to the whole country. For example, there has been localised research in parts of England (Garthwaite et al 2015), research scoping provision across Scotland (Sosenko et al, 2013) and quantitative research covering Britain due to a lack of data on Northern Ireland (Loopstra et al, 2015, 2018).

What does rising food bank use and the accompanying political, public and academic interest tell us about the UK welfare state? This chapter locates these post-2010 trends in the context of a longer history of social policy, and discusses the important sea change that they represent when compared to previous policy reforms. The chapter begins by exploring evidence of and responses to hunger before the proliferation of food banks, and then goes on to examine the nature of contemporary hunger and responses to it. Recent welfare reforms and the accompanying rise of food banks are examined as part of a long-term trajectory of a shrinking welfare state and the growing prominence of charities in the UK's welfare sector. The chapter ends with reflections on the social justice implications of increasing reliance on food charity in the UK. In particular, it addresses questions about the need for systematic policy responses and the implications for future practices of food charity.

To examine the rise of food banks in the UK, and particularly the interaction between food banks and changing social policies, the concept of 'food insecurity' is employed in this chapter. It is defined as 'limited, inadequate or insecure access to food due to financial resource constraints' (Tarasuk, 2001: 2). Experiences of food insecurity range from anxiety about food supplies running out, to qualitative compromises on both diet and social aspects of food behaviour, to more severe experiences of going without food, up to going whole days without eating (Wunderlich and Norwood, 2006). These more severe experiences of food insecurity have been identified as driving food bank use (Loopstra and Tarasuk, 2012, 2015) but mild and moderate food insecurity are also issues of growing concern in the UK (Bates et al, 2017).

The definition used in this chapter reflects a continuum of experiences, and food insecurity can also manifest in experiences of social exclusion. These have been highlighted in other definitions – for example, Anderson (1990) explicitly points to the importance of the social acceptability of food and the ways in which food is obtained. This is an important dimension for this chapter because it enables questions to be asked about the appropriateness of food banks as a response to food insecurity and what adequate and acceptable assistance looks like. It is important to note that the term 'hunger' is used in this chapter both to refer to severe food insecurity and in discussion of historical understandings of this and related issues in the UK.

Hunger in the UK from the 20th century to the 2000s

Many commentators have compared the rise of food banks in the UK during the 2010s to the breadlines that appeared during the Great Depression (Gardiner, 2017). They have suggested that while food insecurity was not eradicated after this time, it is more visible now than at any point since the economic slump of the 1930s, before the establishment of the modern welfare state. The 1930s were marked by high levels of unemployment and hunger marches, where protestors decried their destitution, government inaction and welfare reforms that reduced unemployment benefits, terminated access for those claiming for longer than six months and introduced a means test (Vernon, 2007). Malnutrition was widespread during this period. In particular, the story of Minnie Weaving – a mother who died of pneumonia due to undernourishment – sparked debate about the inability of the welfare state to ensure that the country's citizens did not starve to death (Vernon, 2007).

These conditions were documented in studies by Seebohm Rowntree and other social researchers throughout the early part of the 20th century (Glennerster et al, 2004). Rowntree devised an essential income standard based on the value of a basic basket of food. He used this measure to establish that a significant proportion of the population did not receive enough income to meet their most basic food needs. He observed that the many people who did not meet his standard included both those in work and those who were out of work and receiving unemployment benefits. This contributed to the recognition of economic conditions as the key driver of poverty (Glennerster et al, 2004). His work also contributed to growing calls for the government to provide an adequate safety net which ensured that people's basic needs were met. In his 1942 report on social insurance, Sir William Beveridge used this research to provide evidence that people did not have enough money for basic subsistence, arguing that the 'abolition of want requires a re-distribution of income through social insurance and by family needs' (Beveridge, 1942: 7). Beveridge's report is considered to be the foundation for the modern welfare state in the UK, and highlights that one of its key aims was ensuring that basic food needs were met.

Poverty – and thus hunger – disappeared from view in the 1950s (Glennerster et al, 2004). During the 1960s, new methods of defining poverty, with a focus on relative measures, were established, and there was particular concern about social exclusion (Glennerster et al, 2004). However, some path-breaking research conducted from the 1970s to the 1990s showed that experiences of food insecurity could still be found in homes across the UK. While early work by Townsend focused on broader experiences of poverty and social exclusion, it documented experiences of food insecurity in the first survey of poverty and social exclusion in 1982. This detailed that 13 per cent of adults reported missing out on meals several times during the year because of a lack of money; 3 per cent reported not being able to afford to eat two meals a day (Lansley and Mack, 2015).[2] In interviews conducted with low-income lone parents in the 1990s, Dowler and Calvert highlighted the important role that material circumstances played in driving poor nutrition for lone parents and sometimes their children. Food was often seen as a flexible budget item compared to paying bills, leading to poorer diets, especially for parents (Dowler and Calvert, 1995). During 2003–05, a large-scale study was conducted into dietary intakes among materially deprived households (Nelson et al, 2007b). This included a measurement of household food insecurity using the United States Department of Agriculture (USDA) Household Food Security Survey Module. It found that among the adults surveyed, 29 per cent were food insecure, meaning that they had reported experiences of running out of food, skipping meals and experiencing hunger due to a lack of financial resources (Nelson et al, 2007a).

The history of responses to hunger in the UK

Whenever hunger is recognised in communities, there tends to be local mobilisation to respond to it. Soup kitchens – places that distribute hot food free of charge – have a long history of serving poor working families, the unemployed and homeless in the UK, though they have always had their critics (Croll, 2011). Generally, they also disappeared from view after the 1930s and the establishment of the welfare state, which reduced the role for charities in welfare provision. Throughout the 20th century, charitable initiatives to feed people did not disappear, but they primarily served the visibly poor and hungry – people asking for food ('begging') on the streets.

In response to the growing recognition of the issue of homelessness, such initiatives increased in number, and a new form of 'soup run' developed in the 1990s, where churches and social groups came into metropolitan areas to serve food from mobile premises or to distribute sandwiches (Shelter, 2005). The mobile delivery of food to homeless people became an issue of political debate in the mid-2000s, when there were moves to ban the activity (Shelter, 2005). Opponents of these initiatives argued that they promoted dependency on the free food, drinks and other items distributed, and that they did not fit with systematic responses to homelessness. However, providers of soup runs argued that they provided critical care to some of the most vulnerable people in society (Shelter, 2005).

Despite evidence of food insecurity and hunger within low-income households, initiatives targeting hunger within this group largely did not exist (Lambie-Mumford et al, 2014). Local food programmes tended to focus on access to nutritious food in deprived communities, cooking skills, social isolation and increasing nutritional knowledge (McGlone et al, 1999). Such programmes were primarily public health programmes or social initiatives run by churches in the forms of cafes or community kitchens. Food distribution through these projects served as a means either of drawing people to the programme (for example, for social interaction) or of education. In recognition of poorer diets among low-income people, many programmes targeted this demographic but they were not intended to alleviate hunger (McGlone et al, 1999).

Thus, the establishment and proliferation of national-scale organisations that facilitate or coordinate food banks with the aim of alleviating hunger since 2010 is a new phenomenon (Lambie-Mumford et al, 2014). Their professionalisation, coordination and nationwide scale make these initiatives distinct from those of the past, which were more ad hoc and localised, and operated relatively out of view of policymakers and the media. Why has this trend emerged now, and does it signify a failure of the welfare state to fulfil its aim of preventing 'want'? The next section looks at historical policy responses to the problem of food insecurity before the chapter moves on to examine evidence of shortfalls in the system today.

Evolution of policy responses to food insecurity

Despite the role played by hunger and access to food in motivating the development of welfare state provision around the time of Beveridge, since then, household food insecurity has been an implicit – rather than explicit – concern of policy responses to poverty (notably seen as covered by social security payments). Importantly, social security levels are not explicitly tied to the costs of purchasing the items needed to constitute an adequate diet. While such payments were historically linked to the Retail Price Index, this changed to the Consumer Price Index in 2011 (resulting in lower uprating) (Joyce and Levell, 2011). Since 2015, out-of-work benefits have been frozen. As illustrated in a recent report, a single unemployed person will now only receive about one third of what is required to meet a minimum income standard in the UK (Padley and Hirsch, 2017).

There is a strong and consistent link between household income and food insecurity, with policies aimed at enhancing household incomes having been shown to reduce food insecurity in other country contexts (Loopstra, 2018). As such, in national policy terms, the relevance of household income and social security to food insecurity might lead one to expect that this issue would come under the remit of the Department for Work and Pensions (the national government department that oversees social security and pension policy). However, household-level food security is currently the responsibility of the Department for Environment, Food and Rural Affairs (Defra) (Food Chain Analysis Group, 2006). Even here, policymakers only began to apply the notion of food security to the household in the late 2000s. The 2006 evidence and analysis paper published by Defra introduced considerations of access to food and the affordability of food for households, rather than exclusively focusing on food security as an issue of national supply, as had been the case in the past (Food Chain Analysis Group, 2006; MacMillan and Dowler, 2012). However, the department has maintained a focus on proxy indicators such as the percentage of household expenditure on food rather than directly measuring household food insecurity. Even if it were to recognise the importance of household food insecurity and its systematic measurement, Defra lacks the policy levers to address the issue on its own.

In addition, UK poverty measures have not consistently taken account of access to food. Having the resources to access a customary diet was at the forefront of Townsend's (1979) definition of poverty. Questions relating to types of diet and food experiences (including being able to invite friends or family over for a meal, at least two meals a day, fruit and vegetables, and meals with a source of protein) are also established measures in surveys such as Breadline Britain and the Poverty and Social Exclusion Survey (Gordon and Pantazis, 1997; Gordon et al, 2000; Poverty and Social Exclusion Team, 2013). Other indicators of material deprivation for children and pensioners – some of which reference food – are part of the government's annual 'Households below average income' report (Department for Work and Pensions, 2018). These investigate families' ability to afford items such as fresh fruit and vegetables for their children every day; questions for the elderly include asking if they have at least one filling meal a day. However, the full continuum of food insecurity experiences is not explored, and no food experiences are captured for working-age adults. As discussed later in this chapter, while this looks set to change in the future, having had no annual measurement of households' financial access to food until now has impeded the evaluation of how household food insecurity has changed over the past decade, and whether trends have been in line with rising food bank usage. It also means that the impact on food insecurity of changes to welfare entitlements has not been evaluated, as has been done in other countries.

Outside of social security payments, there are a handful of supplementary initiatives designed to facilitate better access to food, which are managed by different government departments. Despite overlaps and the potential for strategic policy approaches to food insecurity across departments, initiatives have remained siloed. This lack of a joined-up approach, focused on a common understanding of the problem of household food insecurity, has resulted in a range of disparate programmes over time. The Department of Health manages the Healthy Start food voucher scheme and the School Fruit and Vegetable Scheme (SFVS), while school meal programmes are managed by the Department for Education and individual local authorities. The Healthy Start scheme replaced the Welfare Food scheme in 2006 and provides vouchers (for formula and cow's milk, and fresh or frozen fruit and vegetables) to pregnant women and children under four years old (Lucas et al, 2015). Families are eligible if their income is below £16,190 a year, they are in receipt of tax credits or out-of-work benefits, or if the mother is aged under 18. The vouchers are worth £3.10 each, and the scheme provides two vouchers per week per child aged under 12 months, and one per week per pregnant woman or child aged 12–48 months (Lucas et al, 2015).

From September 2014, free school meals were made universal for all children in reception class, year one and year two of school (ages five to seven years) (Long, 2015). For older school-aged children, parents do not have to pay for school meals if they are in receipt of income support or out-of-work benefits, tax credits, or state pension credit (Long, 2015). However, the introduction of Universal Credit[3] will bring in means testing for free school meals (over the age of seven) for families in receipt of benefits. The School Fruit and Vegetable Scheme – established after the publication of the National Health Service (NHS) plan in 2000 – also promotes access to healthy foods for children, and provides one portion of fruit or vegetables every day to all children aged four to six who are in state-funded schools (National Health Service, 2015). The 2013 School Food Plan included funding for breakfast clubs in schools in deprived areas. A total of £3.15 million over two years was announced (to be match-funded by the organisation that successfully tenders to deliver the scheme) to provide breakfast clubs in schools where at least 40 per cent of pupils are entitled to free school meals (Dimbleby and Vincent, 2013). The goal was to set up breakfast clubs in 500 schools over the two years of the plan (Dimbleby and Vincent, 2013). However, this policy has been pursued despite a lack of systematic evidence on the effectiveness of breakfast club provision for overcoming child food insecurity (Lambie-Mumford and Sims, 2018).

The rise of food banks in the UK

Context

Following the 2007/08 financial crisis, the effects of the ensuing economic downturn were felt across the UK. Unemployment rose from 1.61 million in April 2008 to a peak of 2.68 million in October 2011, and wages fell by more than 10 per cent in real terms between 2008 and 2015 (Coulter, 2016). Around the same time, food prices in the UK increased sharply, rising 18 per cent in real terms between 2007 and their peak in 2012 (Department for Environment, Food and Rural Affairs, 2014). Defra highlighted that by 2012/13, falling incomes and rising costs of living – including rising food prices – meant that food had become over 20 per cent less affordable for those in the lowest income decile compared to 2002/03. The results of the 2011 Family Food Survey showed that while many households were 'trading down' to cheaper food commodities in response to price increases, those in the lowest income deciles were not, indicating that they were likely to already be buying the cheapest food available (Department for Environment, Food and Rural Affairs, 2012; Dowler and Lambie-Mumford, 2015).

Against this economic backdrop, there was no expansion of social protection for low-income households to shield them from rising food prices and other harmful effects of the economic downturn (Loopstra et al, 2016; Reeves et al, 2017). Instead, the Conservative–Liberal Democrat Coalition government – which was elected in 2010 – embarked on what has been described as one of the most radical, and regressive, sets of changes to social security in the UK since the welfare state was established.

In 2010, the Coalition government announced a sweeping programme of wide-ranging reforms aimed at reducing the national deficit, with a particular focus on cutting welfare costs (HM Treasury, 2010). Budgets for schools, the NHS and pensions were protected but those for local government services, social care and welfare benefits were dramatically reduced (Lupton et al, 2015; De Agostini et al, 2017).

Entitlements were changed for a range of benefit types and claimants, for example: access to housing benefit and local housing allowances was cut off or reduced for people aged 35 or younger; a benefit cap was introduced in 2013 and further tightened in 2017; and since 2015, working-age benefits have been frozen. A number of welfare reforms have also made it harder for claimants to qualify – and maintain their eligibility – to receive benefits. From 2011, a requirement was introduced for Employment and Support Allowance claimants to undergo 'work capability assessments' in order to determine their eligibility for this benefit paid to people who cannot work because of illness or disability. Those placed in the 'work-related activity group' were additionally required to engage in work-related activity, such as job searches, work preparation schemes and practice job interviews, in order to keep receiving benefits (Barr et al, 2015; Dwyer et al, 2016). Similar types of conditions were imposed on lone parents claiming income support who have children aged five or older (Johnsen, 2016). In a further move towards greater conditionality, the Claimant Commitment was introduced in 2013 for Jobseeker's Allowance (JSA) claimants (Department for Work and Pensions, 2013a) and soon extended to everyone claiming Universal Credit. These commitments, determined by Jobcentre advisers, outline the job-seeking actions that claimants must complete in order to be eligible for these benefits. Failure to meet these requirements means that claimants lose their eligibility for benefits altogether or temporarily have their benefits stopped – a practice known as 'sanctioning' (Reeves and Loopstra, 2017). In 2012, reforms to sanctioning practices intensified penalties, stopping benefit payments with immediate effect for a new minimum of four weeks, representing a loss of £300 for a single claimant aged 25 or over (Comptroller and Auditor General, 2016). For more serious offences, penalty periods were extended to a minimum of 13 weeks, and then anything up to 156 weeks (Department for Work and Pensions, 2013b). This programme of austerity and welfare reform has been the backdrop to the rise of food banks in the UK.

Defining 'food banks' in the UK context

A particular terminology has emerged in the UK to describe the new form of food charity and other types of food assistance. The term 'food aid' is used by policymakers and NGOs to refer to initiatives providing short-term help with access to food (Cooper and Dumpleton, 2013; Hansard, 2013). Food aid is defined by Defra (as set out in Lambie-Mumford et al, 2014: iv) as 'an umbrella term encompassing a range of large-scale and small local activities aiming to help people meet food needs, often on a short-term basis during crisis or immediate difficulty; more broadly they contribute to relieving symptoms of household or individual level food poverty and poverty'. While such assistance includes a whole range of initiatives – such as providers of hot meals, soup runs and food programmes for children – 'food banks' have dominated the discourse and debate in the UK in recent years. Food banks have generally come to be defined as charitable initiatives that provide parcels of food for people in emergency situations to take away, prepare and eat (Lambie-Mumford and Dowler, 2014). This provision usually aims to help relieve some kinds of food crisis. While the 'food bank' label is quite high profile, it conceals significant variability between the projects that identify themselves using this term. Such variation might include differences in the food provided, conditions of access and opening times, as well as whether other services are on offer at the project (Dowler and Lambie-Mumford, 2015). Overall, it is difficult for policymakers and researchers to capture the full extent and coverage of the charitable emergency food provision category due to the sheer range of provider types and sizes.

In the context of this international edited collection, an important point to note is that a key defining trait of UK food banks is their direct involvement in the provision of food to individuals in need. This is in contrast to definitions of food banks elsewhere, which are understood more as 'middlemen', collecting and redistributing food to community projects and not themselves being client facing (Berner and O'Brien, 2004; Costello, 2007; Pérez de Armiño, 2016). Also important for international comparison is the fact that organisations involved in the redistribution of surplus food are not usually part of the 'food bank' category in the UK. While some food banks might obtain supplies for provision from surplus food redistribution initiatives, unlike in some other countries, these redistributors are not themselves generally recognised as food banks. However, there are exceptions to this general rule, with some organisations that call themselves 'food banks' and collect and store food distributing it to organisations that then provide it to people in need.[4]

Growth of contemporary food banks

The Trussell Trust Foodbank Network is the largest network of food banks in the UK. This chapter focuses on this network as it represents the largest front-line food charity organisation in the country and collects data from across its membership. Recent work to count the number of food banks operating outside this network suggests that about 60 per cent of food banks in the UK are part of The Trussell Trust's network, with the number of identified independent food banks totalling 651 in 2017 (IFAN, no date).[5] In 2012, The Trussell Trust reported that it was opening two food banks every week (Lambie-Mumford, 2013). This rapid expansion of their network, and accompanying statistics on the growing number of people receiving food from it, played a key role in making hunger and food bank use front-page news in the UK.

To comprehend this growth, it is important to understand how the organisation works. The Trussell Trust Foodbank Network was established as a social franchise in 2004, enabling local faith groups and churches to join the network and replicate its food bank model, which has been running at its first site in Salisbury since 2000 (Lambie-Mumford, 2013). Trussell Trust food banks are established 'from the ground up', with local church and Christian faith groups expressing an interest in starting a food bank. To join the network, such groups pay a start-up fee and commit to paying an annual membership fee. Membership also entails agreement to the aims and vision of The Trussell Trust, collecting and reporting data, and following the trust's prescribed model (The Trussell Trust, 2016).

Trussell Trust food banks share some characteristics with food banks (or food pantries) operating in Canada, the US and elsewhere in Europe in that they aim to provide a food parcel of mostly non-perishable groceries free of charge to people seeking assistance. However, The Trussell Trust requires that individuals first obtain a referral voucher from a front-line care or health professional in order to receive food (Lambie-Mumford, 2017). Referral vouchers are held by local front-line organisations with which food banks have established relationships, and thus voucher holders vary from area to area. They can include Jobcentre Plus offices, local authorities, Citizens Advice Bureaux, general practitioner (GP) practices, social workers and schools. Referring agencies fill in standardised referral vouchers to gather basic household socio-demographic information. They are also asked to select the main reason why the client requires a food parcel from a list that includes benefit changes, benefit delays, low income, no recourse to public funds, delayed wages, debt and homelessness.

While The Trussell Trust gives a certain figure on its website for the number of food banks in the network, in practice, a single food bank may constitute one site or multiple distribution sites. Some are run by a single church or faith centre, while others operate as a local network of churches or community groups, with each partner operating a food bank distribution centre. As of 2018, The Trussell Trust's foodbank network consisted of 428 'food banks', running over 1,200 client-facing food bank distribution centres.[6]

Corresponding rise in public and policy interest

The growth of food banks has sparked reaction from all sectors, including NGOs, the media, and the private and public sectors. There has also been considerable political reaction at the local, devolved and national levels (for example, Hansard, 2013). Some politicians have identified the rise of food banks as an important symbol of a failing welfare state (Dugan and Owen, 2014). In response to these criticisms, the government has instead suggested that the rise in food bank use is driven by the supply of food banks, and has praised initiatives that have risen to the challenge of meeting the needs of their local communities (Conservative Home, 2012). This implies that need has not changed. Due to the lack of government recognition of the problem, public reactions to the rise of food banks have yet to translate into substantive policy responses driven by elected members of councils, assemblies or Parliament. At the national level, there has so far been no formal policy response from the government. While elected officials in devolved and local governments have worked on various initiatives, such as grant funding or food strategies, these have been local and often short- or medium-term responses (Dowler and Lambie-Mumford, 2015). In the absence of a state response to rising need, charitable food initiatives such as food banks are left to respond as best they can to the need that they face in their local communities.

However, there have been several notable interjections into the policy debate. In 2014, a flagship report was published by some of the UK's most high-profile poverty NGOs working in collaboration (Perry et al, 2014). The same year saw the publication of the findings of the Parliamentary Inquiry into Hunger and Food Poverty (All-Party Parliamentary Inquiry into Hunger and Food Poverty, 2014; Forsey, 2014). In 2015, the Fabian Society published the report from its Commission on Food and Poverty (Tait, 2015). All of these provided unique evidence about the previously under-researched field of hunger in the UK. They symbolised a public acknowledgement of the will to address the issue of hunger, and every one of them outlined actionable recommendations designed to reduce the need for emergency help with food from projects such as food banks.

Emerging evidence on food bank use

As the number of people using food banks has grown, certain research questions have become key: who is receiving help from food banks and what is driving their use? Data collected through Trussell Trust referral vouchers provide headline figures on the main reasons why people are referred. However, the classifications are crude – low income, benefit problems and benefit delays, among others – and do not provide insight into the household circumstances or socio-economic characteristics of those who are referred. Some of the first insights into the wider circumstances surrounding food bank use in the UK came from the reports highlighted in the previous section of this chapter. In the report by Perry et al (2014), respondents who were interviewed described experiencing reductions in benefit payments and sometimes payments being stopped altogether, but also noted the recent loss of earnings or changes in family circumstances. Importantly, chronic low income was rarely the reason that people turned to food banks, though these respondents regularly struggled to make ends meet; rather, it was an acute crisis that generally led to food bank referral. People commonly expressed feeling uncomfortable with the idea of receiving food assistance but felt that they had no other choice. Inadequate incomes meant that they were vulnerable to income crises, pushing them into desperate circumstances that sometimes made using food banks unavoidable (Perry et al, 2014). Evidence gathered from food aid providers through the All-Party Parliamentary Inquiry into

Hunger and Food Poverty confirmed the importance of these factors but also identified 'complex problems' (Forsey, 2014), such as debt, addiction and family breakdown.

Academic research has also examined who is using food banks and why. Garthwaite et al (2015) conducted an ethnographic study of food banks in the North-East of England between November 2013 and March 2015. The study included interviews with 42 men and women who were using food banks. All interviewees were of working age, either with or without children, but most were not working. Ethnographic observations of the food banks and information shared in interviews suggested that many of the people receiving help experienced mental health problems. Some interviewees described poor mental health as the cause of their job loss, while others gave it as the reason that they had failed to meet conditions of benefit receipt (such as the Claimant Commitment), resulting in a benefit sanction. Experiences of food insecurity seemed to further exacerbate mental health issues. The insufficiency of incomes to cover basic food costs was evident from reports of going without food, having to seek out the cheapest foods and offers, not being able to afford meat, fruit or vegetables, and not being able to afford foods recommended for their health conditions (Garthwaite et al, 2015).

More recently, a survey of households receiving help from Trussell Trust food banks in nine regions across England, Wales and Scotland was conducted over the period of October to December 2016 (Loopstra and Lalor, 2017). This enabled analysis of the population of households using these sites, and how they compare to households in the general population. The survey revealed that almost none of the households using food banks included adults of pension age. The most common type of household using food banks was single, working-age adults, followed by lone parents and their children. As proportions of all people living in low-income households in the UK, lone parents and their children were over-represented in food bank use, whereas pensioners were under-represented. This may be because pensioners are less likely to be food insecure and have been protected from welfare reforms but it may also reflect personal resistance to using food banks or trouble accessing them in this particular demographic.

In this survey, almost 70 per cent of the households using food banks were also receiving out-of-work benefits, with disability benefits being the most common type. Compared to general data on claimant characteristics in the UK, disability claimants deemed fit for work and JSA claimants were over-represented in their use of food banks. About a third of the sample had no educational qualifications, and a further third had only attained GCSE/O-level qualifications. About 15 per cent of respondents were not born in the UK, generally matching the overall population of the country, and less than 5 per cent were asylum seekers. A recent study of people using food banks in inner London reported similar socio-demographic and financial characteristics (Prayogo et al, 2017).

Importantly, in contrast to those who have traditionally been served by meal programmes (for example, people sleeping rough), food bank users were predominantly living in rented accommodation – either social housing or privately rented (Loopstra and Lalor, 2017). Just over 6 per cent were sleeping rough or staying in a night shelter at the time of the survey, though an additional 7.5 per cent were living in temporary homelessness accommodation provided by a council. These findings are generally consistent with the idea that, through food banks, food aid has expanded to reach a new demographic in the UK (Power et al, 2017).

This emerging evidence base shows how the characteristics of households using food banks tend to reflect the low-income groups that have experienced the most profound impacts of changes and reductions in welfare entitlements – specifically, people with disabilities, lone parents, families with children and working-age adults. These findings also match quantitative policy studies that have examined how patterns of food bank use across local areas relate to cuts in spending on welfare entitlements and local services, benefit sanctions, and unemployment (Loopstra et al, 2015, 2018). However, although acute financial crises resulting from welfare changes are a key reason for food bank referral, the findings of these studies on food insecurity also suggest that meeting food needs has been a long-term struggle for many of the households using food banks.

Contemporary food insecurity

The problem of food insecurity needs to be understood in the population more broadly, not just among those using food banks. Food insecurity has not been regularly monitored in the UK population, so it is difficult to identify whether it has been rising over the past decade. However, recent national surveys have shown that the prevalence of household food insecurity is, indeed, many times higher than the number of people recorded using Trussell Trust food banks, raising questions about how much hunger has been hidden in the UK over the years (Taylor and Loopstra, 2016). For example, in 2016, the Food Standards Agency (FSA) included the USDA Adult Food Security

Module in the fourth wave of its Food and You survey (Bates et al, 2017). This found that 13 per cent of UK adults were only marginally food secure, meaning that they have problems at times or anxiety about accessing adequate food, but the quality and quantity of their food are not substantially reduced. It also found that 8 per cent of UK adults had low or very low food security, meaning that they had compromised on the quality, variety and desirability of their diets in the past 12 months or, in the cases of very low food security, that their food intake was reduced because they lacked money for food. While the FSA survey did not publish findings relating to children, Unicef recently produced a report based on food insecurity measures included in the Gallup World Poll. Using the Food and Agriculture Organization (2015) Food Insecurity Experience Scale, it showed that 9 per cent of UK children under the age of 15 lived with a respondent who was moderately food insecure during 2014–16, and an additional 10.4 per cent – the highest proportion anywhere in Europe – lived with someone who was severely food insecure (Pereira et al, 2017).

Judging by the general characteristics of severe food-insecure households in the UK, households using food banks appear to be those in more acute circumstances. They have very high rates of severe food insecurity (for example, higher than 78 per cent), are predominantly receiving out-of-work benefits and have very low levels of income (Loopstra and Lalor, 2017). This observation matches UK and international research suggesting that food banks are used as a coping strategy of last resort by individuals experiencing food insecurity (Loopstra and Tarasuk, 2012).

Contextualising welfare reform and food banks in a longer welfare history

Recent social policy reforms can certainly be viewed as part of a 40-year trajectory of neoliberalising social policy changes that have eroded welfare entitlements and service provision over time. However, the evidence discussed in the previous section of this chapter does suggest that the step change in social policy reform since 2010 has played a critical role in the growth of food banks in the UK. Two aspects of these policy shifts are particularly important: the increasing reliance on charities to respond to need in local communities; and drastic welfare reforms and austerity policies since 2010.

Generally, since the 1970s, the effects of neoliberalism on UK social policy have included increasingly individualised notions of risk and care, increased conditionality, and communitarian and contractarian interpretations of dependency and solidarity (Dean, 2008; Ellison and Fenger, 2013). These conditions over the last 40 years form the context in which recent reforms and policy changes have taken place. However, the nature and scale of reforms since 2010 represent a more radical change in social policy. Analysts have drawn attention to the scale of the changes introduced over the last ten years through policies of austerity and welfare reform. They have reported the largest cuts in public finances ever seen and some of the most extensive reforms to state benefits since the introduction of the welfare state in the 1940s (Taylor-Gooby and Stoker, 2011; Beatty and Fothergill, 2013). As highlighted earlier in this chapter, evidence that these reforms are linked to the rise of food banks suggests that low-income households have been unable to buffer these changes. Benefit delays, cuts in entitlements and acute income shocks arising from sanctioning have resulted in households not having enough money for food and other basic living necessities.

Significant changes in political interpretations of the causes of and best responses to poverty have fuelled policy shifts since 2010. Specifically, there has been a marked departure from a focus on the structural causes of poverty. Instead, there is now increasing emphasis on notions of personal responsibility for individual circumstances of poverty, tied up with a resurgence of discourses around 'deservingness' (Ellison and Fenger, 2013; Pantazis, 2016). At the same time, responses to poverty have been reinvented, with a growing emphasis on conditionality attached to state provision, consequent reductions in entitlement levels and an increasing role for non-state providers. Welfare diversification policies under successive New Labour governments (1997–2010) and the Coalition government's 'Big Society' platform (2010–15) both resulted in the professionalisation and expansion of the role of the voluntary sector – and growing expectations of its role – in meeting need in local communities (Fyfe, 2005; Carmel and Harlock, 2008; Alcock, 2010). Since 2010, these conditions have led to an increasing reliance on charities to plug the gaps in state provision. Food banks are a prime embodiment of these shifts in terms of both the nature of provision (as examples of modern charities filling the gaps) and the nature of the needs they meet (increasingly resulting from the retrenchment and inadequacy of the state safety net).

The increased role for the charitable sector in meeting need in local communities is reflected in the nature of food bank initiatives. In a study of The Trussell Trust foodbank network, Lambie-Mumford (2017) documented how the network approaches its work strategically, particularly when it comes to organisational growth, corporate partnership working and food sourcing. The organisation is streamlined, with a range of professionalised processes to respond to perceived need and assume responsibility for food insecurity in practice.

As highlighted earlier in this chapter, the franchise model operated by The Trussell Trust involves franchisees paying an upfront fee and then being required to work in particular ways and be audited annually. In return, they can use Trussell Trust branding and receive training and ongoing support from staff at regional and national levels. There are strategic approaches to both network growth and food sourcing, and national coordination is a key part of the network's offer. Through partnerships with supermarket chains, The Trussell Trust is able to hold collection days at branches throughout the country, with individual food banks collecting at their local stores. The organisation also fosters other types of corporate relationships, such as corporations sending retail partner staff to work as volunteers, and sharing expertise in the form of mentoring or consultancy.

In summary, recent shifts in social policy – which have implemented individualised interpretations of the causes of and best responses to poverty – have had a direct impact on both the need for food banks in the UK and their particular shape. On the basis of the available evidence, it can be said that policy change since 2010 has been particularly formative, and has signified a marked shift in political approaches to poverty.

Social justice implications of the increasing need for food assistance

The UK is at an important juncture for social policy. The growth in food bank provision and increasing reliance on food charity to plug gaps in the welfare system raise urgent questions about what happens next. This section examines the social justice implications of the UK's current reliance on ad hoc charitable provision.

Food charity creates 'other' social protection systems, which are not based on rights or entitlements, but instead defined by exclusion. Emergency food provision is an identifiably 'other' system of food acquisition given that it lacks key features of food shopping – the socially accepted method of food acquisition (Meah, 2013). The food offered through food charity is largely sourced (by projects) and exclusively acquired (by recipients) from outside the marketplace, and recipients lack (consumer or citizenship) rights within such provision systems. Emergency food systems are not only identifiably 'other', but experientially so as well (Garthwaite, 2016). Feelings of embarrassment and stigma, the religious function of the spaces in which this food is often provided, and the discourses of the 'needy' and 'hungry' all serve to alienate and socially exclude those in need of assistance with food (Lister, 2004). Importantly for social policy research, these systems are not universal or guaranteed. Food charity is unaccountable to those that it serves and accessibility is highly varied. Such provision is therefore an ad hoc charitable initiative defined by and perpetuating exclusion.

This ad hoc nature has important implications for the effectiveness of charitable food assistance as a response to hunger. There is very little evidence that food bank users have their food needs met over the long term, as indicated by high rates of severe food insecurity persisting even among those who use food banks (Loopstra and Tarasuk, 2012; Loopstra and Lalor, 2017). This suggests that the availability of this assistance does not prevent people from going without food. However, even if immediate and basic subsistence needs can be met through food banks, unreliable access and the lack of entitlement to food from this source likely means that feelings of anxiety about access to food – an important dimension of food insecurity – also go unaddressed.

The discrepancy in the numbers of people who experience food insecurity and the numbers of people accessing food banks across high-income countries, including the UK, also raises questions about whether this is an available and/or chosen strategy for households experiencing food insecurity (Loopstra and Tarasuk, 2015; Taylor and Loopstra, 2016). Given that so many food-insecure people do not seek their help, food banks' ability to reduce food insecurity at the population level is limited.

Conclusions

When looking to the future of experiences of food, poverty and emergency food provision in the UK, the persistent lack of a policy response or effective policy framework taking responsibility for food insecurity is particularly concerning. With reforms to welfare provision still unfolding (Hood and Waters, 2017) – notably, in the form of Universal Credit – the drivers of food bank use are likely to persist, if not become worse. At the same time, food prices are continuing to rise and the general cost of living is predicted to increase (Office for National Statistics, 2017), suggesting that food insecurity may well remain at current levels or even grow further.

Given the important link between changing social policies and experiences of food insecurity and food bank use, it is clear that social policy will continue to play a critical role in these issues – whether that is solving or exacerbating them. Any solution will require the government's Department for Work and Pensions to recognise food insecurity and treat it as a policy priority. However, given the way in which these issues cut across governmental remits, a solution could be strengthened by interdepartmental policy strategies, as called for by various lobbying groups (Tait, 2015). As this chapter has shown, issues of rights and entitlements are critical in questions of food access and charitable emergency food provision. Adequate social protection has a vital role to play in protecting people from the harshest effects of poverty. Successfully addressing food insecurity will necessarily involve revisiting the current drivers and priorities of social policy reforms and, ultimately, defending the potential of the welfare state (Farnsworth and Irving, 2015).

Notes

[1] See: http://endhungeruk.org/

[2] This survey was repeated in 2012. In that year, 28 per cent of adults reported often or sometimes skimping on food for themselves because of a lack of money, and 3 per cent reported not being able to afford two meals a day. Surveys conducted in 1990 and 1999 showed lower figures (Lansley and Mack, 2015).

[3] Universal Credit is a major reform in the administration of social security, designed to incorporate all social security entitlements into one payment. The reform has also seen changes to levels of entitlement and conditionality (see: www.gov.uk/universal-credit).

[4] For example, the Oxford Food Bank (see: http://oxfordfoodbank.org).

[5] It is also important to note that this chapter does not talk about the role of FareShare – a surplus food redistribution charity that provides food to community projects helping vulnerable people, for example, housing projects, lunch clubs and social supermarkets. This chapter focuses on The Trussell Trust as an example of front-line charitable emergency food provision.

[6] See Editor's notes at bottom of the following webpage: www.trusselltrust.org/2018/11/27/foodbanks-christmas-2018/

References

Alcock P. (2010) 'Partnership and mainstreaming: voluntary action under New Labour', Third Sector Research Centre Working Paper 32, Accessed 2017, www.birmingham.ac.uk/generic/tsrc/documents/tsrc/working-papers/working-paper-32.pdf

Allen, C. (2016) 'Food poverty and Christianity in Britain: a theological re-assessment', Political Theology, 17(4): 361–77.

All-Party Parliamentary Inquiry into Hunger and Food Poverty (2014) Feeding Britain: A strategy for zero hunger in England, Wales, Scotland and Northern Ireland, London: All-Party Parliamentary Group on Hunger.

Anderson, S.A. (1990) 'Core indicators of nutritional status for difficult-to-sample populations', *Journal of Nutrition*, 120(11): 62.

Barr, B., Taylor-Robinson, D., Stuckler, D., Loopstra, R., Reeves, A., Wickham, S. and Whitehead, M. (2015) 'Fit-for-work or fit-for-unemployment? Does the reassessment of disability benefit claimants using a tougher work capability assessment help people into work?', *Journal of Epidemiology & Community Health*, 70(5), http://dx.doi.org/10.1136/jech-2015-206333

Bates, B., Roberts, C., Lepps, H. and Porter, L. (2017) 'The Food & You survey wave 4', www.food.gov.uk/sites/default/files/media/document/food-and-you-w4-combined-report_0.pdf

Beatty, C. and Fothergill, S. (2013) 'Hitting the poorest places hardest: the local and regional impact of welfare reform', www4.shu.ac.uk/research/cresr/sites/shu.ac.uk/files/hitting-poorest-places-hardest_0.pdf

Berner, M. and O'Brien, K. (2004) 'The shifting pattern of food security support: food stamp and food bank usage in North Carolina', *Nonprofit and Voluntary Sector Quarterly*, 33(4): 655–72.

Beveridge, W. (1942) *Social insurance and allied services*, London: His Majesty's Stationery Office.

Boyle, D. (2014) 'Almost ONE million Britons visit food banks following 162 percent jump in the number of people seeking emergency help', www.dailymail.co.uk/news/article-2605661/Almost-ONE-million-Britons-seek-food-bank-help-following-162-percent-jump-number-people-seeking-emergency-food-help.html

Cameron, H. (2014) 'The morality of the food parcel', *Practical Theology*, 7(3): 194–204.

Carmel, E. and Harlock, J. (2008) 'Instituting the "third sector" as a governable terrain: partnership, procurement and performance in the UK', *Policy & Politics*, 36(2): 155–71.

Comptroller and Auditor General (2016) 'Benefit sanctions', www.nao.org.uk/wp-content/uploads/2016/11/Benefit-sanctions.pdf

Conservative Home (2012) 'Food banks ARE part of the Big Society – but the problem they are tackling is not new', www.conservativehome.com/localgovernment/2012/12/council-should-encourage-food-banks.html

Cooper, N. and Dumpleton, S. (2013) 'Walking the breadline: the scandal of food poverty in 21st century Britain', https://oxfamilibrary.openrepository.com/bitstream/handle/10546/292978/rr-walking-readline-food-poverty-britain-300513-en.pdf;jsessionid=BCB8FB0D452C2112506FE649997509BE?sequence=1

Costello, H.E. (2007) 'Hunger in our own backyard: the face of hunger in the United States', *Nutrition in Clinical Practice*, 22(6): 587–90.

Coulter S. (2016) 'The UK labour market and the "Great Recession"', in M. Myant, S. Theodoropoulou and A. Piasna (eds) *Unemployment, internal devaluation and labour market deregulation in Europe*, Brussels: European Trade Union Institute, pp 197–227.

Croll, A. (2011) 'Starving strikers and the limits of the "humanitarian discovery of hunger" in late Victorian Britain', *International Review of Social History*, 56(1): 103–31.

De Agostini, P., Hills, J. and Sutherland, H. (2017) 'Were we really all in it together? The distributional effects of the 2010–15 UK Coalition government's tax–benefit policy changes', *Social Policy & Administration*, https://doi.org/10.1111/spol.12344

Dean, H. (2008) 'Social policy and human rights: re-thinking the engagement', *Social Policy and Society*, 7(1): 1–12.

Department for Environment, Food and Rural Affairs (2012) 'Family food 2011', https://assets.publishing.service.gov.uk/government/uploads/system/uploads/attachment_data/file/193804/familyfood-2011report.pdf

Department for Environment, Food and Rural Affairs (2014) 'Food statistics pocketbook: 2013 – in year update', https://assets.publishing.service.gov.uk/government/uploads/system/uploads/attachment_data/file/315418/foodpocketbook-2013update-29may14.pdf

Department for Work and Pensions (2013a) 'Claimant Commitment to spell out what jobseekers must do in return for benefits', www.gov.uk/government/news/claimant-commitment-to-spell-out-what-jobseekers-must-do-in-return-for-benefits

Department for Work and Pensions (2013b) 'Jobseeker's Allowance: overview of revised sanctions regime', Accessed February 2018, www.gov.uk/government/uploads/system/uploads/attachment_data/file/238839/jsa-overview-of-revised-sanctions-regime.pdf

Department for Work and Pensions (2018) 'Households below average income: an analysis of the UK income distribution: 1994/95–2015/16', https://assets.publishing.service.gov.uk/government/uploads/system/uploads/attachment_data/file/691917/households-below-average-income-1994-1995-2016-2017.pdf

Dimbleby, H. and Vincent, J. (2013) 'The School Food Plan', https://assets.publishing.service.gov.uk/government/uploads/system/uploads/attachment_data/file/251020/The_School_Food_Plan.pdf

Dowler, E. and Calvert, C. (1995) 'Diets of lone-parent families', *Social Policy Research*, 71: 1–4.

Dowler, E. and Lambie-Mumford, H. (2015) 'How can households eat in austerity? Challenges for social policy in the UK', *Social Policy and Society*, 14(3): 417–28.

Dugan, E. and Owen, J. (2014) 'The real cost-of-living crisis: five million British children "sentenced to life of poverty thanks to welfare reforms"', www.independent.co.uk/news/uk/politics/the-real-cost-of-living-crisis-five-million-british-children-face-life-of-poverty-thanks-to-welfare-9442061.html

Dwyer, P., Jones, K., McNeil, J., Scullion, L. and Stewart, A. (2016) 'First wave findings: disability and conditionality', www.welfareconditionality.ac.uk/wp-content/uploads/2016/05/WelCond-findings-disability-May16.pdf

Ellison, M. and Fenger, M. (2013) 'Social investment, protection and inequality within the new economy and politics of welfare in Europe', *Social Policy and Society*, 12(4): 611–24.

Farnsworth, K. and Irving, Z. (2015) 'Austerity: more than the sum of its parts', in K. Farnsworth and Z. Irving (eds) *Social policy in times of austerity: Global economic crisis and the new politics of welfare*, Bristol: Policy Press, pp 9–42.

Food and Agriculture Organization (2015) 'Voices of the hungry', www.fao.org/economic/ess/ess-fs/voices/en/

Food Chain Analysis Group (2006) 'Food security and the UK: an evidence and analysis paper', https://webarchive.nationalarchives.gov.uk/20130404001020/http://archive.defra.gov.uk/evidence/economics/foodfarm/reports/documents/foodsecurity.pdf

Forsey, A. (2014) 'An evidence review for the All-Party Parliamentary Inquiry into Hunger in the United Kingdom', https://feedingbritain.files.wordpress.com/2015/02/food-poverty-appg-evidence-review-final.pdf

Fyfe, N.R. (2005) 'Making space for "neo-communitarianism"? The third sector, state and civil society in the UK', *Antipode*, 37(3): 536–57.

Galluzzo, M. (2014) 'The truth about food banks: dependency or welfare crisis?', www.channel4.com/news/food-banks-key-questions-hunger-austerity-welfare-cuts

Gardiner, J. (2017) 'Are the 2010s really like the 1930s? The truth about life in the Great Depression', www.theguardian.com/society/2017/mar/04/2010s-like-1930s-look-facts-unemployment-healthcare

Garthwaite, K. (2016) 'Stigma, shame and "people like us": an ethnographic study of foodbank use in the UK', *Journal of Poverty and Social Justice*, 24(3): 277–89.

Garthwaite, K.A., Collins, P.J. and Bambra, C. (2015) 'Food for thought: an ethnographic study of negotiating ill health and food insecurity in a UK foodbank', *Social Science & Medicine*, 132: 38–44.

Glennerster, H., Hills, J., Piachaud, D. and Webb, J. (2004) *One hundred years of poverty and policy*, York: Joseph Rowntree Foundation.

Gordon, D. and Pantazis, C. (1997) 'Measuring poverty: breadline Britain in the 1990s', in D. Gordon and C. Pantazis (eds) *Breadline Britain in the 1990s*, Bristol: Summerleaze House Books.

Gordon, D., Levitas, R., Pantazis, C., Patsios, D., Payne, S., Townsend, P., Adelman, L., Ashworth, K., Middleton, S., Bradshaw, J. and Williams, J. (2000) 'Poverty and social exclusion in Britain', www. jrf.org.uk/sites/default/files/jrf/migrated/files/185935128x.pdf

Hansard (2013) 'Food banks', https://publications.parliament.uk/pa/ cm201314/cmhansrd/cm131218/debtext/131218-0003.htm

HM Treasury (2010) *Spending review 2010*, London: Crown Copyright.

Hood, A. and Waters, T. (2017) *Living standards, poverty and inequality in the UK: 2016–17 to 2021–22*, London: Institute for Fiscal Studies.

IFAN (Independent Food Aid Network) (no date) 'Mapping the UK's independent food banks', www.foodaidnetwork.org.uk/mapping

Johnsen, S. (2016) 'First wave findings: lone parents', www. welfareconditionality.ac.uk/wp-content/uploads/2016/05/ WelCond-findings-lone-parents-May16.pdf

Joyce, R. and Levell, P. (2011) 'The impact in 2012–13 of the change to indexation policy', IFS Briefing Note 120, www.ifs.org.uk/bns/ bn120.pdf

Lambie-Mumford, H. (2013) '"Every town should have one": emergency food banking in the UK', *Journal of Social Policy*, 42(1): 73–89.

Lambie-Mumford, H. (2017) *Hungry Britain: The rise of food charity*, Bristol: Policy Press.

Lambie-Mumford, H. and Dowler, E. (2014) 'Rising use of "food aid" in the United Kingdom', *British Food Journal*, 116(9): 1418–25.

Lambie-Mumford, H. and Sims, L. (2018) 'Feeding hungry children: the growth of charitable breakfast clubs and holiday hunger projects in the UK, *Children and Society*, 32: 244–54.

Lambie-Mumford, H., Crossley, D., Jensen, E., Verbeke, M. and Dowler, E. (2014) *Household food insecurity in the UK: A review of food aid*, London: Department for Environment, Food and Rural Affairs.

Lansley, S. and Mack, J. (2015) *Breadline Britain: The rise of mass poverty*, London: Oneworld Publications.

Lister, R. (2004) *Poverty*, Bristol: Policy Press.

Long, R. (2015) *School meals and nutritional standards: SN/SP/4195*, London: House of Commons Library.

Loopstra, R. (2018) 'Interventions to address household food insecurity in high-income countries', *Proceedings of the Nutrition Society*, 77(3): 270–81.

Loopstra, R. and Lalor, D. (2017) *Financial insecurity, food insecurity, and disability: The profile of people receiving emergency food assistance from The Trussell Trust foodbank network in Britain*, London: The Trussell Trust.

Loopstra, R. and Tarasuk, V. (2012) 'The relationship between food banks and household food insecurity among low income Toronto families', *Canadian Public Policy*, 38(4): 497–514.

Loopstra, R. and Tarasuk, V. (2015) 'Food bank usage is a poor indicator of food insecurity: insights from Canada', *Social Policy and Society*, 14(4): 443–55.

Loopstra, R., Reeves, A., Taylor-Robinson, D., Barr, B., McKee, M. and Stuckler, D. (2015) 'Austerity, sanctions, and the rise of food banks in the UK', *British Medical Journal (BMJ)*, 350, https://doi.org/10.1136/bmj.h1775

Loopstra, R., Reeves, A., McKee, M. and Stuckler, D. (2016) 'Food insecurity and social protection in Europe: quasi-natural experiment of Europe's great recessions 2004–2012', *Preventive Medicine*, 89: 44–50.

Loopstra, R., Fledderjohann, J., Reeves, A. and Stuckler, D. (2018) 'Impact of welfare benefit sanctioning on food insecurity: a dynamic cross-area study of food bank usage in the UK', *Journal of Social Policy*, 47(3): 437–57.

Lucas, P.J., Jessiman, T. and Cameron, A. (2015) 'Healthy start: the use of welfare food vouchers by low-income parents in England', *Social Policy and Society*, 14(3): 457–69.

Lupton, R., Burchardt, T., Fitzgerald, A., Hills, J., McKnight, A., Obolenskaya, P., Stewart, K., Thomson, S., Tunstall, R. and Vizard, P. (2015) 'The Coalition's social policy record: policy, spending and outcomes 2010-2015', http://sticerd.lse.ac.uk/dps/case/spcc/RR04.pdf

MacMillan, T. and Dowler, E. (2012) 'Just and sustainable? Examining the rhetoric and potential realities of UK food security', *Journal of Agricultural and Environmental Ethics*, 25(2): 181–204.

McGlone, P., Dobson, B., Dowler, E. and Nelson, M. (1999) *Food projects and how they work*, York: Joseph Rowntree Foundation.

Meah, A. (2013) 'Shopping', in P. Jackson (ed) *Food words*, London: Bloomsbury Academic, pp 197–200.

Moore, S. (2012) '2012 has been the year of the food bank', www. theguardian.com/commentisfree/2012/dec/19/2012-year-of-the-food-bank

Morris, N. (2013) 'Hungrier than ever: Britain's use of food banks triples', www.independent.co.uk/news/uk/home-news/hungrier-than-ever-britain-s-use-of-food-banks-triples-8882340.html

Mould, C. (2014) 'The £100,000 raised by readers for *Mirror*'s Christmas Appeal will make a massive difference to hungry families', www.mirror.co.uk/news/uk-news/100000-raised-readers-mirrors-christmas-2985176

National Health Service (2015) 'The school fruit and vegetable scheme', www.nhs.uk/LiveWell/5aday/Pages/Schoolscheme.aspx

Nelson, M., Erens, B., Bates, B., Church, S. and Boshier, T. (2007a) *Low income diet and nutrition survey, volume 3: Nutritional status, physical activity, economic, social and other factors*, London: Stationery Office.

Nelson, N., Erens, B., Bates, B., Church, S. and Boshier, T. (2007b) *Low income diet and nutrition survey, volume 1: Background methods, sample characteristics*, Norwich: Stationery Office.

Office for National Statistics (2017) *Statistical bulletin: Consumer price inflation, UK: December 2017*, London: Office for National Statistics.

Padley, M. and Hirsch, D. (2017) *A minimum income standard for the UK in 2017*, York: Joseph Rowntree Foundation.

Pantazis, C. (2016) 'Policies and discourses of poverty during a time of recession and austerity', *Critical Social Policy*, 36(1): 3–20.

Pereira, A.L., Handa, S. and Holmqvist, G. (2017) *Prevalence and correlates of food insecurity among children across the globe*, Florence: UNICEF Office of Research.

Pérez de Armiño, K. (2016) 'Erosion of rights, uncritical solidarity and food banks in Spain', in G. Riches and T. Silvasti (eds) *First world hunger revisited: Food charity or the right to food?*, Basingstoke: Palgrave Macmillan, pp 131–45.

Perry, J., Williams, M., Sefton, T. and Haddad, M. (2014) 'Emergency use only: understanding and reducing the use of food banks in the UK', www.cpag.org.uk/sites/default/files/Foodbank%20Report_web.pdf

Poverty and Social Exclusion Team (2013) 'Going backwards: 1983–2012', www.poverty.ac.uk/pse-research/going-backwards-1983-2012

Power, M., Doherty, B., Small, N. and Teasdale, S. (2017) 'All in it together? Community food aid in a multi-ethnic context', *Journal of Social Policy*, 46(3): 447–71.

Prayogo, E., Chater, A., Chapman, S., Barker, M., Rahmawati, N., Waterfall, T. and Grimble, G. (2017) 'Who uses foodbanks and why? Exploring the impact of financial strain and adverse life events on food insecurity', *Journal of Public Health*, 40(4): 1–8.

Reeves, A. and Loopstra, R. (2017) '"Set up to fail"? How welfare conditionality undermines citizenship for vulnerable groups', *Social Policy and Society*, 16(2): 327–38.

Reeves, A., Loopstra, R. and Stuckler, D. (2017) 'The growing disconnect between food prices and wages in Europe: cross-national analysis of food deprivation and welfare regimes in twenty-one EU countries, 2004–2012', *Public Health Nutrition*, 20(8): 1414–22.

Register of All-Party Parliamentary Groups (2017) 'Foodbanks', https://publications.parliament.uk/pa/cm/cmallparty/171220/foodbanks.htm

Shelter (2005) 'SHP practice briefing: food for thought: soup-runs and soup kitchens', https://england.shelter.org.uk/__data/assets/pdf_file/0004/220693/GP_Briefing_Food_for_thought.pdf

Sosenko, P., Livingstone, N. and Fitzpatrick, S. (2013) 'Overview of food aid provision in Scotland', Herriot Watt University, www.webarchive.org.uk/wayback/archive/20170706161002/http://www.gov.scot/Publications/2013/12/8757

Tait, C. (2015) *Hungry for change*, London: Fabian Society.

Tarasuk, V. (2001) *Discussion paper on household and individual food insecurity*, Ottawa: Health Canada.

Taylor, A. and Loopstra, R. (2016) *Too poor to eat? Food insecurity in the UK*, London: Food Foundation.

Taylor-Gooby, P. and Stoker, G. (2011) 'The Coalition programme: a new vision for Britain or politics as usual?', *The Political Quarterly*, 82(1): 4–15.

The Trussell Trust (2016) 'What we do: The Trussell Trust partners with local communities to help stop UK hunger', www.trusselltrust.org/what-we-do/

The Trussell Trust (2017) 'UK foodbank use continues to rise as new report highlights growing impact of Universal Credit rollout on foodbanks', www.trusselltrust.org/2017/04/25/uk-foodbank-use-continues-rise/

Townsend, P. (1979) *Poverty in the United Kingdom*, Berkeley, CA: University of California Press.

Vernon, J. (2007) *Hunger: A modern history*, Cambridge, MA: Belknap Press of Harvard University Press.

Wells, R. and Caraher, M. (2014) 'UK print media coverage of the food bank phenomenon: from food welfare to food charity?', *British Food Journal*, 116(9): 1426–45.

Williams, A., Cloke, P., May, J. and Goodwin, M. (2016) 'Contested space: the contradictory political dynamics of food banking in the UK', *Environment and Planning A: Economy and Space*, 48(11): 2291–316.

Wunderlich, G.S. and Norwood, J.L. (2006) *Food insecurity and hunger in the United States: An assessment of the measure*, Washington, DC: National Research Council of the National Academies.

8

Conclusion: food charity in Europe

Hannah Lambie-Mumford and Tiina Silvasti

Introduction

This edited collection provides the first comprehensive study of the rise of food charity across Europe. This concluding chapter pulls together the findings of all the individual case studies to analyse what comparisons can be drawn regarding the growth of this type of charitable provision across the continent over the last few decades. The aim of this book is to use food charity as a lens through which to examine changing responses to poverty in the context of shifting social policies, and the data provided by the case studies have demonstrated just how important a lens food charity is in this regard.

As this chapter outlines, a comparative study of the rise of food charity across Europe highlights several key things. First, the food charity landscapes in different countries vary widely; although they have common characteristics that can be categorised (see the typology later), this provision is ultimately difficult to quantify. Second, across the cases, there have been particular spikes in food charity provision at times of economic crisis and state welfare retrenchment. Third, regardless of the historical role of the third sector in the various welfare regimes, since the neoliberal wave, charities have come to play increasingly important roles in the provision of care in every country studied, whether in place of traditionally state-provided support or support from the family.

While this book has a particular focus on the social policy aspects of the rise of food charity, the case studies clearly highlight the importance of supply-side factors in the shape and scale of emergency food provision. This reveals how other policy measures – particularly in the domains of agriculture or the environment – may have an impact on social policy as directing surplus food to food charities impacts on the nature, scale and embeddedness of food aid as a response to food poverty. In particular, the case studies demonstrate the significance of the European Union (EU) Food Distribution Programme for the Most Deprived Persons of the Community (MDP) and – after 2013 – the Fund for European Aid to the Most Deprived (FEAD) in institutionalising the practice of redistributing surplus food through food charity. The implications of these findings for social justice are profound. The case studies demonstrate the detrimental effects of reduced social rights in two areas: first, the impact on food charity users' experiences of poverty and exclusion; and, second, a significant shift further away from welfare practices based on systems underpinned by universality and entitlements towards systems of ad hoc provision that are vulnerable, unreliable and exclusionary.

In addition to providing an important step forward in our knowledge about the rise of food charity in Europe, this book also serves to highlight just how much we do not yet know about this phenomenon. It is clear that further rigorous comparative work is required, particularly to explore the true scale of food charity, its operations and the drivers of need for help with food across the continent.

This book brings together leading researchers from across the breadth of Europe – both geographically and in terms of different welfare regimes – to explore the driving forces behind the rise of food charity. It provides a comprehensive social policy analysis of this contemporary phenomenon in different countries, exploring in particular the role of welfare state retrenchment and the responsibility that charity is assuming in its wake. This final chapter provides a comparative analysis of several key themes across the case studies. These are: the nature and scale of food charity; relationships between changes in welfare provision and the growth of food charity, as well as the shifting role of charity more generally; the role of food supply in shaping food charity; and the social justice implications of changing welfare states and the growth of food charity. The chapter ends by setting out the implications of this evidence base for future research and policy analysis.

Food charity in Europe: nature, scale and public discourse

The case studies provide valuable insight into the nature and scale of food charity across contemporary Europe. This part of the comparative analysis examines what food charity looks like in practice across the countries studied, the scale of its current operations and the different ways in which public discourses have reacted to the presence of food charity in different countries.

What is food charity in Europe?

As outlined in the Introduction, one of the key tasks of this book is to establish some coherence in the terminology applied to food charity. It is clear from the cross-country analysis that terms are used in slightly different, and even awkwardly overlapping, ways. Words like 'deliverer', 'distributor' and 'provider' are used to describe different kinds of operations working at different scales and in different ways. In order to gain some comparative clarity, it is helpful to return to the definition of food charity provided in the Introduction:

> This book adopts a broad definition of charitable food provision. This refers to all voluntary initiatives helping people to access food that they would otherwise not be able to obtain. It therefore covers a variety of provision, including projects that provide food parcels, food banks (of all kinds), soup kitchens, meal projects and social supermarkets. In these projects, food may be provided at low or no cost, with its distribution facilitated by a range of organisations (faith or non-faith) involved in delivery at various scales of operation (local, regional and national).

A food charity project is therefore the end link in the chain that gives food to people in need. Importantly, these projects are distinct from 'mid-layer' food redistribution projects, where 'redistribution' to food charity projects is broadly defined to include surplus food redistribution, the redistribution of other food donations (including from individual citizens through food drives) or the channelling of financial donations to support food charity operations.

While food charity projects may collect surplus food or donations, and store food themselves (which is notably the case in Germany and the UK), they may also – or instead – use a mid-layer organisation to source food. The case studies highlight the importance and reach of such organisations, particularly in Italy, Spain, the Netherlands and Slovenia, where the practice of surplus food redistribution is more embedded. These organisations' main role is to redistribute surplus food, which is sourced through EU schemes, as well as other corporate food surplus donations. However, they may also collect and distribute financial donations, and provide training and other support.

The case studies confirm both overlap and divergence in the use of the term 'food bank'. In the majority of cases (the Netherlands, Italy, Spain and Slovenia), it is used to describe a mid-layer organisation concerned with food collection, storage and redistribution. However, in the remaining cases, this term is either not used (in Germany, the *Tafel* initiative is the most prominent label) or used differently (in the UK and Finland, it refers to a project that provides food directly to recipients).

In addition to highlighting the presence of distinct layers in different European food charity systems, the case studies also draw attention to the incredibly wide variety in the nature of food charity projects themselves. Many of the case studies mention established food charity projects that have a wide reach. These projects may have been set up to provide social support, of which food is just one aspect (for example, Caritas in Italy, Spain and Slovenia), or they may have food charity as a principal function and provide other signposting or help in addition to food (for example, *Tafel* in Germany and The Trussell Trust food banks in the UK). However, beyond these established national food charity organisations, it is clear that a plethora of other projects – either working independently or as part of smaller networks – exist in all the countries studied.

From this analysis, we were able to develop a typology of food charity. Taking the umbrella definition of food charity outlined earlier, the European food charity examined in this book falls into the categories of 'emergency' and 'non-emergency' support (as identified in the US by Mabli et al [2010]). These can then be referred to as charitable emergency food provision (Table 8.1) and charitable food assistance (Table 8.2), respectively.

Charitable emergency food provision includes projects that help with an acute food crisis and includes food parcel and prepared food provision. The key characteristics of charitable emergency food provision are:

- The provision is free.
- The provision is intended to meet an acute 'hunger/lack of access to food' need and intended to be temporary. The intension of emergency provision is critical here – there may, in fact, be chronic use but the project is intended to provide only emergency help.
- The provision is outside the mainstream market.

Charitable emergency food provision – most notably, food parcel provision – has been the predominant focus of the chapters included in this book but it is also important to set out in more detail the work of charitable food assistance initiatives. Charitable food assistance, as non-emergency food charity, refers to projects offering ongoing help with food access, helping hungry or vulnerable people. The key characteristics of this kind of provision are:

- providing ongoing support, which may be intended to support ongoing access to a vulnerable or hungry population but is not designed to meet an acute need;

Table 8.1: Charitable emergency food provision examples

Types of project	Broad description	Labels used	Points of variation	Country examples
Food parcel provision	Provide an amount of food ('parcels of food') for people to take away, prepare and eat	Food bank, food pantry, food project	People may be given a pre-prepared parcel or may be able to choose freely from foodstuffs, people may/may not be able to state dietary requirements The amount of food may vary as may the type of food and whether it is fresh or long-life	'Breadlines' in Finland Food parcel provision by Caritas (Italy, Spain, Slovenia) *Tafel* (Germany) Food Pantries (the Netherlands) The Red Cross (Slovenia) 'Delivery projects' (Spain).
Prepared food provision	Provides pre-prepared food for people to eat on site or take away	Soup run, soup kitchen, breakfast clubs aimed at child hunger relief (as opposed to childcare), school holiday programmes	Food could be eaten on or off site Could be prepared by the project or be pre-prepared food (for example, supermarket sandwiches)	'Consumption projects' in Spain 'Give me 5 for a Smile' (Slovenia) Soup kitchens (Germany, Spain, the UK).

Table 8.2: Charitable food assistance projects

Types of project	Broad description	Labels used
Subsidised food 'shopping'	The aims of these projects are usually about easing access to food Where costs are nominal these may be seen as alternatives to food parcel projects but they often also allow people to access the service for a longer period of time	Social supermarket, food co-operative, food pantries (in the UK)
Subsidised prepared food	May be about promoting access to food and/or a social function of bringing people together or providing a gateway to services for those that may be in need of further support	Community cafes, lunch clubs

- subsidised (free or reduced cost), with the aim of easing access to food and reducing costs;
- may have 'market' characteristics (supermarket food, monetary exchange) but still outside the primary food market; and
- ways of working would include a membership system, food co-ops, nominal/voluntary contributions and community cafes/lunch clubs.

It is also important to set out the wider 'food aid' context in which this food charity typology fits. Food charity often also sits alongside state-provided support with food in a bigger landscape of assistance, as set out in Figure 8.1.

Figure 8.1: Typology of 'food aid'

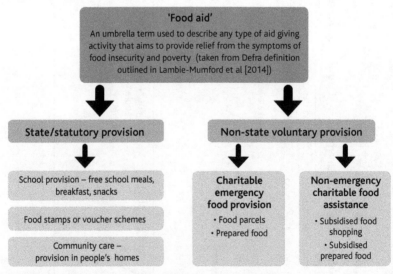

Note: Defra = Department for Environment, Food and Rural Affairs.

It is important to acknowledge that this typology is an ideal type, meaning that it is formed from characteristics and elements of the food aid phenomenon presented in the case studies but is not meant to necessarily correspond to all of the characteristics of any one particular case study. Following this typology and the evidence on the nature of food charity systems in Europe, it also becomes possible to develop a representation of European food charity systems, as outlined in Figure 8.2.

Table 8.3 sets out key information on the food charity landscapes of the case-study countries. Food charity across all the countries clearly

Figure 8.2: Food charity system diagram

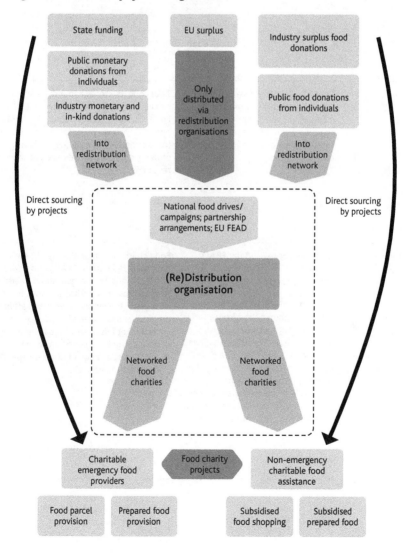

Table 8.3: Food charity landscapes across case-study countries

Country	Prominent food charity projects and mid-layer organisations	Brief description of food charity landscape
Finland	FEAD food is distributed by 22 partner organisations, including the ELCF, FBOs and NGOs. *Yhteinen pöytä* is an emerging second-tier organisation that coordinates activities with parishes and municipalities. It is being piloted in several city regions and aims to establish best practice for food aid delivery in Finland.	There is no national umbrella organisation for food aid. The largest operators are the ELCF, other FBOs and NGOs, for example, associations for unemployed people. They provide food parcels to take away or meals to eat at their premises.
Germany	*Tafel* (the National Association of German *Tafel* trains members and manages private donations, for example, from large private donors such as Mercedes), Caritas, Diakonie.	*Tafel* collects, stores and provides food directly to people in need and may provide other goods or social services alongside food. It also operates through other large organisations (for example, Caritas). Soup kitchens and other projects do exist but are talked about and researched less.
Italy	Together, Caritas and the FBAO account for 70 per cent of all charitable food handed out. Seven organisations form a network that redistributes food from the FEAD programme: FBAO, Caritas (Caritas Italy), *Croce Rossa Italiana* (Red Cross Italy), *Comunità di S. Egidio* (Community of Sant'Egidio), *Banco delle opere di Carità*, *Associazione Banco Alimentare Roma* (Food Bank Association Rome), and *Associazione Sempre Insieme per la Pace*.	Food charity is dominated by the national food bank federation (FBAO) and Caritas. The FBAO is a mid-level organisation, redistributing food to providers. Caritas provides food to recipients through its centres and affiliated projects, and Emporia of Solidarity – a social supermarket initiative where people 'buy food' using electronic points on a card. In addition, there are also a range of other independent and undocumented projects.

Food sources	Access routes to food assistance	Rise and scale of food charity (food charity statistics from national organisations)
Most of the food is donated directly from retailers and the food industry to the charities without the involvement of a second-tier organisation. Food provision based on the FEAD programme is coordinated by the Finnish Food Authority, which delivers the food to partner organisations who then distribute it to recipients. More coordinated practice – with *Yhteinen pöytä* providing regionally centralised food collection and short-term storage – is under development.	There is no means testing. Charities are free to evaluate applicants' need for food. It is generally known that municipal social workers guide people in need of help to the appropriate charities, even if these charities are not part of the official social security system in Finland.	The first breadlines and food banks were set up in the mid-1990s because of the deep recession. Since then, charitable food provision has become established and now covers the whole country. There are no reliable statistics on charitable food aid provision. FEAD food was provided to 284,352 people at least once during 2017. The Church Resource Agency estimates that around 100,000 people receive food aid every year.
Tafel redistributes surplus but also runs food drives and takes monetary donations. It does not take food from the FEAD programme. Those funds are instead used to support social inclusion initiatives.	For support through *Tafel*, people need to 'prove' their need – often through benefit documents. People can also be signposted by state agencies.	*Tafel* began in the early 1990s. The period 1993–2003 saw moderate growth (330 projects established). The period 2003–10 saw a rapid increase alongside welfare reforms (up to 877 projects). There has been consolidation since 2010 (at 934 projects). In 2017, the 934 *Tafel* projects had 2,100 outlets servicing 1.5 million users.
Surplus food – including food from the FEAD programme – as well as food drives.	Caritas counselling centres assess applicants' need for help with food.	There was a 47 per cent increase in food aid provision between 2010 and 2013 – from 2.8 million to 4.1 million individuals. The FBAO has 21 regional agencies operating at the local level. Caritas has registered 3,816 food distribution centres and 353 soup kitchens, with the latter serving over 190,000 recipients. Other, undocumented projects also exist. FEAD food is distributed to 219 second-tier organisations and then to 11,554 front-line agencies. In 2015, this food was distributed to 2.8 million people.

(continued)

Table 8.3: Food charity landscapes across case study countries (continued)

Country	Prominent food charity projects and mid-layer organisations	Brief description of food charity landscape
Netherlands	Association of Dutch Food Banks.	The Association of Dutch Food Banks is the most prominent group of mid-level organisations that distribute food to 'food pantries'. There are other independent initiatives, including Muslim food banks and food banks for the elderly or children.
		One food parcel – matched in size to individual household composition (with a value of €35) – is provided per week for up to three years.
Slovenia	Red Cross Slovenia, Caritas and the Lions Club.	The Red Cross and Caritas provide food parcels and manage redistribution logistics. The Lions Club is another key mid-layer food redistribution organisation that also gives food to the Red Cross and Caritas. There are many other local ad hoc food charity projects and other initiatives such as donations for school lunches (Give Me 5 For A Smile!).
Spain	The Spanish Red Cross and FESBAL – 'food bank' is a registered trademark associated with FESBAL, and projects have to abide by its guidelines.	Nationally coordinated food redistribution through the Spanish Red Cross and FESBAL – they both distribute food to smaller charities and provide food directly to people in need. Various third sector organisations and informal charities collect food from food banks to hand out. There are other independent initiatives that provide food from different sources or money for food. Social discounting projects like social supermarkets also exist.
		FESBAL distributes food to collaborating entities which might be 'consumption projects' (soup kitchens and so on) or 'delivery projects' (where people take the food away).
UK	The Trussell Trust Foodbank Network. Fareshare is the most prominent second-tier redistribution organisation sending food to a range of emergency and non-emergency food charity projects, though, in many cases, it does not supply Trussell Trust food banks.	Food banks have come to dominate the discourse and landscape of food charity in the UK as a result of the prominent Trussell Trust projects. Food banks are recognised as outlets that provide emergency food parcels (containing a prescribed combination of foodstuffs and sized to household composition) for people to take away, prepare and eat. Other food charity projects do exist, including independent food banks, soup kitchens and other forms of community provision.

Notes: ELCF = Evangelical Lutheran Church of Finland; FBOs = faith-based organisations; NGOs = non-governmental organisations; FBAO = Food Bank Foundation; FESBAL = Spanish Federation of Food Banks

Food sources	Access routes to food assistance	Rise and scale of food charity (food charity statistics from national organisations)
Mostly surplus redistribution organised at a regional level, though individual projects collect donations locally. Food projects in the Netherlands do not receive food assistance through the FEAD. These funds are instead used to support social inclusion for elderly people on low incomes.	People are referred by a social worker or other professional, and their discretionary income is calculated to confirm that they qualify. In 2018, the monthly income assistance threshold was €130 per household plus €85 per person in the household.	The first food bank was established in 2002. In 2014, there were 453 food pantries, rising to 530 by 2017. The number of people receiving help was on the increase until 2014, when it started to fall; it has remained stable since 2016. As of 2017, 168 food banks were operating in conjunction with eight regional distribution centres, sending food to 453 food pantries to be handed out. In 2017, 132,500 people received help from food banks.
Mostly surplus redistribution including EU MDP/FEAD, though there are some public food drives, for example, the school lunch scheme.	People are required to prove their need by showing evidence that they are in receipt of social assistance or being referred by social services.	Red Cross provision spiked in 2013 at the time of the economic crisis and the implementation of welfare reforms. In 2017, the Red Cross distributed food to 129,035 people, and Caritas to 94,884 people. The Lions Club delivered food for 2 million meals.
FEAD food redistribution but also corporate philanthropy and public support from individual citizens – around 25 per cent of food sourced by food banks comes through twice-yearly national 'Great Food Drives' collecting food donations from individuals at supermarkets. Food banks also receive other kinds of corporate support beyond surplus food.	Distributors must provide the food banks with information on the final recipients of food.	There are 56 food banks sending food to thousands of projects. Currently, 6,000 registered projects receive food from food banks. This is down from 9,000 in 2008, which the authors ascribe to the introduction of various conditions placed on projects that receive food through the FEAD programme. FESBAL distribution has increased from 60,000 tons of food in 2008 to 151,527 tons in 2018.
Private food donations from individuals as part of local or national food drives are a key source for food banks. Fareshare handles the redistribution of food industry surplus. The EU FEAD funding is used to provide financial support for breakfast club initiatives.	In The Trussell Trust model – and independent initiatives based on it – people have to be referred to a food bank by a professional (for example, state social security adviser, health worker or community worker).	In 2016/17, The Trussell Trust Foodbank Network – the UK's largest food bank organisation with 1,300 food banks – gave food to adults and children 1,182,954 times – an increase from 128,697 in 2011/12.

shares some commonalities. The provision is primarily charitable and, for the most part, run by volunteers, though there may be some funded staff. In all countries, there are organisations operating at one or both of two tiers in the structure of food charity, with the first tier comprising client-facing food charity projects, and the second tier comprising food redistribution initiatives. To access food, recipients have to be assessed to confirm that they are in need – either by the providers themselves (for example, Caritas, *Tafel* and operators in Slovenia) or through referral processes (the UK, Germany, Slovenia and the Netherlands). Yet, it is not entirely clear how rigorously or consistently these referral and assessment processes are applied, and there appears to be a wide variety of approaches. For example, the Netherlands sets an income threshold for eligibility, while Finland has no officially validated procedure for assessment at all, so practices vary between operations.

Therefore, while it has been possible to draw out key insights into the overarching nature of food charity in Europe, there are significant gaps in knowledge and issues of incomparability across the case studies. These include matters relating to what food is handed out (in terms of the kind, amount and whether this is standardised), how it is handed out and why people are seeking help from charitable food projects.

The scale of food charity in Europe today

It is clear from the case studies that data on food charity – in terms of the scale of provision and need for help – are patchy at best, and what are available are not robustly comparable. Several case-study authors highlight problems with the data available and advise caution with its use (in Chapters 1, 2, 5 and 7). However, as demonstrated by Table 8.1, collectively, these case studies do play an important role in gathering together existing data for the first time.

The reliance on food charities and mid-layer organisations for data is clearly problematic. Some public food aid distribution channels – for example, the FEAD programme – release annual reports. However, there are numerous independent charitable operators that rely on private donations, and it is very difficult, if not impossible, to obtain precise figures about their activities. Food provision is often counted per parcel/meal provided, not per person, so the exact scale in terms of unique individuals is impossible to discern. Available information also varies in specificity, depth and breadth, and has not necessarily been designed to provide systematic data for national analysis (Lambie-Mumford and Dowler, 2015). There are also important ethical and logistical questions about how appropriate it is for these data to be collected by charities and the level and nature of information that is collected about the people that they help.

Public discourses surrounding food charity

The case studies make interesting observations about public and political discourse surrounding the rise of food charities in the countries on which they focus. The authors report positive public responses to the notion of reducing food waste through the redistribution of surplus to food charity projects (in Chapters 1, 5 and 6). In this context, food waste recovery through charities is regarded as an act of environmental responsibility; as such, it provides a positive interpretation of charitable surplus food provision.

Elsewhere, reactions have varied. In the Netherlands, the public response has been characterised by moral outrage at the need for food charity projects (see Chapter 4). In Germany and the UK, there appear to be correlations between neoliberal (UK) and neo-social (Germany) shifts, with the common consequence that the charitable endeavour of food charity is seen as a positive intervention. That said, in both countries, the rise in need for emergency food was originally greeted by a sense of public outrage (Chapters 2 and 7). In Finland, the public discourse is contradictory. Charitable food aid is interpreted as an illegitimate form of social security in the framework of Nordic welfare state policies. Yet, it is accepted as philanthropic kindness that it is appropriate for faith-based organisations (FBOs) to provide (see Chapter 1).

Food and poverty or 'food poverty': theoretical and empirical debate

As outlined at the start of this chapter, the focus of this edited collection is primarily on the nature of responses to poverty in Europe, specifically using food charity as a lens through which to explore how such responses have changed as a result of shifts in social policy. Access to food is treated throughout this volume as a key aspect of poverty, one that is worthy of independent investigation and vital in understanding the impact of wider policy shifts.

Within this theoretical and conceptual context, the case studies highlight that 'household food insecurity' and 'food poverty' have variable relevance as specific policy issues across the case-study countries. Some authors use both concepts to discuss their country cases, for example, Slovenia and Spain (in Chapters 5 and 6). The concept of food poverty is favoured in Finland and Italy (see Chapters 1 and 3); as noted in the Introduction, the term 'food security' also means 'food safety' in these languages. 'Food insecurity' is used in the UK (Chapter 7).

However, the relationship between these concepts and the wider concept of poverty is also given more detailed reflection in the case-study chapters. As Arcuri et al point out in Chapter 3, the idea of food poverty per se has varied relevance in food charity practice: 'even if the largest share of services that Caritas provides entail food distribution, it points out that food poverty is not a specific target to be addressed and should rather be part of a broader definition of poverty'. In Chapter 2, Kessl et al make a similar intellectual argument for keeping attention on the broader concept of poverty, suggesting that a focus on food alone could be counterproductive in understanding how to protect standards of living and overcome poverty most effectively. The theoretical and empirical work in this book serves to reinforce the importance of situating discussions of food charity within this overall context of poverty. It is essential for research to maintain a focus on the relationship between food experiences and poverty, and not lose sight of socio-economic structural determinants.

The rise of food charity and the political economy of welfare in Europe

Table 8.4 sets out each case study's findings on the link between changing political economies of welfare and the rise of food charity across Europe. From the evidence presented throughout these chapters, it would appear that there is, indeed, a link between changes to social rights and entitlements, as well as increased emphasis on non-state providers, on the one hand, and the rise of food charity, on the other. This appears to manifest itself not only in the timing of food charity expansion, but also in actual practices – particularly in relation to post-neoliberal-wave governments being active in facilitating food charity projects and celebrating the role played by these particular civil society actors. It would therefore appear that while specific policies and timescales have differed, reductions and increased conditionality in state entitlements have played an important role in determining the need for and shape of help with food – in the form of widespread food charity – across Europe.

There are some further commonalities across case-study countries. In Finland, in the Netherlands and – at least early on in the

Table 8.4: Charting changes in welfare provision and the rise of food charity across the case studies

Country	Welfare shifts	Rise in food charity
Finland	Economic recession in the 1990s was the catalyst for neoliberal change in economic and social policies. As a result, basic social security benefits remained frozen for more than ten years. In addition, activation policy measures were implemented to connect unemployment benefit to work-related obligations. Failing to meet the requirements of the activation model results in cuts to unemployment benefit.	Need for food aid was initially triggered by the recession of the early 1990s, and the first charitable activities started in the middle of that decade. Levels of basic social security benefits – for example, labour market support, sick leave allowance and income assistance – remain too low to provide a decent standard of living, maintaining the need for food aid.
Germany	The 2003–05 *Hartz-Gesetze* reforms embedded neo-social policies.	The increase in food charity happened alongside the introduction of these reforms. The period 1993–2003 saw moderate growth (with a total of 330 projects established). After the welfare reforms were introduced, there was a rapid increase during 2003–10 (up to a total of 877 projects), and there has been consolidation since 2010 (a total of 934).
Italy	Austerity measures have involved cuts in welfare expenditure, which was already at a low level, and caused increasing regional differences in state provision.	There was a 47 per cent increase in food aid provision between 2010 and 2013 – up from 2.8 million recipients to 4.1 million.
Netherlands	Since the 1990s, and more intensely since 2013, there has been increasing emphasis on individual responsibility and the role of non-state actors. There have been cuts to levels of entitlements and the introduction of more bureaucratic processes to access social security, which have resulted in income reductions.	Since the initial establishment of food charity in 2002, there has been evidence of local governments increasingly playing facilitative roles as regards the work of food charities, and that people are 'falling through the cracks' of more conditional welfare assistance.

(continued)

Table 8.4: Charting changes in welfare provision and the rise of food charity across the case studies (continued)

Country	Welfare shifts	Rise in food charity
Slovenia	The Social Assistance Act 2006 made welfare provision more conditional and focused on individual responsibilities. A further round of reform and welfare spending cuts was initiated in 2009 – in the wake of the economic crisis – with the Social Assistance Benefits Act. This came into force in 2012 at the height of the effects of the economic crisis, when unemployment rates had doubled.	Red Cross provision spiked in 2013.
Spain	Over the last decade, social security provision has stagnated and there is evidence of strain on family support networks, which have traditionally been a key aspect of the Spanish welfare system. The third sector has stepped in. Post-crisis, there has been a tightening of access to social security. Delays in processing applications and payments are common, and policies vary widely across different municipalities.	Distribution by FESBAL increased from 60,000 tons of food in 2008 to 151,527 tons in 2018.
UK	In 2010, the UK government began the largest overhaul of the social security system since the establishment of the welfare state. Reforms have involved capping and freezing social security payment levels, increasing conditionality, and tightening criteria for eligibility. At the same time, funding for public services – including local authorities and family support centres – has been cut across the board.	The largest increases in food charity followed these reforms, and there is mounting evidence linking welfare reform with the rise of food charity. In the year 2016/17, the UK's largest food bank organisation, The Trussell Trust foodbank network, distributed 1,182,954 food parcels to adults and children across the country, up from 128,697 in the year 2011/12.

development of food charity – in the UK, there is an emphasis on people 'falling through the cracks' of the welfare system. This implies that bureaucratic processes – as well as conditionality and criteria for entitlement – are an important factor in the need for help with food (see Chapters 1 and 4). Chapters 3 and 6 emphasise the significance of decentralised welfare processes in Italy and Spain, leading to wide variations in entitlements and support for those in need across those countries. Additional pressure on public finance for welfare is also reported in Italy and Slovenia in the form of EU regulations on spending and deficits, exacerbated by the financial crisis (see Chapters 3 and 5).

The changing role of (food) charity in welfare

The findings presented across the case studies suggest that regardless of the historical role of the third sector in different welfare regimes, since the neoliberal wave and the economic crisis of the late 2000s, charities are now playing different and more prominent roles in the provision of care, whether in place of support traditionally provided by the state or the family. Data from Germany, the Netherlands and the UK suggests that since the 1990s – and in particular more recently – neoliberal thinking in support of privatised modes of care has fostered increasing political approval of charity, including food charity, playing a role in this area. In these countries, charities are assuming responsibility for support and provision that the state would previously have been expected to provide (see Chapters 2, 4 and 7). In Spain, where the family has historically played a particularly prominent role in social support, evidence suggests that this support is becoming exhausted. In response, charities – including those providing food – are playing ever more important roles (see Chapter 6). Italy provides another interesting example of where charities have always played a prominent role in social assistance given the fragmented nature of state welfare. In Chapter 3, Arcuri et al observe that the role of charity in Italy – spearheaded by food charities – is shifting from a single focus on provision to an additional focus on advocacy and lobbying for improved public social policies. Seeing rising levels of need, charities are becoming increasingly aware of their inability to solve the root causes of poverty in the country.

There is also important evidence across the case studies of changing welfare practices, which increasingly incorporate food charity projects. This means not only that food charity projects are more and more present and prominent in the various welfare landscapes, but also that the ways in which the projects interact with state welfare providers in practice have been changing over time.

Evidence from across the case studies highlights increasing state support or involvement in food charity practices. Most commonly, this is in the form of formally or informally referring people in need from state agencies or professionals to food charity projects, as reported in Finland, Germany, the Netherlands, Slovenia and the UK (Chapters 1, 2, 4, 5 and 7). There are also reports of local authorities giving financial or in-kind (such as logistical) support to food charity projects across the countries studied, including Finland, the Netherlands, Spain and the UK (see Chapters 1, 4, 6 and 7). In Finland, the Ministry of Social Affairs and Health maintains that food charity is not part of the social security system; however, at the same time, it allocated €1.8 million to food aid projects in 2016/17. In Germany, the Minister for Family Affairs is automatically appointed as the patron of *Tafel*. Kessl et al (in Chapter 2) sum up the situation all across Europe: 'Existing welfare states as public systems of poverty reduction are being complemented by a private–public system of poverty relief, which has been established in the shadow of formal state institutional arrangements.'

The role of food supply and agro-economic policies in shaping food charity

As previously mentioned in this chapter, this book set out to focus particularly on the social policy aspects of the rise of food charity. However, analysis of the data provided by the case studies clearly highlights the importance of supply-side factors in the shape and scale of emergency food provision. In particular, the countries studied demonstrate the significance of the MDP and – after 2013 – the FEAD in institutionalising surplus food redistribution through food charity.

In all cases except the UK, surplus food redistribution is the most common method for food charity projects to secure food. While all authors report that projects source additional food in other ways, redistribution of surplus food is shown to play a major role. Food charity projects in Finland, Slovenia, Italy and Spain source food through the FEAD. In the UK, the programme is used specifically to provide financial support to breakfast clubs in primary and secondary schools in England for pupils who are entitled to free school meals (European Commission, 2019). In Germany and the Netherlands, the operational programmes of the FEAD focus not on food initiatives, but instead on social inclusion programmes. In each country where

FEAD food stocks are used in food charity – or have a history of such use – this was found to be a determining factor in the shape of food charity (see Chapters 1, 3, 5 and 6). These chapters highlight how the scale, organisation and regulated nature of participation in the FEAD scheme have resulted in the prominence and institutionalisation of the redistribution of surplus food through food charity.

Following participation in EU redistribution schemes, Good Samaritan legislation – making the redistribution of surplus food easier – was introduced in Italy in 2016 and Slovenia in 2017. In Finland, food supervision authorities have loosened the regulations on directing expiring food from grocery stores to charities by relaxing the rules concerning expiration dates. Furthermore, in the Netherlands, the government's coalition agreement refers to the EU Council publication that calls on states to make the redistribution of surplus food easier, highlighting the importance of EU agricultural policy (Council of the European Union, 2016).

This book began with an assertion that as a group of researchers in the area of food charity, the authors have observed that food waste and experiences of limited access to food are distinct phenomena, with different determinants and requiring different responses and solutions. This research was framed to focus on food charity provision (first tier). However, it has become clear through the comparative analysis that, in fact, food sourcing practices at the second, mid-layer, tier – especially surplus food redistribution and food waste recovery through charitable food provision – constitute an important determinant of the scale, nature and embeddedness of first-tier food charity projects.

The Introduction cautioned that where issues of food waste and experiences of limited access to food are not treated distinctly, there is a real danger of conflating environmental policy questions – about how to reduce food waste – with discrete social policy questions – about both the need for assistance with food and the best and most appropriate social responses to experiences of poverty. The analysis of the case studies serves to confirm the truth of this warning. In particular countries – notably, Italy and Slovenia – the conflation of these areas has become embedded in policymaking through Good Samaritan Acts (see Chapters 3 and 5). In Finland, there is a legislative initiative proposing a ban on large shops throwing away or destroying unsold food and an obligation for retailers to donate such food to charities. The rationale behind the legislation is to tackle food waste and food poverty in tandem.

In policy analysis terms, the importance of the MDP and the FEAD indicates that there is crossover between policy spheres. First, the MDP programme, as a part of the Common Agricultural Policy (CAP), bought up agricultural overproduction surplus to balance market fluctuations. This surplus food was later delivered as food aid. In this way, emergency food aid was used as a kind of market support for European agriculture. From 1987 to 2013, this manoeuvre worked to stabilise food supply for many of the charitable actors and thus helped to establish charitable food aid provision in many European countries. Second, some recent EU–wide environmental policy initiatives, such as the zero–waste initiative (in 2017) and the circular economy (in 2019), have a tangible impact on social policy practices in relation to extensive and embedded food charity in terms of state funding or support through surplus food provision to food charities. As observed in the Introduction, while there is no common EU social policy, initiatives that have come out of the CAP – in the form of the MDP and later EU guidelines regarding food waste (Council of the European Union, 2016) – have, in effect, served to homogenise private welfare practices in several member states in the form of surplus food redistribution through food charity. This policy sphere crossover is also apparent at a domestic level – for example, in the Netherlands, Slovenia, Italy, Finland and, more recently, the UK (Defra, 2018). Here, decisions made in the sphere of public policy concerning the environment – namely, surplus food redistribution incentives – are impacting on the scale and nature of food charity in the practice of both private and state social welfare. These decisions also serve to legitimise charity as a response to need, providing an 'illusion of a just system' and proving hard to argue against (a moral 'buy one, get one free').

Another reason why it is important to acknowledge that these initiatives originate in environmental policy spheres is that this highlights the fact that these policies stem from the problem of food surplus and how to avoid waste. Surplus food redistribution policies did not begin with the problem of lack of access to food, or any assessment that the provision of surplus food was the best response. As the evidence provided in this book (in Chapters 1 and 3) and many others (for example, Riches, 1997) shows, an ad hoc system of private food charity reliant on unpredictable redistribution practices would not be the evidence-based policy solution presented in response to the problem of the systemic lack of access to food. Furthermore, the redistribution of surplus food through food charity is a downstream response to overproduction and does not represent environmental policy seeking to question the upstream production processes and construction of consumption practices resulting in the current scale of waste.

The social justice implications of welfare retrenchment and the rise of food charity

The social justice implications of the increasing need for and provision of charitable assistance with food are profound. This section of the concluding analysis discusses the implications of the book's findings for entitlements, equality and fairness, as well as for the future of food charity practice, policy and research more generally.

In the first instance, the comparative analysis highlights how changes to social rights brought about by neoliberal policy shifts have had direct consequences on food charity assistance in terms of both practice and rising need. The authors of all the case studies highlight the role played by increased conditionality and reduced levels of entitlements in driving increased need. Several case studies also demonstrate how neoliberal assumptions and practices are embedded within food charity, for example, means testing as part of requirements to 'prove' one's need for food assistance (at projects in Germany and Slovenia) or via referral criteria (in the Netherlands and UK). Yet, food charities also appear to make efforts to play a role in social policy. For instance, the worsening of need in Italy has prompted Caritas to monitor the inadequacy of social assistance (see Chapter 3). In the UK, The Trussell Trust has always regarded advocacy and lobbying as part of its role (see Chapter 7). In Finland, the Evangelical Lutheran Church of Finland (ELCF) has regularly put poverty issues on the political agenda (see Chapter 1).

The case studies highlight a variety of ways in which exclusion is embedded within the need for and practice of food charity assistance. Chapters 2 and 6 set out how exclusion from consumer society is embodied in both the need for and receipt of charitable food assistance. Experiences of exclusion and shame on the part of food aid recipients are discussed in Chapters 2 and 5. Chapter 4 observes the irony of the moral outrage that dominated public discourse in the Netherlands about the rising need for food charity when compared with the relative lack of reflection on the implications of the form of such charity, specifically, the fact that it is redistributed surplus food.

The case studies in this book demonstrate that food charity projects across Europe are assuming responsibility for helping people who lack adequate access to food. At a structural level, the shift of this responsibility appears, from this analysis, to be a function of states no longer assuming full responsibility for social protection. This is seen in the regressive social policy shifts that have occurred following the neoliberal wave – whether through reduced entitlements (in the

UK, Germany, Slovenia and Finland), increased conditionality (in the Netherlands, Germany, the UK, Slovenia and Finland) or the failure to pursue more comprehensive social protection (in Spain and Italy). As welfare states retrench – or at least policy fails to adequately respond to need – in practice, food charity projects are assuming responsibility for care. As Van der Horst, Pijnenburg and Markus argue in Chapter 4, there is an iterative process at play here. As charitable initiatives step in to fill gaps left by state provision, and the political discourse praises the efforts and impact of charitable social assistance, food charity could be further exacerbating state retrenchment by taking on this role.

Conclusions

This edited collection provides the first comprehensive study of the rise of food charity across Europe. Using food charity as a lens through which to examine the changing dynamics of poverty and the social policy responses to it, the book acts as a key social policy text on the nature of responses to poverty in the context of shifting social policies and changing welfare states.

While this book represents a significant step forward in understanding the rise of food charity across Europe over recent decades, it also serves to highlight the significant gaps in knowledge. Further systematic comparative study is required in several key areas. In the first instance, it will be important to develop and test the typology of European food charity and mid-layer organisations set out here. It will also be crucial to obtain a more systematic and reliable understanding of the scale of food charity provision, its operation and the reasons people are seeking food assistance. For future social policy analyses, it will also be important to gain a better understanding of the practices and relationships between states (at local and national levels) and food charities. This is especially urgent because this cross-case analysis suggests that a charity economy – including food charity – is growing and taking shape rapidly, at least partly in the shadow of institutionalised welfare systems (see Chapter 2).

This is an important juncture at which to take stock of the implications of the rise of food charity across Europe. Researchers in social policy and other areas are now beginning to ask about the longevity of these projects as part of welfare landscapes. This collection provides urgently needed social policy insight into the drivers of the growth of food assistance and the nature of the charitable responses developing across Europe. The findings indicate a pressing need to radically reassess social policy priorities – and the consequences of environmental policies – if the ever-increasing provision of food charity is to be abated or reversed.

References

Council of the European Union (2016) 'Food losses and food waste, 10730/16', http://data.consilium.europa.eu/doc/document/ST-10730-2016-INIT/en/pdf

Defra (Department for Environment, Food and Rural Affairs) (2018) 'Environment Secretary announces new scheme to reduce food waste and Natural England Wildlife targets', https://deframedia.blog.gov.uk/2018/10/01/environment-secretary-announces-new-scheme-to-reduce-food-waste-and-natural-england-wildlife-targets/

European Commission (2019) 'FEAD in your country', https://ec.europa.eu/social/main.jsp?catId=1239&langId=en&intPageId=3630#navItem-1

Lambie-Mumford, H., Crossley, D., Jensen, E., Verbeke, M. and Dowler, E. (2014) 'Household food insecurity in the UK: A review of food aid', London: Department for Environment, Food and Rural Affairs.

Lambie-Mumford, H. and Dowler, E. (2015) 'Hunger, food charity and social policy – challenges faced by the emerging evidence base', *Social Policy and Society*, 14(3): 497–506.

Mabli, J., Cohen, R., Potter, F. and Zhao, Z. (2010) *Hunger in America 2010: National report prepared for Feeding America*, New Jersey, NJ: Mathematica Policy Research Inc.

Riches, G. (1997) *First world hunger*, London: Routledge.

Index

Note: Page numbers for figures and tables appear in italics.